# Digital Culture

CHARLIE GERE

REAKTION BOOKS

*For Stella*

Published by Reaktion Books Ltd
33 Great Sutton Street, London EC1V ODX, UK

www.reaktionbooks.co.uk

First published 2002, second edition 2008
Copyright © Charlie Gere 2002, 2008

Printed and bound in Great Britain
by CPI/Antony Rowe, Chippenham, Wiltshire

British Library Cataloguing in Publication Data:
Gere, Charlie
    Digital Culture. – Rev and updated ed.
    1 Digital electronics – Social aspects   2. Computers and civilization
    I. Title
    303.4'834

ISBN: 978 1 86189 388 8

# Contents

The second edition of a book offers the author the chance to reflect on changes that have taken place since the first edition was published. In the case of *Digital Culture* this means trying to think about some of the most dramatic and important transformations that are the result of the increasing ubiquity and importance of digital technologies. I believe that the underlying argument of the book – that people (in the 'developed' world at least) increasingly live in a 'digital culture' – holds true. Indeed I would suggest that this is more clearly the case than when I started writing about the subject back in the mid-1990s. To some extent our culture is becoming so thoroughly digital that the term *digital culture* risks becoming tautological.

One of the concomitants of our current digital culture is the sense of rapid change. Everything is of course always changing all the time. Change appears to be a given of existence, whether it is manifested in the universal tendency towards entropy, or in the glacially slow drift of evolutionary change. The only thing that never changes is that everything always changes. Mostly this process of change is slow enough to be imperceptible, other than in retrospect, or by implication. But for the beings that Nietzsche so dismissively characterized as 'some clever animals' in a 'remote corner of the universe' things appear to be changing very fast, perhaps too fast. The reason for this rapid change is the animals' extended and augmented capacity to manipulate their environment through their technological prostheses, from flint tools through to computers. It is this capacity alone that distinguishes the clever, human animals from the other, less clever, species that share the same world. The human is only human in so far as it is technical. Technology is not a product of human beings. It is a precondition of their existence. It is technology that has enabled humans to be clever, or at least to think of themselves as such. It is also technology that appears to have brought them potentially to the brink of their own annihilation, whether through nuclear war or global warming, which is not clever.

It is the increasingly rapid development and complexity of technology that is making things change so rapidly. Our technologies are always in the process of changing us and our relationship with our environment. The difference is the rate at which this change is taking place. For the first few million years of hominoid and human tool use, change would have been more or less imperceptible. Then, within the last twenty to thirty thousand years, developments started to pick up pace. By the time we arrive at the modern era, technology is developing at an incredible rate (for those of us in the 'developed' world at least). Finally, the last one hundred or so years have seen more and more rapid technological change and development than in all of previous human history. If it was possible to plot this rate of development on a graph, with technological complexity on the vertical axis and time on the horizontal, then the likely result would be a line that barely crept above the base line until it almost reached the further edge, at which point it would curve dramatically, until it was almost vertical. It would show that the rate of technological development is exponential, in that it grows in relation to its size. One of the results of this accelerating rate of growth is that it is increasingly hard, if not impossible, for us to fully grasp what is going on.

Though most of us are aware of other technological developments and issues – for example, questions of nuclear power and nuclear weaponry, industrial production and its effects on the environment, diminishing energy reserves and the search for renewable and sustainable sources of energy – our most vivid encounter with technology and experience of its capacity for change is likely to be through our media, which are changing and developing in extraordinary and unprecedented ways. This is particularly true of digital media, such as the Internet and the World Wide Web, mobile telephony, digital video, which either enable us now to do things we did before more often and more easily, or to do things we could previously barely imagine. More dramatically they are in the process of transforming not just our world, but our very selves, how we understand who we are. They are changing everything, including the idea of 'media' itself (already a problematic and contentious term). And this is the problem: almost by definition any radical transformations brought about by the media are impossible to fully grasp at the time they are taking place. This is because how we understand the world is structured by and accessible through our media (if you use the term in the broadest sense, to include, for example, language). There is not, indeed there cannot be, a point outside of our media from which we can have some kind of privileged un- or premeditated perspective on any aspect of our existence, let alone that of media itself.

Consider how someone in Europe in the late fifteenth century might have understood the development of printing. However educated he or she might have been it is unlikely that they could have grasped the full implications of this new media technology, or the dramatic effects it would have on Western and, eventually, global culture and society. His or her way of thinking would have evolved within and for a particular 'media ecology', and thus would not be fit for comprehending new emerging media conditions. It is surely far more likely that, in the late fifteenth century at least, printing would still have been regarded as an extension or more efficient scribal practice, a kind of prosthesis or substitute for the production of texts by hand, not as the means for a wholesale transformation of the intellectual environment. We are perhaps at a similar moment in our understanding of the transformations being wrought by our new technologies.

But this is to fall into the trap of thinking of current technological and media change in terms of earlier such transformations. Much as military planners are always said to be making preparations to re-fight the last war, rather than the new one they are going to be confronted with, we can only understanding new media in terms of old. It is possible that the ability to fully grasp the implications of the transformations wrought by printing only occurs when print culture itself has began properly to be superseded by electronic, 'post-print' culture. If we were capable of understanding the changes around us, then they would not truly be changes, but merely developments of the present situation. All we can do therefore is to map the changes we see in the hope of maintaining our grasp on our rapidly changing situation. This is what I hope *Digital Culture* offers.

# What is Digital Culture?

In the early years of computing, when computer memory space was scarce, programmers used abbreviations as much as possible. This involved, for example, encoding years using only the last two digits. Thus '1965' would become simply '65' (or rather, its binary equivalent). To the early programmers this must have seemed of little or no significance, and as computer memory became cheaper and more widely available there was no longer any need for such parsimony. But, as the new millennium approached, some experts began to propose that this apparently insignificant aspect of early computing might have produced an unwelcome legacy. It was suggested that, when the clocks rolled over to the new millennium, any system still using the two digit method of encoding dates would not recognize that it was 2000, and think, for example, that it was 1900, with all sorts of unforeseeable consequences. The problem was that many operating systems and programs still used the shorter convention, despite it no longer being necessary, and that many of the early computer programs continued to run, often deeply embedded in the older mainframe computers still used by institutions such as banks.

This realization generated much doom-watching and apocalyptic scenario-constructing, often emanating from those who would most benefit. Consultancy services to combat the possible effects of the 'Millennium bug', the 'Year 2000 problem' or the 'Y2K bug', as the issue was variously called, proliferated. ('Y2K' was the preferred designation among computer experts, which seemed to suggest that the love of abbreviation, which caused all the problems in the first place, was now a part of computer culture.) Among the possible consequences was the breakdown of banking computer systems, leading to people being unable to access their money and therefore to possible social unrest, as well as broader national and global consequences relating to interruptions to the flow of finances. It was also suggested that similar outcomes might result if the systems governing the distribution of welfare provision were to be affected. Lifts, medical equipment, air conditioning systems, elevators, were all potentially at risk, as indeed were electricity grids, traffic control systems, air control systems and any other system that used digital technology (which in effect meant almost every aspect of a developed nation's technical infrastructure). Most chilling of all was the suggestion that nuclear missiles might be confused by consequences of the bug and launch themselves. This was vociferously denied by those in charge of such weapons, and did indeed seem fairly improbable. Nevertheless the consequences of computer breakdown on the human element in nuclear defence was potentially catastrophic enough for the Pentagon to invite Russian military observers into the Peterson Air Force Base over the New Year period to observe the American early warning observation systems and to be on hand should any problems arise.

That there might be rioting on the streets, aeroplanes dropping from the skies and even accidental nuclear war as a direct result of the coming of the third Christian Millennium seemed almost too pat. For those inclined to apocalyptic beliefs the millennium bug presented a plausible mechanism by which Armageddon would be put in train. Even for those without such beliefs the coincidence of the bug and the symbolically charged date was unnerving. Those with libertarian leanings, which included many in the computer industry, seemed to welcome the consequences, as it enabled them to fulfil fantasies of self-reliance away from government intervention. Meanwhile governments around the world attempted to forestall any problems, though with varying degrees of enthusiasm and investment. In the end, as we know, nothing happened. The New Year came and went without incident. Whether this was because of or despite the various preparations and warnings is open to debate. There is an entirely plausible view that the whole issue was hyped up, largely by those with a vested interest in selling their knowledge of computer systems. Whatever the truth of the matter many of the doom-mongers and those who had listened them too assiduously ended up looking rather foolish. The unfortunate Eckhart family of Lisbon, Ohio, who had spent several years stockpiling food, conducting surprise drills, practising with firearms, studying rudimentary dentistry and field medicine and converting their savings into gold, found that the most apocalyptic result of the millennium was being gently mocked by *Time* magazine for their bunker mentality.

Not that this is any reason to be complacent. Putting aside the contempt such survivalist foolishness always incites and the *schadenfreude* that accompanies the humiliation of self-proclaimed experts, the issues that emerged in the context of the millennium bug scare, concerning our increasing reliance on overly complex, sometimes archaic systems, remain a definite cause for concern. But the bug did far more than highlight such problems. It was an apocalypse in another sense, an *apo-kalyptein* – an uncovering or disclosing of what had previously been hidden. Like a lightning flash over a darkened scene, it made briefly visible what had hitherto been obscure; the almost total transformation of the world by digital technology. It is hard to grasp the full extent of this transformation, which, in the developed world at least, can be observed in almost every aspect of modern living. Most forms of mass media, television, recorded music, film, are produced and, increasingly, distributed digitally. These media are beginning to converge with digital forms, such as the Internet, the World Wide Web, and video games, to produce a seamless digital mediascape. When at work we are also surrounded by such technology, whether in offices, where computers have become indispensable tools for word processing and data management, or in, for example, supermarkets or factories, where every aspect of marketing and production is monitored and controlled digitally. Much of the means by which governments and other complex organizations pursue their ends rely on digital technology. Physical money, coins and notes, is no more than digital data congealed into matter. By extension, information of every kind and for every purpose is now mostly in digital form, including that relating to insurance, social services, utilities, real estate, leisure and travel, credit arrangements, employment, education, law, as well as personal information for identification and qualification, such as birth certificates, drivers licences, passports and marriage certificates.

This pervasion of digital technology through our lives is part of a broader set of phenomena. The last 30 years have seen both the rise of globalization and the domination of free market capitalism, the increasing ubiquity of information and communications technologies, and the burgeoning power and influence of techno-science. Digital technology is an important and constitutive part of these developments, and has, to some extent, determined their form. The computerization of banking, international currency exchange and trading has greatly aided the rise of globalization and financial liberalization. The possibilities of convergence and integration that digital technology offers has led to it to dominate technical developments in media and communications. Computers are also the essential means by which the vast amounts of data that large techno-scientific projects require are managed and manipulated. The concurrent development of science, media and capital under the aegis of digital technology produces a kind of fast-forward effect in which everything appears to take place at an accelerated rate and to produce dramatic change in a very short time. This excites both euphoria and terror, not least because of the shocking pace at which things happen. One has barely enough time to register one set of events and its possible consequences when another makes it irrelevant. At the same time these events offer extraordinary challenges to the preconceptions through which our existence is negotiated. These include, for example, the annihilation of physical distance and the dissolution of material reality by virtual or telecommunication technologies, or the apparent end of the human and the rise of the so-called posthuman as a result of advances in Cybernetics, robotics and research into consciousness and intelligence.

Given how important digital technology has become to our lives it is useful to know what the word 'digital' actual means. In technical terms it is used to refer to data in the form of discrete elements. Though it could refer to almost any system, numerical, linguistic or otherwise, used to describe phenomena in discrete terms over the last 60 or so years, the word has become synonymous with the technology which has made much of the aforementioned possible, electronic digital binary computers. To some extent the terms 'computer technology' and 'digital technology' have become interchangeable. Computers are digital because they manipulate and store data in digital, binary form, zeroes and ones. But, as the above indicates, the term digital has come to mean far more than simply either discrete data or the machines that use such data. To speak of the digital is to call up, metonymically, the whole panoply of virtual simulacra, instantaneous communication, ubiquitous media and global connectivity that constitutes much of our contemporary experience. It is to allude to the vast range of applications and media forms that digital technology has made possible, including virtual reality, digital special effects, digital film, digital television, electronic music, computer games, multimedia, the Internet, the World Wide Web, digital telephony and Wireless Application Protocol (WAP), as well as the various cultural and artistic responses to the ubiquity of digital technology, such as Cyberpunk novels and films, Techno and post-pop music, the 'new typography', net.art and so on. It also evokes the whole world of wired capitalism dominated by high-tech companies such as Microsoft and Sony and the so-called 'dot.coms', companies based on the Internet, which, for a while, seemed to present the ideal model for twenty-first-century business, as well as, more generally, the ungraspable complex of corporate business which, enabled by high technology, operates on a global level and sometimes appears to wield more power than nation states. It also suggests other digital phenomena, such as the new paradigms of computer-controlled and supposedly clean 'virtual war', or the computerization of genetic information as in endeavours such as the Human Genome Project, in which the transmission of inherited characteristics becomes a digital matter in itself. Thus the apparently simple term digital defines a complex set of phenomena.

From this it is possible to propose the existence of a distinctive digital culture, in that the term digital can stand for a particular way of life of a group or groups of people at a certain period in history, to invoke one of Raymond Williams' useful definitions of culture as a keyword.[1] Digitality can be thought of as a marker of culture because it encompasses both the artefacts and the systems of signi-fication and communication that most clearly demarcate our contemporary way of life from others. A useful confirmation that this culture exists is the number of recent books that have as their starting point the central and determining fact of the dominance of the digital, either in technological or philosophical terms. As an indication, David Abrahamson of Northwestern University recently published a bibliography of books and articles concerning 'Digital Culture, Information Technology, the Internet, the Web' in the on-line *Journal of Magazine and New Media Research*; it contains 450 items, the vast majority of which were published in the last five years.[2] Nor are these technical works in the usual sense. They range from sociological analyses of information society, first-hand accounts of experiences with the Internet, philosophical discussions concerning aesthetics, ethics and ontology, works of cultural theory and political analysis. It even includes, perhaps as an indication of the vitality of digital culture, a book entitled *The Joy of Cybersex: A Guide for Creative Lovers* by Deb Levine. Many of these books refer in their titles to digital culture or to some variation on that theme, such as cyberculture, electronic culture or the information age/society. Others allude to digital aesthetics, digital arts, or even 'being digital'.

If the proliferation of work of this sort seems to confirm the existence of a distinctive digital culture, it also highlights one of the main problems with how it is understood. The discourse of digital culture, as represented by much of this work, appears to be animated by two interconnected beliefs. One is that such a culture represents a decisive rupture with what has preceded it, and the other is that digital culture derives from and is determined by the existence of digital technology. Both these beliefs seem reasonable at first sight, and in the most practical sense, both are true. The existence of a distinct digital culture is only recognizable in the light of recent technological developments, and gives every appearance of being distinctly different to what came before. But, as this book will attempt to demonstrate, as a culture it is neither as new as it might appear, nor is its development ultimately determined by technological advances. It would be more accurate to suggest that digital technology is a product of digital culture, rather than vice versa. As Gilles Deleuze points out, 'the machine is always social before it is technical. There is always a social machine which selects or assigns the technical elements used.'[3] Digital refers not just to the effects and possibilities of a particular technology. It defines and encompasses the ways of thinking and doing that are embodied within that technology, and which make its development possible. These include abstraction, codification, self-regulation, virtualization and programming. These qualities are concomitant with writing and, indeed, with language more generally, and, inasmuch as language, written or spoken, is digital in that it deals with discrete elements, then almost all human culture may be said to be digital.

But such a claim does not explain the emergence of our contemporary digital culture, nor the particular form it has taken. Digital culture in its present specific form is a historically contingent phenomenon, the various components of which first emerge as a response to the exigencies of modern capitalism, and then are brought together by the demands of mid-twentieth century warfare. The Second World War was the catalytic event out of which modern electronic digital binary computing emerged and the Cold War the context in which it developed to assume its current form. But technology is only one of a number of sources that have contributed to the development of our current digital culture. Others include techno-scientific discourses about information and systems, avant-garde art practice, counter-cultural utopianism, critical theory and philosophy, and even subcultural formations such as Punk. These different elements are as much a product of the paradigm of abstraction, codification, self-regulation, virtualization and programming as the computer. Digital culture has been produced out of the complex interactions and dialectical engagements between these elements.

This, then, is both the subject and theme of this book. It is written out of the belief that it is not possible to understand digital culture unless one can distinguish the heterogeneous elements out of which it is composed. It is important moreover to understand the context in which they develop, and how they interact to produce that culture. As the book's title suggests, the focus is decidedly on the cultural, rather than, for example, the sociological. Important as they undoubtedly are, issues such as changes in the workplace brought about by new technology are not the concern here. Nor is the aim simply to write a history of digital culture, in the sense of a linear account of a progression of cause and effect, leading, inevitably, to our current situation. It is, rather, an attempt to 'blast a specific era out of the homogenous course of history'[4] and to 'grasp the constellation which this era has formed with a definite earlier one',[5] or in this case a number of earlier ones, including nineteenth-century capitalism, twentieth-century warfare, the post-war avant-garde, the counter-culture, post-modern theory and Punk.

The above quotes come from Walter Benjamin's 'Theses on the Philosophy of History', in which he expounds his idiosyncratic combination of Marxist historical materialism and Jewish mysticism as the basis for thinking about history in revolutionary terms. For Benjamin the homogenous empty time of historical progress is contrasted with the 'the time of the now' (*jetztzeit*), which is 'shot through with chips of Messianic time'.[6] For Benjamin, an unbeliever, this meant the ever-present promise of revolution in the face of fascist ascendancy. While not comparable to Fascism, the dominance of digital technology is not without its threatening aspects. If, as Max Weber suggested, industrialization and the rise of capitalism lead to the 'disenchantment of the world', the process by which rationality and legality replace more mystical forms of knowledge and authority, then its supersession by the so-called information or post-industrial society results in a radical re-enchantment. As with the aestheticization of politics under Fascism the world is placed under a kind of spell, an enchantment, in which we are beguiled by the effects of new technologies and media, and what they seem to promise, and thus fail to see how they are part of an apparatus of dominance, control and exploitation.

The spell cast by these technologies owes much to their apparently magical qualities. Their ineffable, immaterial capabilities suggest a whole array of supernatural figures, such as angels, ghosts and golems. These spectral emanations are accompanied, and interceded with, by a panoply of priest engineers, software wizards, techno-gurus, charismatic leaders and futurologist soothsayers. It is against the technological enchantment practised by these figures that this book is written. In particular it is a response to the soothsayers of the digital age, the futurologists, futurists and techno-utopians whose message of combined technological and social progress charms us into complacency. By returning to the past as the constellation out of which the present is constructed we can exorcize this charm. As Benjamin remarks it is only by remembrance that we can strip 'the future of its magic, to which all those succumb who turn to soothsayers for enlightenment'.[7]

# 1. The Beginnings of Digital Culture

In the late 1930s Alan Turing, a fellow of King's College, Cambridge, published a paper entitled 'On Computable Numbers with Application to the *Entscheidungsproblem*'.[1] It was a response to part of one of a number of proposals by the German mathematician David Hilbert. Hilbert wished to cast all mathematics in an axiomatic structure, using the ideas of set theory. From the beginning of the twentieth century on, he proposed a number of programmes that would achieve his aim. In the 1920s he put forward his most ambitious of these programmes, in which all mathematics was to be put into an axiomatic form, the rules of inference to be only those of elementary logic. He proposed that a satisfactory system would be one which was consistent, in that it would be impossible to derive both a statement and its negation, complete, in that every properly written statement should be such that either it or its negation should be derivable from the axioms, and decidable, in that any statement or its negation should be provable by an algorithm. The completeness part of this programme was shown to be unworkable by the German mathematician Kurt Gödel who, in 1931, demonstrated that there was no system of the type Hilbert proposed in which integers could be defined and which was both consistent and complete. The impact of this discovery, which is known as 'Gödel's incompleteness theorem', was great and its importance goes beyond mathematics to encompass broader questions of systems and systemization. The decidability part of the programme was also undermined by the simultaneous work of Gödel and Turing. In order to approach the question Turing imagined an entirely conceptual machine, which could be configured to be in a number of different states. He based this idea on the typewriter, which can be configured to write in either upper or lower case. The difference was that Turing's machine could be configured in an infinite number of states. He also imagined his machine having a writing head, like a typewriter key, which could write and erase marks on an infinite tape. The tape would contain spaces that were either marked or blank. The writing head could move up and down the tape in either direction. It could also read whether the space on the position contained a mark or was blank. The machine could be configured to undertake a number of different actions according to what it found. With the appropriate configuration almost any mathematical problem could be solved, but certain problems were effectively unsolvable with such mechanical processes. By devising his universal machine Turing proved that mathematics was not decidable. Turing's virtual machine worked for him inasmuch as, as a kind of philosophical toy, it enabled him to conceptualize and solve the problem with which he was concerned. He also went some way in conceptualizing the modern computer, by positing a binary machine that could be configured in any number of different states.[2] Turing was able to use his purely theoretical ideas about calculating machines during the War when he developed methods and technologies for decrypting German U-Boat signals. This work in turn led to some of the first modern electronic binary digital computers. Turing's *Entscheidungsproblem* paper is widely regarded as one of the first conceptualizations of such machines, and one of the keystones of the development of digital technology. But it is fascinating as much for the past to which it alludes, albeit unconsciously, as for the future it anticipates. In a sense it contains, *in minutiae*, many of the elements from which digital technology and digital culture developed.

Turing's thought experiment is of particular importance for the development of modern computers in that it was intended to be a universal machine. Though a number of electronic calculators had been produced these were mostly dedicated devices, capable only of specific hardwired operations. In contrast, Turing's imaginary device was, in theory at least, able to be programmed to undertake any mathematical problem. The idea of a universal machine had already been imagined by predecessors such as Charles Babbage and Ada Lovelace, and work by George Stibitz, Konrad Zuse and Claude Shannon and others made its practical realization more feasible, but Turing's particular vision had a conceptual coherence lacking before. As mentioned before, Turing was able to conceive of the idea of the universal machine through the example of the typewriter, which can be configured in two different states, upper and lower case, using the same keyboard. On one level Turing's use of the typewriter was merely expedient: it was a readily available tool that Turing himself used, albeit erratically.[3] He was undoubtedly concerned simply to find some device that could act as a model in conceptualizing a solution to the problem he was addressing. It is almost certain that Turing had little interest in the social and cultural implications of his choice. Yet the technology he chose, and that was so readily available to him, was in fact deeply embedded in a network of social and cultural meaning, one derived from contemporary capitalism. Thus it is possible to see how capitalism offered the context in which the computer could develop.

## THE DIVISION AND ABSTRACTION OF LABOUR AND CAPITAL

Invented in the late nineteenth century, as a response to the burgeoning information needs of business, the typewriter standardizes and mechanizes the production of language, reducing the elements out of which it is composed to abstracted signs (illus. 1).[4] In this it is a paradigmatic product of the system in which it was developed. Like the typewriter and, by extension, Turing's device, the operations of capitalism are fundamentally predicated on abstraction, standardization and mechanization, to ensure that it can operate as a universal machine, capable of treating disparate phenomena as equal and interchangeable. This is found in its emphasis on the exchange value of commodities, rather than their use value, the introduction of credit, paper money, and 'fiduciary' money, the division of labour into discrete and repeatable parts, and the standardization of components. This abstraction enables the flow of goods, money, and people crucial to capitalism's continuous quest for expansion and profit. It also allows for the integration of machinic assemblages, including physical machinery, such as the steam engines and spinning jennys of the early nineteenth century, and factories, in which workers were bound to machines and their work is regulated like machine-like processes. One result of this is that under capitalism signification is no longer anchored to stable, embodied meanings. Goods are no longer valued for their material

1 A Remington typewriter, after 1874.

and embodied usefulness, but instead for their exchange value. The value of money no longer refers to its intrinsic worth as metal, or what it might represent in stocks of gold. Wealth is in liquid form rather than tied to ownership of land. The complex web of feudal social relations is replaced by the 'cash nexus'. Workers are regarded as abstract labour power. Thus signification itself becomes autonomous, and signifiers move independently from the world of material objects. As Karl Marx analysed in the first section of *Das Kapital*, the commodity is at the heart of capitalism's capacity to operate in abstract terms. Marx shows how, in order to be circulated, commodities have to be considered in terms of their exchange value. This is a form of 'semiotization' in that the commodity's physical and material character ceases to be of account in relation to its capacity to circulate, as a sign, within a capitalist society.[5] As long as a commodity is circulating thus it can be considered in terms of its comparative value against other commodities. Labour too is considered a commodity in that it too is exchanged for money.

Turing's imaginary device not only invokes the typewriter, one of the paradigmatic information technologies of nineteenth-century capitalism, but also, in the tape and writing head assemblage, the very model of the assembly line. Moreover, the algorithmic method which his machine was intended to automate is itself a model of the division of labour, which, as both Adam Smith and, later, Marx realized, lies at the heart of efficient capitalist production. Smith begins *The Wealth of Nations* with his famous description of the manufacture of pins, an operation divided, according to Smith, into eighteen different parts, each of which can be undertaken by a separate labourer.[6] In this manner a far greater number of pins can be produced per person than if one worker undertook the whole process of manufacture for each pin. The division of labour also allows each individual action to become a repeatable and interchangeable sign. Codified in this manner, the operations of production can be more easily understood and controlled. This can

2 A Jacquard silk-weaving hand-loom, the first machine to use punched-card programming, 1810.

help reduce reliance on expensive skilled labour, and living labour altogether.

This can be seen in one of the first (and most celebrated) examples of automation, in which the division of labour was embodied in a machine (illus. 2). Joseph-Marie Jacquard's pattern-weaving loom of 1804 controlled the lifting of each of the warp threads for each pass of the shuttle through a system of wooden cards punched with holes. The actions of the human weaver were codified and converted into marks on the wooden card, which were then 'read' by the machine in order to repeat them. The Jacquard Loom can be understood as an early attempt to reduce the costs and difficulties of employing living labour, by embodying the labour process in fixed capital. Though embedded in an artisanal paradigm, it anticipates not only automation but the whole development of labour management in which workers' actions become discrete and interchangeable, and in which individual skill ceases to be of account.

One of the first theoreticians of labour management was the mathematician Charles Babbage (illus. 3). In a number of works,

3 The computer pioneer Charles Babbage (1791–1871) in 1860.

studying the postal system, the railways, and especially in his *On the Economy of Machinery and Manufactures*,[7] Babbage examined ways of making manufacturing efficient, economic and rational. Following the work of Smith he promulgated the economic advantages of the division of labour, as well as the increased use of machinery in manufacturing. This directly inspired the work for which he is now most famous, his development of early computing machines. From 1822 right up to his death in 1871 Babbage was engaged in building, or trying to build, machines, the 'Difference' and 'Analytical' engines (illus. 4), that are recognizably prototypical computers. His initial reasons for building the 'Difference Engine' concerned the efficient production of mathematical tables, used both at sea and in industrial production. Babbage had come across the table-making project of Baron Gaspard de Prony in France, which had employed the division of labour advocated by Smith in *The Wealth of Nations*. Prony had divided the work of generating such tables into a number of small simple tasks distributed among many human 'computers'. Babbage realized that this technique could be automated and persuaded the government to fund the Difference

Engine, which was comparatively simple, being intended only to calculate and print out such tables. The second, the 'Analytical Engine', had it been completed, would have been programmable, and able to calculate any formula, and to compare numbers and decide how to proceed with the operation it was performing. The engines were modelled on industrial machinery and built using the same techniques. But they also invoked the newly emerging digital technologies of control. Babbage intended employing the punched cards used by Jacquard in his loom as a method of programming his Analytical Engine. What Babbage hoped to achieve for his Analytical Engine is less extraordinary than some of the ideas of his colleague Ada Lovelace (illus. 5). She remarked that the Analytical Engine 'can arrange and combine its numerical quantities exactly as if they were *letters* or other *general* symbols'. She also suggested that the engine might compose elaborate and scientific pieces of music of 'any degree of complexity or extent'. Remarking on the use of punched cards as used in the Jacquard Loom she wrote 'We may say most aptly that the Analytical Engine weaves algebraical patterns just as the Jacquard-loom weaves flowers and leaves'.[8] Though Babbage did not think of employing his engines in pursuit of efficient manufacturing, he embodied a link between calculating machinery and rational industrial management that has never since been broken. Both his calculating machines and his management theories were responses to burgeoning capitalism, which was producing the need for ways of dealing with ever-greater amounts of information, and for more efficient and rational ways of producing profits. These twin needs, information processing and rationalization, have permanently linked the development of calculating machinery with the development of modern capitalism, in all its protean forms. Indeed one might argue that, though manufacturing processes did not generally use machinery for control purposes until the twentieth century, processes of mass production and the division of labour clearly evolved within a paradigm of machine logic, one later developed by Frederick Taylor and Henry Ford.

At a deeper level Babbage's dream of a machine capable of responding without prompting from outside resembles the very basis of the market. As formulated by Adam Smith in *The Wealth of Nations*, this became the canonical expression of the ideology of classical capitalism. Central to Smith's argument was the notion

5 Babbage's protégée and programming pioneer Ada Lovelace (1816–52), c. 1844.

of the market as a self-regulating system. *The Wealth of Nations* can be, and has been, read as the description of a vast self-regulating machine, that of a free market, which with the minimum of state interference, relies on the famous 'invisible hand',[9] which would lead to commodities finding their appropriate value. The computer-like nature of free-market capitalism led the historian Fernand Braudel to suggest that the 'market', the system by which goods are exchanged for money, was 'the first computer mankind ever had, a self-regulating machine that would itself ensure the equilibrium of economic activities'.[10] Such ideas were already being embodied in machines at more or less the same time as Smith was writing *The Wealth of Nations*. His contemporary James Watt developed a number of modifications to contemporary steam technology that enabled more work to be done with the consumption of less fuel. Among these was the 'Governor', a device based on a mechanism seen on a mill by Watt's partner Matthew Boulton. The Governor is a device that steam pressure causes to rotate centrifugally. If it rotates fast enough it is designed to rise. In doing so it will release the pressure causing to rotate. Thus it governs the pressure generated by the steam engine. The Governor is the first practical self-regulating technology, and acted as a paradigm for later conceptions of self-regulation such as those of Norbert Wiener, the developer of the concept of Cybernetics. The publication of *The Wealth of Nations* and James Watt's production of his first large machines coincide almost exactly, though this can only be considered as, in the words of Otto Mayr, 'evidence of the interdependence of the socio-intellectual with the technical activities of a culture', rather than evidence of any determinate influence in either direction.[11]

Steam power also inspired the development of thermodynamics, one of the paradigmatic scientific discourses of the nineteenth century. Thermodynamics dominated not just science and technology, but even conceptions of labour and political economy. It also made its mark in theology, philosophy, and popular culture. But latent within it the beginnings of another paradigm can be discerned, that of information, which would come to take a similarly dominant role in the twentieth century. The first law of thermodynamics was codified by the German scientist Hermann von Helmholtz, then 26 years old, in a famous lecture given at the Berlin Physical Society in 1847. Helmholtz constructed a full mathematical formulation of the concept, which could be applied to mechanics, heat, electricity, magnetism, physical chemistry and astronomy. In essence Helmholtz stated that energy can be neither created or destroyed, and that there was a fixed amount of energy in the universe. This formulation was crucial not just in the development of thermodynamics, but in the move from a general conception of the universe in mechanistic terms inherited from Newton, to one in which energy is the dominant aspect. Rudolf Clausius and William Thomson (later Lord Kelvin of Largs) independently developed the second law of thermodynamics. Clausius's version of the second law states that energy may not lose quantity but it does tend to lose quality. Clausius realized that, without outside aid, heat could only move from a hot reservoir to a cold one and not vice versa. Clausius coined the term 'entropy', from the Greek for transformation, to describe what he saw as the universal tendency towards equilibrium, or in other words towards a situation in which energy is distributed equally in a system. In a lecture of 1894 the German physicist Ludwig Boltzmann, inventor of statistical mechanics, compared entropy to 'missing information'. In this passing statement he prefigured the relation between entropy and information that would comprise a vital aspect of how information came to be understood. In the next century this insight would become the basis of Information Theory and be of crucial importance to the development of telecommunications, computers, genetics, and Cybernetics.[12]

Capitalism can operate as a self-regulating system because of the emergence of the 'money commodity'. The latter serves as a form against which all other commodities can be valued and which allows for universal exchangeability and thereby abstraction. By the late-eighteenth and early-nineteenth century much of the money in circulation was in paper form, as cheques or banknotes, known as 'fiduciary' money. From this it was a short step to 'fiat' paper money, notes that are issued on the fiat of the sovereign, and are legal tender representing so many units of a currency, but are not promises to pay something else, such as a precious metal. Though nominally connected to the value of a material substance, gold or silver, fiduciary paper money started the process completed by fiat money, of turning money into a pure sign. The concept of paper money led to extended debates in the nineteenth century that concerned not just questions of finance, but wider issues relating to the nature of signs in general. The idea that a sign could stand for and act in place of what it is supposed to represent was a cause of anxiety. An American cartoon of the 1870s showed a rag doll next to a notice declaring that it is 'a real baby by Act of Congress', being offered a piece of paper upon which is written 'This is milk by Act of Congress', while on the wall there are a number of pictures, including one of a house inscribed with 'this is a house and lot by act of the architect', one of a cow, similarly declaring 'this is a cow by act of the artist'. Beneath is a banknote saying 'this is money by Act of Congress'. Here it is possible to see prefigurings of both our current concern with virtuality and simulacra and of the anxieties such concepts generate. The transformation of money into sign enabled capitalism's development and expansion, by greatly facilitating the operations of credit and the transfer of capital. Only recently with the increasing use of e-money and the concomitant rise of e-commerce has the dematerialization of money been fully realized, but, as the above suggests, it is immanent within, and necessary for, capitalism's operation.

Such abstraction resonated with developments in areas such as mathematics and logic. The work of self-taught mathematician George Boole in formulating symbolic logic would become a crucial element in the future development of information technologies.

Boole made a number of brilliant contributions to mathematics, but his most famous was to be found in his books *The Mathematical Analysis of Logic*[13] and *An Investigation of the Laws of Thought*.[14] In these works he successfully applied algebraic methods to logic, thus allowing logical relations to be calculated in a mathematical manner. One of Boole's insights was that his algebraic logic worked using only two numerical values, 1 and 0, which could stand respectively for the universe and nothing. Within Boole's system it is possible to deduce any result from these terms, the variables $x$, $y$, $z$ etc. and the standard operators, $+$, $-$, $\times$. Boole's symbolic logic was highly influential on later generations of logicians and mathematicians, and indirectly contributed to the conception of the modern digital computer. More directly, Boole's logic also contributed to the development of binary switching systems for telephone switchboards before the Second World War and, after, to the building of logical circuits. Much of the work examining the applications of Boolean logic to telephone switching relays was undertaken by MIT student Claude Shannon, who was also largely responsible for the post-war development of Information Theory.

Boole's work in Symbolic Logic was, in fact, anticipated by the seventeenth century philosopher Gottfried Leibniz, who was one of the most important and influential thinkers of his period, and whose interests ranged across science, mathematics, politics and metaphysics. Starting with his *Dissertatio de arte combinatoria* of 1666,[15] he was concerned with the dream of a perfect, logical language. To this end Leibniz worked on a number of schemes involving the use of numbers to represent concepts, which could then be manipulated to determine whether statements were true or false. This was paralleled by his interest in calculating machines, which he built, and which he saw as being able to undertake some of these logical processes of induction, as well as his development of binary notation. His ambitious programme for logic proved to be unrealizable in both practical and philosophical terms. It also marked a return to formalism that was problematic to other philosophers of the time, reacting as they were to the formal logic of Aristotelianism. Though after his death his work in logic and language was largely neglected in favour of other aspects of his work, he is now seen as having anticipated many of the developments surrounding computing. His intention to formalize thought in a logical system clearly anticipates both the development of programming languages and of Artificial Intelligence. This, along with his interest in calculating machines, has led to his being regarded as a kind of grandfather of the computer age. His interest in the formal structure of thought can also be seen as anticipating contemporary projects such as Structuralism that themselves are concerned with structure. Though Leibniz's ideas clearly prefigured many current developments, he did not, in fact, make any direct contribution to the history of the computer. Apart from other factors, his considerations on logic and language were mostly in private papers, which were not widely known to the late nineteenth century, by which time many of the ideas he discussed had been developed further independently.

## ABSTRACTION, COMMUNICATION AND REPRESENTATION

The necessity of enabling the circulation of signs of various sorts led to the development of increasingly sophisticated information and communication technologies. Some of these developed out of the demands of contemporary warfare. In the late eighteenth century, field armies had grown larger, weapons had become more elaborate and administrative needs increased accordingly. 'Napoleonic warfare required an apparatus of command, control and communications more advanced than anything previously attempted.'[16] One result was the development of more complex and flexible systems of communication than had previously been possible or necessary, leading, eventually, to the first electric digital technology. The electric telegraph (illus. 6) was developed more or less simultaneously in

6 'The Telegraph' song-sheet cover. Written and performed by George Leybourne (1842–84, also known as 'Champagne Charlie') in the 1860s.

the 1820s and '30s, by the British scientists Sir Charles Wheatstone and Sir William Fothergill Cooke, and the American painter, Samuel Morse. Morse developed an intricate code involving sending short signals for numbers, which could then be looked up in a codebook. Morse's colleague Alfred Vail developed a far more practical system involving sending combinations of short and long signals to represent letters of the alphabet. This was named (rather unfairly) Morse Code. The electric telegraph and Morse Code were first widely adopted as a solution for the 'crisis of control' in what was then possibly the most complex system ever built, the railways. Both in Britain and the United States the early railways were troubled by large numbers of accidents as well as problems with efficiency, mostly owing to the difficulty of coordinating different trains on the same line. The telegraph offered a means of coordinating and organizing the railways, thus initiating one aspect of what James Beniger calls the 'control revolution',[17] which for Beniger represents the nineteenth-century beginnings of the 'Information Society', commonly supposed to be a more recent phenomenon.

The combination of railway and telegraph was also an important component of the beginnings of modern commodity capitalism. Increased communications both encouraged the growth of markets, and changed the nature of those markets. In the United States in particular, the telegraph, along with the railroad, enabled a radical shift from local markets' conditions of supply and demand to national markets', in which the price of goods responded to national conditions. As James Cary points out, the telegraph evened out markets in space, and placed everyone in the same place for purposes of trade, thus making geography irrelevant.[18] In effect the telegraph was responsible for the development of widespread futures trading, trading in time, rather than arbitrage or geographical price differences. But in order for such a condition to be realized other conditions needed to change. According to Cary 'the development of futures trading depended on the ability to trade or circulate negotiable instruments independently of the actual physical movement of goods.'[19] What was traded was information rather than actual products. To begin with this meant the warehouse receipts from grain elevators along the railroad line, which were traded instead of the grain itself. In order to facilitate this kind of trade, products had to be standardized and homogenized so that they could be bought and sold without inspection. Cary continues to suggest that this process of divorcing the receipt from the product can be thought of as 'part of a general process initiated by the use of money . . . the progressive divorce of the signifier from the signified, a process in which the world of signifiers progressively overwhelms and moves independently of real material objects'.[20]

Other methods of allowing signs to circulate were developed at the same time, including photography. Jonathan Crary points out that the photograph was the most significant, in terms of cultural and social impact, of the 'new field of serially produced objects' that characterized modernity.[21] As he puts it: 'The photograph becomes a central element not only in a new commodity economy but in the reshaping of an entire territory in which signs and images, each effectively severed from a referent, circulate and proliferate.'[22] Crary explicitly compares the photograph to money, both being homologous forms of social power in the nineteenth century, and 'totalising systems for binding and unifying all subjects within a single global network of valuation and desire'.[23] (The capacity to produce a number of images from the same negative made the photograph more mobile, but only in a limited sense. Other technological solutions were needed to allow photographs to be reproduced in large quantities, and thus to circulate widely and freely. Attempts to transmit pictures by telegraph were made as early as 1843, but were not of high enough quality to succeed commercially. In the last quarter of the nineteenth century a number of methods for cheaply producing printing blocks from photographs were developed, which were rapidly and enthusiastically adopted by newspapers. The most famous and successful of these techniques was halftone, developed by Frederick Ives of Philadelphia in 1883 and refined by Max and Louis Levy a decade later.)

According to Crary the development of photography is enabled by a rupture in understanding concerning the physiology of vision, in which the corporeality of the observer becomes of account in the act of seeing. This also laid the ground for research into the 'persistence of vision'. This derives from work done in the early nineteenth century into after-images, which showed that images persisted in the optic nerves after what was being looked at was no longer visible. One result of this research was a proliferation of optical devices, which exploited persistence of vision to create the illusion of movement. These included the kaleidoscope, the phenakistiscope, the zoetrope (illus. 7) and the thaumatrope. These devices are digital in that they divide the continuous motion involved in an action into discrete elements. They clearly anticipate and prepare the ground for the cinema, which relies exactly on the persistence of vision they exploit, but also the coming of digital media, which would employ similar techniques involving discrete elements.

The invention of the telegraph and photography, along with the accompanying sense of the general dematerialization of signs, led to anxiety about the relation between language and meaning. The early nineteenth century saw a plethora of books and magazine articles about ciphers, secret writing, and cryptography, a phenomenon Shawn James Rosenheim has identified as the beginnings of what he calls 'the cryptographic imagination', which, for him, underpins literary modernity. Perhaps the most visible cultural manifestation of interest in the cryptological is the development of the detective story.[24] This genre, which first emerged in the early nineteenth century, concerns the decoding of cryptic signs, usually by a gifted individual. Exemplary of the genre are the Sherlock Holmes stories by Conan Doyle and the works of Edgar Allan Poe. Poe's fiction in

7 Zoetrope, c. 1860 – one of the earliest digital visual technologies.

particular evidences a fascination with a world full of signs that can be decoded and an anxiety, or even despair, about the ability to uncover the true nature of things.

The later nineteenth century saw the development of new digital office technologies, intended to manage the increasing, and increasingly complex, amount of information with which business was confronted as a result of its massive expansion under the aegis of monopoly capitalism. These included machines for calculation, sign production and tabulation, such as cash registers, calculating machines, filing systems, tabulating machines and typewriters. Each of these devices answered the need of an increasingly complex capitalist system to produce, circulate and control signs and to render other phenomena into signs, for those purposes. Calculators, such as the Comptometer developed by Felt and Tarrant (illus. 8), the Adder-Lister from Burroughs Adding Machine Company, and cash registers, such as those developed by National Cash Register, helped businesses and shops manage their affairs in ever faster and more intricate markets. Many of the companies responsible for manufacturing and marketing these devices were later involved in the burgeoning computer industry that emerged after the Second World War. Most famous was C-T-R or the Computing-Tabulating-Recording Company, which Thomas Watson Sr joined after he was fired from his position as general manager at National Cash Register, and which was renamed in 1924 by Watson, International Business Machines, or as it is still known today, IBM.

The tabulating machine (illus. 9) was developed in response to one of the main issues of industrialization. One of the results of the Industrial Revolution was a great movement of population from agrarian communities to urban centres. This had the effect of producing both a new kind of individual and a new mass society.

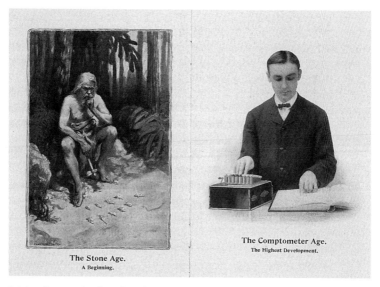

The Comptometer Age.
The Highest Development.

The Stone Age.
A Beginning.

8 Advertisement for the Felt and Tarrant Comptometer, c. 1915.

The new free-floating individuals were no longer subject to the old forms of power, and new decentralized techniques of control and discipline were needed. Michel Foucault writes of the power of examination and documentation as an essential part of the mechanisms of discipline.[25] Subjects began to be defined by a 'whole series of codes of disciplinary individuality that made it possible to transcribe by means of homogenization the individual features by the examination'.[26] This process, which enables 'the formalization of the individual within power relations', makes it possible to 'classify, form categories, to determine averages, to fix norms'.[27] It also allows the circulation, comparison and transmission of such data, within institutions and disciplines. This had two effects, the constitution of the individual as a describable, analysable object and his or her placing within a comparative system.

Through such means people became, for the purpose of social control, discrete signs, both individual and homogenous, about whom information could be transmitted, circulated, manipulated

9 The Hollerith tabulating machine, 1890s.

and compared. Perhaps the largest scale example of such endeavours is the Census, the ten-yearly enumeration of a country's population. The first censuses took place in the United States in 1790 and in Britain in 1801. By 1880, in America at least, the problem of gathering and collating the large amount of information required was proving insurmountable, at least by the means then available. These were the conditions that provoked the development of the tabulating machine, one of the major technical developments on the way to the modern electronic computer. A young engineer, Herman Hollerith, designed a system using punched cards similar to the sort used by the Jacquard Loom and proposed by Charles Babbage for his Analytical Engine. Each person was represented by a card. Facts about them were noted by holes punched in the card. The power of Hollerith's system was that the information could be tabulated and sorted and counted mechanically. Complex concatenated sorts could be undertaken, cross-tabulating different data. Hollerith's tabulating machine is an exemplary product of the disciplinary,

10 Vannevar Bush and the Differential Analyser (a powerful analogue calculator), 1920s.

panoptic society described by Foucault. Within his system people are made visible as pieces of digital data. They are individuals, but their individuality is rationalized and normalized in a system of signs that also homogenizes them as a mass, and makes them interchangeable and manipulable as data. Widely adopted by insurance companies and railways, Hollerith's machine is the first direct ancestor of the modern computer. The tabulating machine industry became one of the bases of the future computing industry via companies such as IBM, and it was also one of the technologies exploited in the 1920s and '30s during research into the possibilities of calculating machines for scientific research. Hollerith's invention also helped found a connection that continues unabated to this day, between digital technology and methods of surveillance, control and discipline.

Hollerith's invention enabled the management of large amounts of data with an unprecedented degree of efficiency. It made possible great advances in the development of sophisticated calculating machines, such as Vannevar Bush's Differential Analyser (illus. 10), designed at the Massachusetts Institute of Technology in 1930, of which Alan Turing was aware. In the following decade the very first digital electronic calculating machines, as well as Turing's conceptualization of the universal machine, described above, were

developed. In Germany Konrad Zuse (illus. 11) built a digital calculating machine called the Z1 in 1938, while in 1939 in the United States
John V. Atanasoff and his student Claude Berry built the ABC or
Atanasoff-Berry Computer, also electronic and digital. In 1939, building on his experience in using IBM accounting machines, Howard
Aiken, with the collaboration of IBM, started to develop a calculating machine, the Harvard-IBM Automatic Sequence Controlled
Calculator, also known as the Harvard Mark I, which was to be
followed by three more machines, the Marks II, III and IV. In the
same year George Stibitz built his Complex Number Calculator,
which used Boolean logic to calculate. None of these machines were
computers in the modern sense, in that they lacked the capacity to
store data, or in some cases were hard-wired to perform one task.
But all were close to the modern conception of the computer.

It was in this period that Turing published his *Entscheidungsproblem* paper, which anticipated the future development of digital
technology. At the same time two other essays were published that
were unwittingly prescient about the future of digital technology
and culture. One was by the German Marxist philosopher and critic
Walter Benjamin, called 'The Work of Art in the Age of Mechanical
Reproduction',[28] and the other was an entry for the *Encyclopédie
française* written by English novelist Herbert George (H. G.) Wells,
entitled 'The Idea of a Permanent World Encyclopedia'.[29] In his essay

11 Konrad Zuse and
colleague at work
on one of the first
digital computers in
his parents' front
room, late 1930s.

Wells proposed what he called a Permanent World Encyclopaedia, involving the 'collection, indexing, summarising and release of knowledge'[30] by a 'centralised world organ' working on a 'planetary scale' to pull the mind of the world together'.[31] Wells saw the technical means to realize this idea in the newly developing field of micro-photography. For him the capacity for endless reproduction and wide circulation afforded by photography was a 'way to world peace that can be followed without any very grave risk of collision with the warring political forces and the vested interests of today'.[32] Thus for Wells the technologies of reproduction offered the possibility of going beyond the antagonisms of contemporary politics and towards a global community united under a 'common ideology'. By contrast Benjamin saw mechanical reproduction as a means of resistance, rather than unification. In his essay he suggested that the mechanical reproduction of works of art detaches them from the domain of tradition and enables them to be reactivated for different purposes.[33] For Benjamin this meant art could stop being based in ritual and tradition and instead be based in politics, thus, in particular, enabling a deritualized art to combat the fascist aestheticization of politics through the politicization of aesthetics.[34] (Benjamin's more antagonistic vision of technology's potential political role reflected his status as a German Jew, for whom the threat of Fascism and Nazism was real and immediate. Three years later, at the age of 48, he died at the Franco-Spanish border, while fleeing Nazi-occupied France.)

## THE CONSEQUENCES OF THE SECOND WORLD WAR

Though it is likely that a universal digital computing machine would have emerged in time, circumstances forced its development more rapidly than might have been the case. By the 1930s war was clearly imminent. Its nature was clearly going to be dictated, in part at least, by recent technological advances in ballistics, telecommunications and weapons of mass destruction. Radio, for example, with its ability to transmit messages through the air without the aid of wires, had been invented in the 1870s by Marconi. This presented an unprecedented set of challenges. In conjunction with the greater mobility made possible by the development of the internal combustion engine, it transformed warfare. Commanders and troops could signal to each other without the necessity of laying physical lines of communication. In theory at least this greatly increased the flexibility and capacity of movement of armies. But this freedom came at a price: the enemy could easily intercept any signal broadcast by radio. In the beginning of this century European governments began to see both the possibilities and dangers of radio communication and prepare appropriate ways of tackling them. Attention began to be paid to cryptography and cryptoanalysis, the sciences of encoding and decoding messages (illus. 12). Among those involved in this work was Alan Turing. It was Turing's mathematical expertise, rather

12 A three-ring Enigma cypher machine in its wooden transit case, 1930s. It was used by the Germans during WWII to encode and decode secret transmissions to U-boats.

than his ability to imagine machines, that brought him to Bletchley Park, the British Government's top secret centre for analysing encoded signals intercepted from the enemy. There his interest in both the abstract world of mathematics and the practical one of mechanical and electrical engineering served him well. Through the commitment and intelligence of Turing and others the German codes used in radio transmissions were broken (illus. 13).[35] The extraordinary demands of complex cryptoanalysis led to radical and innovative solutions involving mechanized calculating devices, capable of running through possible solutions with unprecedented speed (illus. 14). A number of such devices were built during the War, and by the end engineers had started to explore the possibilities of electronics. The problem with these machines was not in the electronics, but in the mechanical components, the relays and those used to ingest the paper tape that contained the data, so that it might be read. The solution was to store data internally, in electronic form. Such work led eventually to the machine that might be considered to be the first proper digital computer, the Manchester Mk 1 (illus. 15). It was built and designed by researchers working at the Royal Society Computer Laboratory, then housed at Manchester University. It exploited a method of storing data using cathode ray tubes, designed by F. C. Williams and T. Kilburn at Manchester

13 The 'Bombe' code-breaking machine at Bletchley Park, 1943.

14 Wrens operating the 'Colossus' computer at the British code-breaking centre at Bletchley Park, 1943.

University. The Manchester machine, which was in service in 1948, has a strong claim to be the first electronic digital computer in the modern sense because of its capacity to store data. Soon afterwards the electronics firm Ferranti (illus. 16) collaborated with Manchester University to produce a properly engineered version of the machine, which became the basis of one of the first commercial computers.

In fact the British developments described above, though possibly leading to the first actual modern computer, were less historically important than similar developments in the United States. This is partly because much of the British work was not known about until later, owing to security considerations, and partly because, after the War, the US was far more prepared to invest in research into computing machinery. Nevertheless, through links within the small community of those interested in such developments on both sides of the Atlantic, the work of Turing and others in Britain became known and appreciated. The importance of this work is in its conception of digital technology being concerned not so much

15 The Manchester Mk 1, June 1949, the first fully electronic stored-program computer in operation, built by Professor Max Newman at Manchester University.

simply with calculation but rather with the manipulation of symbols. In this it anticipated much of how computing would later develop, which would not necessarily have been obvious at the time.

In the United States the impetus to develop digital calculating machines derived from a different set of requirements. The need to generate the unprecedented numbers of ballistic tables, describing the angles at which artillery needed to be fired in different conditions, gave new impetus to pre-war computer projects, and in doing so led to the construction of one of the first modern computers. Before the War such tables were generated by hand. Almost immediately it was finished in 1944, the Harvard Mark I was enlisted for the war effort to calculate ballistic tables. Similar uses were made of Bush's Differential Analyser, and Stibitz's Complex Number Calculator technology, by then incorporated in a series of machines built at Bell Labs, known as the Bell Relay Machines. Later in the War similar machines were used in the Manhattan Project for the unprecedentedly complex calculations involved in the building of the atomic bomb. The twin demands of ballistic tables in the War and the Manhattan Project for building the Atom Bomb led to the building of another candidate for the title of the first modern computer. By 1943 it became evident that the production of ballistic tables had fallen so far behind that new and faster means of production were needed. The Moore School of Electrical Engineering at the University of Pennsylvania was approached, since it was known that several of its staff, including engineers Presper Eckert and John Mauchly, were interested in electronic calculating machines. The Moore School presented an idea for constructing called the Electronic Numerical Integrator and Computer or ENIAC. The 'and Computer' in the name represented Mauchly's belief that the machine should be capable of more general tasks than simply undertaking numerical integration, which is what interested the military authorities.[36]

The construction of ENIAC was further encouraged by the involvement and interest of the Hungarian emigré mathematician John von Neumann, who was involved in the Manhattan Project, and who saw that digital computing might be the solution to the mathematical complexities of A-Bomb design. ENIAC was actually completed in 1945, too late to take any active part in the War. It was vast, expensive and, in comparison to electromagnetic machines, very fast. It was not quite a computer in the modern understanding, since it lacked any data storage. But it was an electronic, digital calculating machine, and as such is an important object in the history of modern computing. One of its most valuable contributions was to demonstrate the far greater speeds achievable with

16 Alan Turing and colleagues working on the Ferranti Mark 1 computer, 1951.

electronic digital means as against those possible with comparable analogue electromechanical technology. Furthermore Mauchly's insistence that it should be a machine capable of more general tasks than those needed for ballistics invoked the idea of the computer as a universal machine, which, despite being implicit in Turing's influential pre-war paper, was not widely appreciated. The ENIAC led to the EDVAC, the 'Electronic Discrete Variable Computer', which was able to store data, and which also inspired a document entitled 'First Draft of a Report on the EDVAC'. In this paper the now standard logical structure of modern computers was first articulated, comprising of a memory unit, storing both data and instructions, an arithmetic unit, input and output units and a control unit. It was the capacity to store data electronically that demonstrated that such devices could be universal machines, which could be programmed to perform different operations. This configuration became known as the 'Von Neumann architecture', after John von Neumann, whose name graced the report as its main author.

The simultaneous development of the Manchester Mk 1 and the ENIAC marks the beginning of the digital age, in that they are the first computers in the modern sense: digital, binary machines capable of storing data and of being reconfigured to undertake different tasks. The proximate cause of their emergence was the War with its unprecedented demands for complex calculation at very great speed. But, as this chapter has shown, they are also the embodiment of capitalist modernity, with its emphasis on abstraction, exchangeability and self-regulation. Turing's conceptual machine, capable of being reconfigured in an infinite number of different states, is the perfect, idealized model of capitalism as a universal machine, in which different phenomena, labour and commodities are homogenized in order to be exchanged, manipulated and distributed.

# 2. The Cybernetic Era

CYBERNETIC DISCOURSES

The Second World War was the catalyst not just for the invention of the modern binary digital electronic computer, but also for the development of a number of remarkable and influential discourses, including Cybernetics, Information Theory, General Systems Theory, Molecular Biology, Artificial Intelligence, and Structuralism. Though emerging out of different contexts these discourses are all concerned with developing abstract and formalized systems, in order to understand the phenomena with which they are concerned. In their different fields and contexts each of these systems was highly influential. Indeed to a large extent they represent, collectively, the paradigm of post-war technological and scientific thinking. Though neither determining nor determined by the invention of the computer, they were part of the same intellectual environment. Furthermore the computer offered both a powerful tool with which to pursue research into these areas as well as a source of metaphors through which to envision such ideas. They in turn dictated much of the way in which computing was understood. They are as important in the development of digital culture as the computer itself. Though many of the ideas are now deemed old-fashioned or problematic, their influence is still strongly in evidence in contemporary culture. This can be seen in current terminology and language, with terms such as the 'Information Society' and 'Information Technology' or the use of 'cyber' as a modish prefix, as in 'Cyberculture' or 'Cyber-feminism'. Such usage demonstrates how deeply the ideas of the post-war cybernetic era are embedded in our current digital culture.

Information Theory was developed by Claude Shannon, an electrical engineer trained at the University of Michigan and the Massachusetts Institute of Technology. Before the War he had worked with Vannevar Bush on the Differential Analyser. A summer internship at AT & T's Bell Laboratories helped formulate the ideas behind his thesis for his master's degree in electrical engineering, 'A Symbolic Analysis of Relay and Switching', which looked at the application of boolean logic using telephone relays. This generated far more interest than his thesis for his PhD in mathematics and, in light of the development of digital technology, has been described as one of the most significant master's theses of the twentieth century. His interest in communications continued in the War with work in cryptography, and on developing ways of scrambling audio signals with Project X at the Bell Labs, as well as his research into anti-aircraft missile control systems. These experiences led him to write a memorandum at Bell, entitled 'Communication Theory of Secrecy Systems', which outlined a mathematical analysis of communications systems. These ideas were expanded and made public in 1949 when Shannon published his book, written in collaboration with mathematician Warren Weaver, entitled *A Mathematical Theory of Communication*,[1] which built on the work of other researchers at Bell Labs, including Harry Nyquist and R.V.L. Hartley. In this canonical work Shannon developed a linear schema of the communication process consisting of the following elements: the source of a message; the device that encodes the message for transmission; the channel along which the message is sent; the device that decodes the message; and the message's destination. In the case of a telephone call these elements would be represented by the person speaking into the phone; the telephone itself; the cable that transmits the message; the telephone at the other end; and the person listening.

One of Shannon's key steps was to separate the technical problems of delivering a message from any consideration of its semantic content. This enabled engineers to concentrate on the message delivery system itself. Shannon's concerns were how to find the most efficient way of encoding what he called information in a particular coding system in a noiseless environment and how to deal with the problem of noise when it occurred. 'Noise' was Shannon's term for the elements of a signal that are extraneous to the message being transmitted. He adopted the term 'entropy' from thermodynamics to refer to the measure of a communication system's efficiency in transmitting a signal, which was computed on the basis of the statistical properties of the message source. Through these means Shannon developed a successful general theory for mathematically calculating the efficiency of a communications system that was applicable to both analogue and digital systems.

After the War Shannon's theory was of great use in the burgeoning development of binary digital computers, in the expansion and technological advance of telecommunications, telegraphy, radio, and television, as well as in servo-mechanical devices using feedback signals, and in computers, for which his emphasis on binary logic made the application of his ideas particularly appropriate. The concept of redundancy was of great help in building efficient communications systems intended to operate in 'noisy' conditions, using 'redundant check bits', elements of data designed to enable double-checking of message transmission. For engineers he presented an abstract model for the successful technical transmission and reception of information. Shannon was reluctant to use the word information in his paper, knowing that it would cause confusion about the purely technical nature and potential applications of his ideas. His reluctance was justified as Information Theory began to be applied in areas outside electrical engineering, including cognition, biology, linguistics, psychology, economics and physics.

These different disciplines sought to apply Shannon's model of communication, with its concepts of entropy, redundancy and noise to their own, less technical fields. Shannon himself did not care for these kinds of applications, and wrote papers explaining the technical nature of his ideas. Nevertheless it is from Shannon's concept of information that we owe the idea of information technology and by extension the information society it helped to bring about.

No such scruples were entertained by Norbert Wiener, one of the principle developers of Cybernetics, which he intended to be understood as a general theory of, as the subtitle of his book on the subject has it, 'control and communication in the animal and machine' with particular concern for issues of feedback and self-regulation. Cybernetics incorporated a great deal of thinking about information, in much the same terms as those Shannon had proposed, as well as elements from a number of other disciplines and areas of interest. During the War Wiener had worked at Bell Laboratories on an electronic gun-sight system, which would compute and predict the path of an enemy plane, thus allowing the gun to be aimed at a probable future location. Wiener's research into concepts of self-regulation as well as other work investigating the random behaviour of particles, called Brownian motion, led him to propose a statistical solution to predicting the plane's path. Like Shannon he recognized that information was bound up with uncertainty. A message is made up of a series of individual elements that make no sense in themselves. Until a message is completed its meaning is uncertain. Only as the sequence unfolds is its meaning made progressively clearer. At any one point along the sequence there is a range of possibilities for what might come next, ranging from the probable to the improbable (though not the impossible; any message that violates the basis of communication, by for example being nonsense, cannot convey any information). Wiener thus developed a statistical method for estimating the most probable path taken by a plane, though whether his ideas were actually successful in enabling more efficient air defence is difficult to ascertain.

Some of the most important concepts for Cybernetics were developed in the so-called Macy Conferences, which were initiated in 1942 with a seminar called the Cerebral Inhibition Meeting, held at the Institute for Advanced Study at Princeton. Organized by the Josiah Macy Jr Foundation's medical director Frank Fremont-Smith, the seminar brought together mathematicians, physiologists and engineers, to discuss the work that Wiener and others were developing and how it might be applied to different disciplines. Among those participating by invitation were Warren McCulloch, the anthropologists Margaret Mead and Gregory Bateson, psychologist Lawrence K. Frank, and psychoanalyst Lawrence Kubie. One of the immediate results of the seminar was a paper, published in 1943 by Wiener and Arturo Rosenblueth, with the help of Julian Bigelow, entitled 'Behaviour, Purpose, and Teleology',[2] which enframed the ideas of negative feedback and teleological behaviour that had been developed in relation to self-regulating systems. The next year McCulloch, along with the brilliant young mathematician Walter Pitts, was to publish a paper entitled 'Logical Calculus of Ideas Immanent in Nervous Activity',[3] which suggested that the workings of the brain could be modelled in terms of a network of logical operations. This paper was extremely influential both in presenting a model for understanding the operations of the brain, and in modelling the operations of machines in terms of mental processes.

The seminar was successful enough to attract funding for a series of conferences from the Josiah Macy Foundation. These ran from 1946 to 1954 and generated a great deal of interest and excitement. Among those attending the first conference was John von Neumann, who was able to bring to the conferences his experiences with digital technology, while applying the formalist ideas of McCulloch and Pitts to his understanding of such machinery. In 1944 von Neumann, along with Wiener, McCulloch, Pitts and Howard Aiken, designer of the Harvard Mk 1 electromechanical computer, had formed the

Teleological Society, to examine 'communication engineering, the engineering of control devices, the mathematics of time series in statistics, and the communication and control aspects of the nervous system'.[4] From the very beginning the Macy Conferences were concerned as much with machinic as with biological systems. Von Neumann was also able to engage his interest in game theory, which enabled the application of methods of mathematical modelling of various phenomena to society in general. In 1944, von Neumann, in collaboration with his colleague at Princeton, the economist Oscar Morgenstern, published a book *Theory of Games and Economic Behaviour*,[5] which proposed the use of such mathematical models for economic processes. The principles of this idea were easily conflated with those of the other researchers in formalizing different kinds of behaviour.

The most well-known expressions of the ideas discussed in the Macy Conferences were the two books written by Norbert Wiener, which sought to define the new science of self-regulating systems of all sorts. In 1948 he published *Cybernetics or Control and Communication in the Animal World*[6] and in 1950 *The Human Use of Human Beings*.[7] In these books Wiener formulated the idea of information and feedback as the bases of a paradigm for understanding biological, machinic and social processes. Wiener's conception of Cybernetics was highly influential both for scientific and humanistic disciplines. Wiener took the term Cybernetics from the ancient Greek *kybernetikos*, meaning 'good at steering' or 'helmsman'. In this he was, without his knowing, anticipated by the nineteenth century French physicist André-Marie Ampère, who suggested the term for the study of the control of government. Wiener was, however, aware of the use of the cognate term 'Governor' in the same century to describe self-regulating machines, such as that developed by Watt for his steam engines, mentioned in the last chapter.

The near-simultaneous development of Cybernetics and Information Theory also encouraged the emergence of other similar ideas.

Before the War the biologist Ludwig von Bertalanffy found that the conventional closed-model system of science was inadequate to account for an organism's relation with its environment. In response he developed an open-system model that allowed for the flow of inputs and outputs with the environment. From these beginnings von Bertalanffy developed the notion of a General Systems Theory, which conflated physics and thermodynamics. His ideas were further supported by the work in physics by Ilya Prigogine. In 1954 von Bertalanffy, along with the mathematician A. Rapaport, the biologist W. Ross Ashby, the biophysicist N. Rashevsky and the economist Kenneth Boulding, started the Society for General Systems Research, which applied the ideas first formulated by von Bertalanffy in biology in the 1930s and '40s to other areas. The yearbook produced annually by the society from 1954 onwards was an influential document particularly for those wishing to apply cybernetic and systems ideas to industrial manufacturing and social systems.

At the same time as Cybernetics and Information Theory were presenting new ways of thinking about communication and feedback, similar ideas were being applied to areas such as Molecular Biology and research into consciousness and intelligence. In 1942, while in exile in Dublin, the physicist Erwin Schrödinger gave a series of lectures entitled 'What is Life?'[8] In these talks he explored what enables living systems to resist the effects of entropy in their lifetimes and in the persistence of hereditary traits. His solution was that chromosomes contained what he described as the 'code-script', or in other words the information needed to develop the living systems of which they are part. Shrödinger's ideas were influential in a number of areas. For example they informed the post-war work of Claude Shannon in developing Information Theory, described above. But their force was felt most strongly in research into heredity. Though peripheral to the scientific work undertaken since the nineteenth century in the development of genetics as a scientific discipline, the notion that hereditary traits can be described in terms of information was instrumental in enabling James Watson and Francis Crick to unravel the structure of DNA and later helped researchers to understand the information-like nature of its operations. The pervasive influence of the information paradigm on such research has become more evident recently with the widespread use of computers to 'map' the structure of DNA in ventures such as the Human Genome Project.[9]

Computers meanwhile were contributing to the development of new understandings of consciousness and intelligence. Alan Turing's experience with calculating machines during the War led him to some radical conclusions later. In 1948 he composed a report for the British National Physical Laboratory on 'Intelligent Machinery'. In 1950 he published an article in *Mind* entitled 'Computing Machinery and Intelligence'.[10] In it he suggested that in the foreseeable future computers would be recognizably intelligent. He proposed a test, which would ascertain whether a computer had in fact achieved such intelligence. This, the so-called 'Turing Test', involved somebody communicating via a teletype machine with an invisible correspondent, who might be either a human or computer. He or she had, by asking questions, to determine which one he was communicating with. If the computer could fool its correspondent into believing it was human, then it might be considered intelligent. To some extent this resonated with the work of various researchers who had begun to think of modelling the brain's operation in logical and formalistic terms. The work of McCulloch and Pitts in the mid-1940s mentioned above was an early example of this. In the late '40s Donald Hebb, in his book *The Organisation of Behaviour*,[11] proposed that the brain could be thought of in terms of a complex set of associations without centralized control. But the emphasis in attempting to understand such mental processes started to shift from a biological, embedded paradigm to one emphasising the disembodied logical processes of the mind, which resonated with the potential capabilities of the digital technology then being developed.

Turing's idea constitutes the conceptual basis of what later became known as Artificial Intelligence or AI. Some of the first practical AI work came out of research concerning air defence. Between 1950 and 1951 Alan Newell, a mathematician from Princeton, was running a project at the McChord Field Air Defense Direction Center in Tacoma, Washington. It concerned simulating radar patterns in order to develop an understanding of man-machine interface issues. In order to undertake the simulation the project used an IBM card-programmed calculator. The use of a computer-like device to simulate data inspired Newell to think of computers as possibly being machines for the manipulation of symbols. Herbert Simon from the Carnegie Institute of Technology found the McChord Field work interesting for the same reasons. Newell and Simon, along with Rand Programmer J. C. Shaw, collaborated on building a program to prove logical theorems, the Newell-Simon-Shaw Logic Theorist, which was completed in 1952. This was arguably the first AI program, *avant la lettre*, since the term Artificial Intelligence had not then been invented.

The term actually came into existence in 1956. It was then that a mathematician at Dartmouth, John McCarthy, organized a conference, 'The Summer Research Project on Artificial Intelligence'. Now referred to as the 'Dartmouth Conference', this is regarded as the beginnings of AI, as well as the point where it gained the name by which it is now known. Among those participating in the conference were Claude Shannon and Marvin Minsky, the latter now recognized as one of the principle theorists of AI. The conference represented a decisive shift from embodied, cybernetic models of machine thought, to disembodied, logical, formalized systems. It was also notable for the great confidence that the early AI researchers had in its possibilities. Following the conference Newell and Simon predicted that a computer would be world chess champion; that a computer would compose aesthetically valuable music; a computer would discover and prove an important unknown mathematical theorem; and that most psychological theories would take the form of computer programs. The last prediction in particular demonstrates the degree to which AI was beginning to influence and affect the understanding of mental processes.

At the same time, though in a different context, Structuralism, which emerged in France in the 1940s and '50s, presented a powerful framework, developed ultimately out of the work of linguist Ferdinand de Saussure, in which different phenomena could be formalized and presented in abstract terms. Among Saussure's important moves was a turn away from the 'diachronic' study of a language in terms of its historical development, which had characterized linguistics in the nineteenth century, towards the 'synchronic' study of a language at a particular moment in time.[12] Saussure also separated the sign into two components, the signifier, which is acoustic, and the signified, which is conceptual.[13] For Saussure the sign itself is arbitrary,[14] and meaning is found in language in the differences between signs, not in any positive terms.[15] Saussure's ideas came to be considered under the title 'structural linguistics'. Saussure separated the signifier from the signified, and showed how the sound of the signified bears no innate relation to what it signifies, but he did not pursue this idea to more radical conclusions, insisting on the connectedness of the signifier and the signified.[16] Nevertheless he showed that language cannot claim any one-to-one relation to what it represents, and must, instead, be considered a code. Saussure suggested that his principles could be applied to a general theory of signs, which he called 'semiology'.

The beginning of modern Structuralism resulted from the meeting of the French anthropologist Claude Lévi-Strauss and the Russian linguist and literary theorist Roman Jakobson, while both were in exile in New York during the Second World War. Before the War Jakobson and the so-called Prague School had applied Saussure's ideas to literary theory. Lévi-Strauss attended lectures given by Jakobson in 1942 on sound and meaning, and Jakobson in turn attended Lévi-Strauss's talks on kinship. It was with Jakobson's encouragement that Lévi-Strauss started the work that would become *Elementary Structures of Kinship*.[17] What Lévi-Strauss found particularly interesting was Jakobson's use of Saussure's ideas in a different discipline. In the 1920s, along with Nicolai Trubetzskoy, Wilém Mathesius, and others, Jakobson had founded the Linguistic Circle of Prague, dedicated to the study of poetic language using the structuralist paradigm of Saussure. Lévi-Strauss realized that such an approach would be fruitful for anthropology. By studying structure separate from content in the manner of Saussure's linguistics, anthropology could become both scientifically rigorous and avoid the racism prevalent in pre-war anthropology, which was dominated by the natural sciences.

The influence of Lévi-Strauss's rethinking of anthropology was immense. It seemed to offer new frameworks of thinking that avoided, among other things, the compromised phenomenological approach of Jean-Paul Sartre. It was quickly adopted and adapted by those working in other disciplines, in particular psychoanalysis, by Jacques Lacan; cultural and literary analysis, by Roland Barthes; political theory, by Louis Althusser and history, by Michel Foucault (though he always strenuously denied being a Structuralist). Other inflections of Structuralism were developed by the psychologist Jean Piaget, who retained an interest in the development of ideas, and thus rejected the concentration on synchronic structures that characterized the Saussurean model. Structuralism emerged in a very different context to Cybernetics, General Systems Theory, Molecular Biology, Artificial Intelligence and Information Theory. The latter were largely the product of Britain and the United States, and reflected current techno-scientific concerns. Structuralism was both a Continental European development and one that took place largely within the social sciences. Furthermore it inherited much of the anti-humanist approach that animated Marxism and Freudian psychoanalysis, two of its forebears. The other information discourses by contrast were largely embedded in a liberal-humanist enlightenment tradition. Nevertheless there were both similarities and connections between Structuralism and the other discourses. All were concerned with systems or structures of relations and connections that could be examined without reference to the particular embodied circumstances of the phenomena concerned. Thus such study could also be put on a rigorously scientific basis. They also all used mathematics and algebra both as tools and as exemplary paradigms of formal analysis. In particular the Semiotic Structuralism promoted by Algirdas Julien Greimas at the beginning of the 1960s attempted to construct a version of structuralist analysis that could claim the same rigour as mathematics.[18] There was also a certain amount of exchange between Structuralism and the other discourses. Jacques Lacan invoked many of Shannon's insights into the process of communication,[19] and also devoted part of one of his famous seminars to the relationship between psychoanalysis and Cybernetics,[20] while Piaget and Lévi-Strauss both engaged in cybernetic models of the processes they were interested in. There was less traffic the other way, though in the early '50s Roman Jakobson worked in the Research Laboratory of Electronics at MIT alongside many of the main proponents of Cybernetics and Information Theory, as well as the linguists Noam Chomsky and Morris Halle.

## CYBERNETICS, COMPUTING AND THE COLD WAR

The Second World War that had presented the catalyst for both the invention of the modern computer and for the development of the various discourses described above. But the pressures of the post-war era presented the context in which both the technology and the discourses were shaped, sustained and developed. International political tensions presented a set of problems for which computing and cognate ideas such as Cybernetics offered potential solutions. Much as nineteenth- and early-twentieth-century capitalism offered the framework for the invention of the modern computer, the Cold War was largely responsible for how it developed and how it was used. The way in which we use and think about computers, as media and communications devices, rather than simply complex calculators, is a result of these Cold War developments.

At the end of the War, as the most powerful and prosperous of the Allied victors, the United States assumed the leadership of the 'Free World'. The assumption of this hegemonic role was part of a realignment of world power along new divisions with the United States and its allies on one side and the USSR and its Communist allies on the other. Accompanying this realignment was a perception that the USSR represented not just an ideological opposition, which might wish covertly to undermine the United States, but a direct military threat. This perception had started to emerge before the War had ended. By 1947 it had taken hold, and constituted a central element in American foreign policy. This was not entirely without justification, inasmuch as Stalin had shown himself to be both a brutal dictator, and possessed of military ambitions, as his grip on Eastern Europe seemed to demonstrate. But the USSR had suffered particularly in the recently ended War and was probably not, at that time, in a position to threaten the United States. It is true that Stalin made no secret of his intentions to build up Soviet offensive capabilities, though the USSR did not actually explode an atomic bomb until 1949. But, in hindsight, even Soviet military ambitions could be interpreted as defensive in intention, rather than offensive. As a country that had been invaded in both 1914 and 1941, with devastating consequences, the Russians had cause to feel the need for secure defences. That the USSR did turn out to be the threat the United States believed it to be, may be a classic case of a self-fulfilling prophecy. The United States created the idea of the USSR as a threat so effectively that it had to become one.

Whether the American perception of the Soviet threat was actually justified, then or later, is of less consequence than how it affected

US strategy. Since Pearl Harbour the United States had developed a particular sensitivity to the threat of unprovoked attacks for which they might not be prepared. Such a threat was, of course, far more potent in the light of the devastating nature of the new weaponry, both in terms of the distance it could cover and its destructive capabilities. It also precluded any kind of direct confrontation with the USSR, which could all too easily lead to global destruction. The United States also developed a strategy of containment, which meant both containing the 'free world' from the communist threat, and containing the communist powers within their own borders. This strategy, which Paul Edwards describes as a 'closed world discourse',[21] meant placing itself on a permanent war footing, and entailed the maintenance of a large standing army, massive investment in weaponry and the development of weapons research. This in turn had a positive knock-on effect on the economy as the 'military-industrial' complex provided large numbers of civilian jobs, and a great deal of investment.

It was the resulting 'Cold War' and its exigencies that provided much of the support for research into computing and information technologies, as well as ideas such as Cybernetics and other systems theories. Computers were crucial in offering a solution to one of the great paradoxes of the Cold War. In the context of nuclear weapons, actual confrontation was not possible. But its impossibility was underpinned by both sides being willing to think it possible, and prepare for it. The doctrine of 'mutually assured destruction' or MAD as it was appropriately named, proclaimed that, so long as both sides knew the other was ready and able to respond in kind, then it would be suicidal to make any kind of pre-emptive attack. But for this strategy to be effective, each side had to be convinced, and be able to convince the other that they were not just willing, but able to retaliate. The problem was that there was no way to properly test this ability, other than by undertaking the very act that the whole arrangement was supposed to prevent. The computer offered a way out of this paradox by giving military planners the means to make simulations of possible scenarios, which could then stand in for actual situations.

Cybernetics was of great interest to the American military not just in terms of modelling scenarios, but also in looking at ways of automating warfare. In particular they were interested in the integration of humans and machines as a way of making the operations of war more efficient and foolproof. Thus much of the research into the possibilities of cybernetic systems was funded by the military, and was aimed at military applications. Indeed, as Edwards points out, Cybernetics became the model for military command in the Cold War.[22] In such arrangements soldiers are merely necessary, though risky, human elements in larger cybernetic systems. It was this interest in such systems that led the military to be the major customer for computers, as well as the principal architect of their development. This happened directly through military-funded projects such as Whirlwind, the computer technology underpinning the SAGE Early Warning System (illus. 17), developed under the guidance of Jay Forrester, one of the main proponents of cybernetic thinking. This has been described as 'the single most important computer project of the post-war decade',[23] and involved the development of extremely powerful and reliable computers, incorporating many innovative technologies. Though immensely costly and complex to construct, SAGE was fully operational by 1961. From start to finish it had taken sixteen years to develop and had cost over a billion dollars. It had also commanded the active collaboration of many of the major commercial computer companies, including IBM.

As a solution to the problems of air defence SAGE was almost completely useless. By the time it was finished it was obsolete as a technology, having been superseded by technologies such as transistors and integrated circuits. In fact it may have never been effective as an air defence technology, at least as far as automatic response and

17 View of the SAGE Air Surveillance Room – Direction Center, 1960s.

control were concerned. It was an unreliable and flawed system, which did not perform well in tests. Edwards suggests that its military shortcomings were well known to those involved, and it may never have been intended to be of any practical use. He points to the decision to place SAGE control centres above ground, and thus vulnerable to attack, as demonstrative of the US Air Force's secret intention always to be first to use nuclear weapons.[24] But, as a symbolic defence SAGE worked well in creating the impression for the public of a powerful and reliable air defence system.[25] The technological developments it helped engender also contributed to commercial computer systems such as IBM's System/360 (their first attempt to build a complete suite of compatible computer systems), the airline ticket booking system SABRE, and an airforce-funded attempt to automate the complex work of machine tool operators.

These projects aside, Whirlwind and SAGE are important for a number of more abstract reasons. Apart from demonstrating the importance the military attached to computer development, it also represented a decisive shift in military thinking from analogue, electromechanical machines to electronic, digital systems. This in turn encouraged an understanding of the computer as more than

66  Digital Culture

simply the calculating element in control systems. Instead it became understood as a more general symbolic machine, concerned with the interactive manipulation of information. In practical terms the work on Whirlwind and SAGE entailed the development of many technologies that later became standard parts of modern computing. Indeed Whirlwind and SAGE can be said to have determined much of the structure both technically and conceptually of contemporary digital technology. Among specific technologies it made possible or helped develop were magnetic memory, video displays, effective computer languages, graphic display techniques, simulation techniques, analogue-to-digital and digital-to-analogue conversion techniques, multiprocessing, and networking.

In particular the SAGE/Whirlwind project was crucial in the development of 'real-time' computing in which messages could be responded to almost immediately. This was an extraordinary advance compared to the batch-processing model most commonly employed in computing at the time, which still used the punched card technology first developed at the beginning of the nineteenth century. 'Real time' computing was clearly a fundamental requirement for any use of computing in the hair-trigger matter of nuclear defence. It also necessitated rethinking not just the technology but also the whole way in which computers were used and understood. It was these kinds of issues and concerns that led to the formation of ARPA, the Advanced Research Projects Agency (later known as DARPA, the Defense Advanced Research Projects Agency). This was a body set up in 1958 by the Eisenhower administration as a response to Sputnik, and the Soviet scientific advance that represented.[26] As a government agency ARPA was unusual, in that it had a broad mandate, and almost no accountability. It was thus able to support high-risk projects over a long time. Partly through the gift from the Director of Defense Research and Engineering of a powerful computer built as backup for SAGE, which was surplus to requirements, ARPA became involved in researching military applications of information processing, and in 1962, the Information Processing Techniques Office (IPTO) was formed under the leadership of J.C.R. Licklider.

One of Licklider's concerns was what he called, in a 1960 paper, 'man-computer symbiosis'.[27] This involved finding ways of integrating the machine with human operators that went beyond the automation model. It involved work not just in AI, but also on time-sharing, interactive computing and networking. In the late '50s John McCarthy, one of the pioneers of Artificial Intelligence, developed the concept of time-sharing. This involved the computer dealing with the work of many users at once by cycling through sections of each user's processes very rapidly. By allotting an infinitesimal amount of time to each task in succession, users could be given the impression that they alone had control of the computer. Time-sharing had a number of important effects on computing, not just in practical technological terms, but also in how it was understood and interacted with. The user now interacted with the computer in terms of a private personal engagement. He or she was given the sense of the machine actually being his or hers personally. This represented a decisive shift in computing, towards a model of one-to-one engagement. Time-sharing required the development of other technologies such as graphic displays, such as the General Purpose Graphics Display System, in effect a graphical user interface which used symbols, thus anticipating the graphical user interface systems employed by Apple and Microsoft several decades later.

Licklider also discovered and funded the work of Ivan Sutherland, who succeeded Licklider as director of IPTO, and who had been a PhD student of Claude Shannon's while at Lincoln Laboratory. Lincoln Laboratory was top-secret facility connected to MIT and responsible for much of the work on SAGE. For part of his PhD Sutherland employed technology developed at Lincoln, such as cathode ray displays and light pens, and, in 1962, built 'Sketchpad' (illus. 18), an interactive graphics program whose influence was immense. It allowed the user to draw straight onto the screen, and to manipulate what had been drawn. This was made possible by storing the images as data in the computer's memory. This meant that they could be manipulated as mathematical data. Sketchpad showed that the computer could be used as a visual medium. But it also introduced the idea of the virtual image or object, which have quasi-real existences. Sketchpad constituted the beginnings of, among other things, computer graphics and virtual reality. Sutherland went on to develop technologies specifically designed for virtual reality, including headsets.

The idea of the computer as a visual tool encouraged Douglas Engelbart, another researcher whose work Licklider and IPTO funded. Engelbart had been inspired by an influential article by the

18 Ivan Sutherland sitting at a terminal running Sketchpad, one of the first and most influential computer graphics programs, early 1960s.

scientist and pioneer of the scientific calculating machine Vannevar Bush. Published in the Atlantic Monthly in 1945, when Bush was acting as a special scientific advisor to President Roosevelt, 'As We May Think'[28] proposed a solution to the increasing demands of information retrieval in the form of a device called 'Memex'. This would allow the operator to input text, drawings and notes through a dry photocopier or through head-mounted stereo camera spectacles. This information could be stored in a microfiche filing system. Several files could be displayed at a time, and a simple code would store linked or related files. Though Bush's concept of the Memex system was in terms of the photo-mechanical technologies then available, he anticipated much of the technology that would later be realized in multimedia and graphical computing. As well as the above ideas, Bush also encompassed data compression, information exchange with other users and voice recognition. Most importantly Bush introduced the notion of 'associative indexing', enabling the user to make trails through the mass of information and record those trails, which can be followed and annotated by other users. It is this capacity in particular that would later come to characterize the areas known as hypermedia and multimedia. Bush's ideas were a crucial influence on a generation of computer scientists and thinkers, pre-eminent among them Engelbart, Theodor (Ted) Nelson and Alan Kay. Engelbart had read 'As We May Think' while serving in the US Army as a radar technician. This, along with his army experience, enabled him to come to a radical understanding of the potential of computers. After the War he was employed as an electrical engineer at Stanford Research Institute, where ARPA funding enabled him to found his Augmentation Research Center (ARC) (illus. 19). ARC was dedicated to researching how computers might be used to augment human intelligence. In its twelve years of existence ARC developed many, if not most, of the techniques we now take for granted in computing. These included word processing, cutting and pasting, separate windows, hypertext (where it is possible to jump from one document to another), multimedia, outline processing, computer conferencing, and even the mouse.

Perhaps the most well known contribution of ARPA to the development of computing is its role in the formation of the Internet, the set of interconnections between computers that now encompasses the world. The idea of establishing such a network had been a concern of Licklider's for some time, and in his 1960 'Man-Computer Symbiosis' paper he described a system of linked computers.

19 The 'experimental pointing device' (a precursor of the modern computer mouse), designed by Douglas Engelbart and the Augmentation Research Center at the Stanford Research Institute in late 1963 or early 1964.

Soon after, in 1962, Paul Baran, of the defence think-tank RAND Corporation, wrote a paper concerning strategies for maintaining communications in event of a nuclear war. In 'On Distributed Communications'[29] he proposed that a communications system should be set up without any centre. Instead a network should be set up composed of equal nodes, so that should any part be destroyed, messages could continue to flow along other routes (illus. 20). In the '60s work was done at RAND, MIT and UCLA looking at the feasibility of building such a communications system using computers, and incorporating the idea of 'packet switching' – sending computer data in small chunks to be reassembled at their destination. (This was an idea developed separately by Baran and an English scientist, Donald Davies, who also coined the term 'packet switching'.) Contrary to legend, the Internet was not developed because of Baran's paper, and thus was not directly conceived as a response to the dangers of nuclear attack. Nevertheless his idea of packet switching solved many of the logistical problems of complex networks. IPTO and ARPA were very interested in Baran's ideas, and had under-taken or sponsored much relevant research. In 1967 they decided to fund a project to develop such a network on a large scale. In Autumn, 1969, four computers, known as Interface Message Processors (IMPs), in UCLA, Stanford, University of California, Santa Barbara and the University of Utah were linked (illus. 21). This

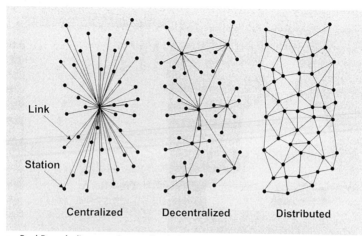

Link

Station

Centralized          Decentralized          Distributed

20 Paul Baran's diagram of centralized, decentralized and distributed networks, reproduced from his famous RAND paper 'On Distributed Communication', 1964.

small network, named ARPANET, was the basis of the future Internet.

In 1970, soon after the implementation of the ARPANET, the Mansfield Amendment to military procurement authorization was passed by the US Congress, partly as a response to Vietnam. In effect this limited Defense Department support for research, through bodies such as ARPA, to projects directly related to defence. This meant that the 'pure' research initiatives into computer applications, such as those described above, could no longer be funded. ARPA later returned to similar kinds of research, particularly in relation to the Strategic Defense Initiative, the SDI, otherwise known as 'Star Wars', the Reagan-administration project to build a defensive shield of rapid missile response to nuclear attack around the US, a plan as ideologically potent and practically useless as SAGE. Elsewhere, the immediate effect of the Mansfield Amendment was dramatic, at least as far as computer research was concerned. DOD computer research funding dropped to nothing, and was not made up adequately from elsewhere in the government. One result of this was that many of the brightest researchers from defence-funded departments gravitated towards the possibilities offered by commercial research, for example in the Xerox Palo Alto Research Center. The Mansfield Amendment represented the end of a golden era of government-funded computer research.

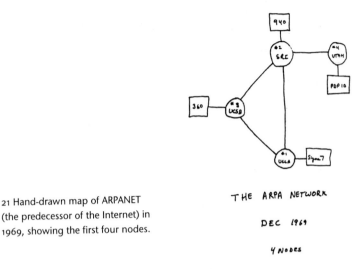

21 Hand-drawn map of ARPANET (the predecessor of the Internet) in 1969, showing the first four nodes.

## CYBERNETICS AND COMPUTING IN CIVILIAN LIFE

The above might suggest that research into and use of Cybernetics and computing was entirely the preserve of the government and the military. But while it is true that much of the research into computing did, at first, take place either in military or government establishments by virtue of funding from such bodies, the methods of organization suggested by Cybernetics and made possible by computers soon migrated from the military to civilian life. Such discourses of control were congenial to those involved with rationalizing industrial manufacture. Frederick Taylor and others had already developed powerful principles for the rationalization of the labour process at the beginning of the century, followed by automation and mechanical control, introduced after the First World War, in particular by Henry Ford in the car industry. In the period between the wars 'technocratic' ideas were also developed which saw science and technology as the solution to various social and political issues. The Second World War greatly advanced the development of systems of production, organization and deployment and also produced a glut of experienced, enthusiastic engineers who were looking for places in which to exploit their new skills and understandings. This led to the wide use of systems approaches to production in all areas of industry. This was manifested in Cybernetics-influenced techniques and theories of 'systems analysis'. With these anything could be analysed as a 'component' within a larger 'system'. Such techniques could be and were applied equally to machinery, military strategy, industrial organization, business planning, urban planning and even government.

The close relationship between computing, military planning and business is made evident in the post-war period. At almost exactly the same period as Jay Forrester, architect of the Whirlwind computer system, the basis of SAGE, left the military to become a professor at the Sloan School of Management at MIT, the President of Ford, Robert McNamara, was appointed President Kennedy's Secretary of Defense. McNamara had originally been a professor at the Harvard Business School. During the War he had applied his business skills to Operations Research problems, in particular the logistics of bombing. After the War he and others involved in such work had applied their experiences to industrial manufacturing at Ford, eventually leading to his assumption of the Ford presidency. In a sense McNamara's career exemplifies the close relation between computing, business and military strategy. Under the aegis of the technocratic, cybernetic culture of Cold War America, such a fit would not seem unusual. Yet McNamara's attempts to apply rational cybernetic solutions to the Vietnam War were disastrous. Nor were the applications of cybernetic ideas in their Cold War form to industry and the economy adequate to predict or deal with the immense disruptions of the 1970s and '80s.

The post-war period also saw the start of the commercial computer industry. Initially its customers were, unsurprisingly, the government and the military. The first computers were vast assemblages, occupying whole rooms, weighing sometimes hundreds of tons, and costing hundreds of thousands of dollars. They were also hard to use and prone to breakdown. Furthermore it was hard to see what uses such machines might have beyond specialized scientific applications. Therefore most, though not all, of the computing machines produced after the War were intended either for military or governmental administrative use, while only a few were meant for business ends, mostly to do with accounting. In general such machines were thought of as large, clever calculators. That they might be put to uses other than crunching numbers was not yet obvious. There was a general perception immediately after the War that there was never going to be a large market for such machines.[30]

Nevertheless the end of the War saw the beginnings of such a market. In Britain Ferranti developed the Manchester Mk 1 as a commercial computer, while the catering firm J. Lyons & Co. commissioned the Lyons Electronic Organizer, or LEO (illus. 22), from the designers of an early experimental machine in Cambridge, to help with their inventories and distribution, and which they subsequently marketed as one of the first business computers. Despite these and other developments the post-war computer industry in Britain did not prosper, while it barely existed in Continental Europe. According to Kenneth Flamm this was because of a failure of the British and other European governments to make adequate funds available to support research and development in the electronics, and a reluctance to see how such technology might find military and governmental applications.[31] Across the Atlantic the situation was very different. The War, which had left European economies and infrastructures devastated, had, through military build up and spending catapulted the United States out of its pre-war economic depression, and to the brink of the longest economic

22 LEO, one of the first commercial computers, built for the Lyons catering company, 1950s.

boom period yet experienced. These circumstances were congenial to the development of a powerful computer industry, particular with the large amounts of Cold-War military investment available for research and development. Involvement with such funded research led Presper Eckert and John Mauchly to leave the Moore School of Electrical Engineering, and start up the first American computer company, responsible for producing UNIVAC, the first computer to achieve a high public profile. Such funding was also crucial in persuading companies such as IBM, already the leader in office technology, to enter the computer market and in allowing them to develop complex technological solutions outside the short-term demands of the market. The entry of IBM into the computer market in the 1950s confirmed that one of the principal uses of computers would be as business machines, a fact already suggested by the takeover of Eckert and Mauchly's company by Remington Rand, the company originally responsible for mass-producing the type-writer in the nineteenth century. The rise of IBM as a computer manufacturer is well documented. Though a comparative late-comer, IBM used its considerable experience in branding, selling and research and development to dominate the computing industry. This dominance was such that, in the '60s, it was characteristic to refer to the relation of IBM and its competitors as that of 'Snow White and the seven dwarfs', reflecting the comparative size of the other firms. (When two of the 'dwarfs', RCA and General Electric, left the computer business in the late '60s this was amended to 'IBM and the BUNCH', with the latter acronym standing for Burroughs, Univac, NCR, Control Data and Honeywell.) IBM took full advantage of government and military funded projects to further its own research into computing, starting with the Defense Calculator, developed during the Korean War, which became the basis of its first proper computer, the 701, and onto work done on the SAGE early warning system, the National Security Agency's STRETCH system, and SABRE, the airline ticket system. Out of these projects came the technological know-how necessary for the commercial products by which the name IBM became almost synonymous with corporate business.

The technology IBM developed, promoted and sold, with the batch-processing, hierarchical style of computing that it encouraged, mirrored the state-regulated balanced economy and social cohesion of the post-war consensus. It is telling that IBM encouraged a mass-production model of programming, rewarding high productivity in terms of lines of code, rather than the elegant solutions to problems preferred by the early 'hackers', the computer devotees at MIT and elsewhere, who became fascinated by the more radical possibilities of digital technology. Nevertheless in the late '50s, '60s and into the '70s, IBM was computing. It not only dominated computing sales at this time, but also defined the image of the computer industry as a corporate endeavour. With IBM computing was a multinational business, the success of which was based on the highly organized and regimented structure of the company, reinforced by the IBM salesmen's obligatory blue suits and white shirts, and their corporate song sheets to be sung at IBM summer camp. This almost Maoist model of collective corporate organization did not make IBM popular among some people working in computing. For those with radical political leanings IBM came to represent the exploitation of the idea of the computer as a tool of corporate control with military connotations, which became increasingly untenable as the '60s wore on. The use of computers as control and communications systems in the Vietnam War brought strongly to the fore the abusive and aggressive potential uses of such technology.[32]

The late '60s were a period of great upheaval and change, of which the hostility to American involvement in Vietnam was one aspect. It was also the beginning of a period of economic change, which would bring to an end the post-war economic boom and with it the combination of mass production, mass consumption and state intervention and support that characterized that era. While it lasted this post-war boom, supported partly by the permanent arms economy of the Cold War, was immensely beneficial for the development of computing. The post-war era also saw the emergence of fields such as Cybernetics, Information Theory and Artificial Intelligence, which presented scientific and philosophical contexts for the technological developments described above. At the same time those developments seemed to confirm the insights arising out of such fields. This powerful concatenation of practice and theory, driven by the paradoxical combination of optimism, prosperity and nuclear terror, gave rise to a kind of heroic age of Cybernetics, in which theories of self-regulation combined with new technologies to give a sense of control and mastery in a complex world. Under the aegis of government and military funded research enormous advances were made in this area. In the 25 years from the end of the War to 1970 computers went from vast, unwieldy and expensive machines, requiring highly specialized knowledge to operate, to something close to the machines we are now familiar with. This was not just a quantitative change, but a qualitative one as well. The development of real-time graphical computing and digital networks, driven largely by the needs of the Cold War, transformed computing entirely and laid the ground for future developments such as the personal computer and the Internet and, by extension, the future shape of digital culture.

# 3. The Digital Avant-garde

## ART AND CYBERNETICS

As the last chapter showed, the post-war era saw the development not just of digital binary computers but a number of discourses and ideas, which together would come to define and determine our current digital culture. These included Cybernetics, Information Theory, General Systems Theory, Structuralism and Artificial Intelligence. Though the emergence of these various discourses neither determined, nor were determined by, the invention of digital technology, they shared many of the same concerns and would become increasingly bound up with the ongoing development of computing. Something similar can be seen in the arts. After the War a number of artists and composers made work and developed ideas that dealt with similar concerns, albeit expressed through very different means. Among them were John Cage, Alan Kaprow, Ray Johnson, members of Fluxus and others involved in Performance and Mail Art, the Nouveau Réalistes, Isidore Isou and the Lettriste movement, those involved with the experimental literature group OuLiPo, and Kinetic and Cybernetic artists and theoreticians such as Roy Ascott, David Medalla, Gordon Pask, Nicolas Schöffer and Hans Haacke. The work these artists were doing reflected the concerns of a world in which information and communications technology and related concepts were becoming increasingly important. This involved exploring questions of interactivity, multimedia, networking, telecommunications, information and abstraction, and the use of combinatorial and generative techniques. Such work was of great importance in relation to the post-war art scene and has crucially determined not only the shape of current artistic practice in relation to digital technology, but also the more general development of digital media. But it is important to emphasize that much of this work was often not primarily about technology in itself, either as a means or a subject. To begin with at least, little, if any, of it was made using computers or other similar technologies. It was not until the late 1950s that computers began to be used to make images or music, and even then this work was mostly undertaken in the spirit of technical research rather than artistic creation. Only by the mid-to-late 1960s did artists start to use technical objects, such as televisions, in their work, and, by the end of the decade, to exploit the possibilities of technologies such as video cameras and computers.

Perhaps the best way to think about the relationship between such work and digital technology is that both were part of the cybernetic culture alluded to above, in which questions of interactivity, feedback, the relationship of organisms with their environment and the transmission and reception of information were of paramount concern. The term Cybernetics is used in this instance to include not just the eponymous theory of Norbert Wiener, but also related discourses such as Information Theory and General Systems Theory, all of which combined to present a powerful paradigm for understanding and operating upon the world. The development of technologies such as the computer, the spread and increasing complexification of systems of communication, and the more general context of a world locked in the potentially fatal systemic stalemate of the Cold War all contributed to the widespread interest in, and adoption of cybernetic thinking. The combination of an increasingly ubiquitous and clamorous electronic mass media and the threat of nuclear holocaust did much to promote a pressing sense of the interconnected nature of things, and a concomitant sense of global fragility. As this chapter will show artists, as much as engineers, scientists or politicians, pursued these interests, even if they did not always explicitly invoke the theories by name. This cybernetic culture is the direct predecessor of our current digital culture, and the contribution it has made to the formation of that culture owes as much to artists as to scientists and researchers.

## JOHN CAGE, INTERACTIVITY AND MULTIMEDIA

It can be argued that the artist who has had the most profound influence on our current digital culture is the composer John Cage. Through his pioneering artistic practice in the '50s and '60s, and through his influence on other practitioners and groups, he fostered interest in a set of concerns that would later become central to the development of digital media and media art. He directly inspired musical movements such as Minimalism, which in its turn had a crucial influence on digital music, as well as art movements such as Fluxus, whose interest in media and telecommunications presaged many current digital art concerns. In particular he opened up space for the development of ideas about interactivity and multimedia, which would not only have repercussions in the art world, but would greatly influence those who, later, came to think about the computer as a medium. This is not to suggest that Cage was, in any sense, a computer artist, or that his work can only be understood in relation to that of those practitioners who might be described as such. In fact Cage's early work does not involve computers at all, and it is not until the 1960s that he started to use them as tools for composition and performance. But in the 1950s he was responding to a similar set of issues and ideas to those that were beginning to be rehearsed in relation to computers.

It may be of some relevance that, during the War, Cage's father, an engineer and inventor, worked on problems of radar detection. As he had done before the War, Cage helped him in his research, which exempted him from the draft, thus enabling him to continue his musical work, and presumably bringing him into contact, albeit tangentially, with many of the technical issues that animated the post-war ideas of Wiener, Shannon and others, who helped develop not just digital and telecommunications technology, but also some of the information discourses described in the last chapter. Though there is no sense that Cage was explicitly interested in the same technical problems as Wiener or Shannon, it is plausible that he was reacting to some of the same concerns about communication and information that informed the others. When he came into contact with their work he evidently found it congenial to his own practice. The publisher John Brockman recalls Cage discussing Wiener's ideas and those of Shannon and Weaver when he encountered him in the mid-1960s, and it is possible that he came into contact with them earlier.[1] In the context of the War and of the increased importance and availability of telecommunications such concerns were, as suggested in the previous chapter, ubiquitous. Cage himself was fascinated by communications technology as shown by his use of radios and record players in compositions during the 1940s. Cage's exploitation of these technologies coincided with the emergence in the late '40s of *Musique Concrète*, which used tape recordings to produce montages of sound, which could be manipulated in a number of ways, and which anticipates many elements of digital musical practice. Among those involved with *Musique Concrète* were the French composers Pierre Schaeffer and Pierre Henry and the French-American composer Edgard Varèse. A little later, in the early '50s, the German composer Karlheinz Stockhausen also started experimenting with tape and electronically generated sound. Later in that decade Max Matthews, an engineer at Bell Labs, produced the first digitally generated music.

The influence of this musical experimentation was profound and extended across both highbrow and popular forms. Cage, Stockhausen and others later greatly influenced the more radical forms of popular music, exemplified by groups such as The Velvet Underground and Kraftwerk. These groups in turn influenced developments such as Techno and other electronic dance music forms. Thus the widespread practice of sampling and the concomitant sonic experimentation to be found in much contemporary pop music may be greatly facilitated by digital technology, but its roots are in the cybernetic culture of the 1940s and 50s. Cage was also an important influence on a later generation of composers, including Philip Glass, Terry Riley, Steve Reich, and LaMonte Young, who took their principal inspiration from 'Minimalist' or, as it was sometimes also known, 'ABC' art, a movement derived from the methodologies of painters such as Kasimir Malevich, whose work reduced visual expression to its essential components. Donald Judd, Carl André and others found in this approach a way of expressing their dissatisfaction with Abstract Expressionism. Minimalism offered instead a form of expression in which the personal and subjective was omitted and in which the artwork referred to nothing but itself. It similarly offered composers a way of creating music in a simple, literal style that eschewed the complexity and sophistication of much contemporary work. Though Minimalism in both its visual and musical forms does not refer overtly to questions of information and communication, its use of the simplest possible elements and its interest in combination and repetition is, arguably, a reflection of such issues. Interestingly most of the Minimalist composers eschewed the use of technology, at least to begin with, preferring to use as simple means as possible. Nevertheless Minimalist music was to be a great influence on various forms of electronic and computer-generated music, both classical and popular.

Like the work of the Minimalist composers he influenced, Cage's work often engaged with the relation between the visual and the audial. This was true of the work he started to develop in the late 1940s and early '50s that also engaged further with issues of communication, order, noise and interaction. Most famous among these is his so-called 'silent piece', *4′ 33″*, which was first performed on 29th August 1952, at the Maverick Concert Hall in Woodstock, in upper New York State, by the pianist David Tudor. Consisting of three short movements of silence this work is one of the canonical moments of the post-war avant-garde. It is open to a number of interpretations. It might be thought of as a provocation, in the avant-garde tradition of attempting to *épater les bourgeois*. It has also, for example been understood as an expression of Cage's interest in Buddhism. According to Cage at least part of the inspiration derived from his experience in the entirely soundproof anechoic chamber at Harvard, where the noise of his own body, the beating of his heart, the rushing of his blood overwhelmed him, demonstrating him that true silence was impossible. What Cage was attempting in the work was not just a provocation, nor simply an expression of transcendent emptiness, but also an attempt to show that any noise could constitute a musical experience. The non-playing of the instrument allowed and made a space for other incidental noises to be listened to, and thus the distinction between noise and music dispensed with.[2]

*4′ 33″* was also inspired by the all-white paintings of Cage's friend Robert Rauschenberg. Cage realized that far from being empty, they act as environmental surfaces, or fields of focus on which dust or shadows may settle.[3] These paintings gave Cage 'permission' to compose a silent piece of music.[4] As Simon Shaw-Miller has pointed out this roots the work in the visual field, as well as making it theatrical.[5] But the importance of *4′ 33″* was how it involved the audience in an unprecedented manner as producers of the music themselves. In this regard its importance is impossible to overstate. It is possibly the most influential avant-garde work of the post-war era, the shockwaves from which continue to be felt today. What Cage achieved, with an astonishing economy of means, was to more or less invent interactivity, or at least to make it available as an artistic strategy. It is now recognized that all works of art require participation from the audience in order to be completed. Furthermore long before $4'33''$ artists were self consciously exploiting this fact. In an essay from the 1960s Umberto Eco talked about what he called 'open work', works which the performer and the audience both help to complete, through different kinds of engagement. 'Open works' are indeterminate and open to different kinds of interpretation. Eco cites the work of Boulez, Stockhausen and Berio, rather than that of Cage, which work he may not have been aware of, as well as the literary work of Mallarmé, Joyce and Kafka, as examples of such open works.[6] (Interestingly, in relation to the previous chapter, in another essay of the same period Eco explicitly connects the issues of communication and indeterminacy within such works with the then recently developed Information Theories of Wiener and Shannon.)[7]

But Cage, by stripping out all the other elements normally associated with a work of art, such as content, foregrounded the very question of interactivity itself. This was particularly resonant in relation to other events of the time. Two months after the premiere of $4'33''$ the United States exploded the first hydrogen bomb. Issues of nuclear defence and deterrence determined the development of interactive technologies, such as those associated with SAGE. Such issues also fostered a climate in which questions of time and attention were of great importance, as well as those of emptiness and the possibility or otherwise of hope. This was made explicit in Rauschenberg's painting 'Mother of God', which preceded the series of white paintings which so influenced Cage's composition of $4'33''$. In this work a white circle is painted over a number of city maps, constituting a grim commentary on the potential of nuclear destruction. Cage's piece would seem to deny the nihilism of Rauschenberg's use of white, by suggesting that empty spaces, whether visual or audial, can become the loci of engagement, interactivity and, thereby, hope. If the beginnings of modern interactive digital technology can be traced in practical terms back to the needs of nuclear defence, then the reconfiguring of that technology as a creative medium owes at least part of its impetus to the work of

Cage, which in turn can be understood as an artistic response to the threat of nuclear destruction. He offered a kind of artistic matrix through which future technological developments could be understood, and, perhaps, be recuperated from their Cold War origins.

## PERFORMANCE AND MULTIMEDIA

Paradoxically *4' 33"* also presaged another aspect of digital media upon which Cage can claim an influence, that which later became known as multimedia. The paradox is that a work of silence and emptiness could possibly suggest the artistic use of multiple media forms. But it is by being totally silent, and allowing the surrounding environment to supply the music, that the silent piece suggests the possibility of anything and everything becoming part of the performance. Historically multimedia can be traced back to any number of beginnings, including Greek tragedy, to various other practices involving combining sounds, words and images, or to Richard Wagner's concept of the total artwork, the *Gesamtkunstwerk*. But again it was Cage who most brilliantly articulated it as an artistic strategy for the post-war era. This was demonstrated in his *Untitled Event*, a collaboration with Merce Cunningham and others that was performed in 1952, the same year as *4' 33"*, and took place at Black Mountain College in Colorado, a small arts institution, founded in the 1930s, which had attracted a number of exiles from the disbanded German Bauhaus as teachers. Cage and Cunningham had already visited the College in 1948 for the Summer School, joining, among others, the artist Willem de Kooning and the architect Buckminster Fuller. For their return visit they produced an extraordinary spectacle. *Untitled Event* was set in a square arena, in which the spectator's seats were arranged in four triangles, dissected by diagonal walkways. On each chair was a white paper cup, which those watching were expected to hold. Overhead there were all-white paintings by Robert Rauschenberg, presumably similar to the works that inspired *4' 33"*. During the performance Cage, dressed in black tie, gave readings from a text about music and Zen, and from the writings of the mediaeval mystic Meister Eckhart, followed by a 'composition with a radio'. While this went on Rauschenberg played old records on a wind-up gramophone while David Tudor played a prepared piano, and, later, poured water from one bucket to another and back again, accompanied by Charles Olson and Mary Caroline Richards reading poetry. Jay Watt played exotic musical instruments, Cunningham and others danced through the aisles, while Rauschenberg projected slides of coloured gelatine and films of the school cook and the setting sun.[8]

This performance was judged a success, by Cage and his collaborators at least, and news of it spread to New York, where a lively experimental arts scene was developing. Four years later, on the course Cage taught at the New School for Social Research in New York, it was a focus of intense discussion. Among the poets, artists, filmmakers and musicians attending were Allan Kaprow, Jackson Mac Low, George Brecht, Al Hansen and Dick Higgins. Kaprow was one of the first to take the possibilities of performance, inspired by Cage's ideas and work, into the public arena, with his *18 Happenings in 6 Parts* of 1959, in which the spectators became part of a performance taking place in a converted loft. This was the first of many such events put together by Kaprow and others, which looked further at the possibilities of performance and installation, or 'Happenings' as they were called, following Kaprow's lead. Kaprow's pioneering work, along with that of Cage, of Jackson Pollock, whose theatricality in making art was a crucial influence, and, in other parts of the world, that of artists such as the Japanese Gutai Group and European artists such as Piero Manzoni, Yves Klein and Georges Mathieu, inspired many artists to engage with these issues and to explore their possibilities in art practice.

Performance Art's heyday was from the late 1950s to the late 1970s and its history encompasses the work of numerous disparate individuals and artists' groups, including Fluxus, which is dealt with in greater detail below, the Vienna Actionists, Gustav Metzger and his Destruction in Art symposium, John Latham, Valie Export, Peter Weibel, Vito Acconci, Chris Burden, Paul McCarthy, Gilbert and George, COUM Transmissions and many others. As this very partial list indicates, Performance Art encompassed many different sensibilities and intentions, and to suggest any unifying tendency, beyond an interest in performance itself in the broadest sense, would be misleading. Some performance art was concerned with explicit social critique. For example its capacity to engage with the corporeal and the material presented artists concerned with questions of gender with an ideal means of exploring such issues. Much performance art was also deliberately confrontational, seeking to shock audiences out of their complacency.

But whatever their individual content or treatments performance works are united by a shared consideration of context and methods. Central to any performance is the question of the space in which it takes place and the means by which it is articulated, often centred on the artist's body as both location and means. Such work concerns the media, in the sense of that which mediates a communication, and how that mediation affects the message. It is no coincidence that modern Performance Art emerged at a time when electronic media were initiating what the Italian philosopher Gianni Vattimo describes as an 'society of generalized communication'.[9] To some extent Performance can be understood as a pre-emptive defensive reaction, emphasizing the corporeal and embodied as well as the ephemeral and the physically located, as a form of resistance to the immateriality, ubiquity and virtuality of mass media and communications, which had taken over so much of art's role as the provider of aesthetic solace and meaning. But Performance can also be seen as rehearsing many issues that later become relevant to electronic and, in particular, digital media. These included questions of interaction, response, feedback, the relationship between the audience and the performance, the methods for combining different media elements and so on. Much of the visual and interactive grammar of modern electronic media, such as television and digital multimedia of various sorts derives from the work of those involved with performance and other, similar areas. Those working in these areas were among the first to explore the possibilities offered by electronic media, first in video and then in digital technology. Many of those involved in developing Performance as an artistic practice are currently involved in media art practice. But, even before the widespread use of technology these practices offered a framework for thinking about multimedia, interactivity and other issues, as well as offering an artistic and poetic matrix through which to think about their use.

### FLUXUS AND MAIL ART

A good example of the poetic engagement with issues of communication was the use of the postal system as an artistic strategy. This was developed by a number of individuals and groups, including the Fluxus collective, whose founders were among the attendees at Cage's sessions at the New School for Social Research. The name for the group was coined by the Lithuanian emigré Georges Maciunas and its members included Higgins, Mac Low, Brecht and Hansen, as well as Robert Filliou, Emmett Williams, Ben Vautier, Daniel Spoerri, Wolf Vostell, Yoko Ono, Nam June Paik, Joseph Beuys, Diter Rot, and LaMonte Young, who all became well known in various capacities. Cage himself was not a member of Fluxus, but acted as a kind of paternal figure and influence. Fluxus's work included performances of various kinds, either involving music or everyday activities and the production of printed material and multiples.[10] Perhaps more than any other art movement Fluxus was about interactive communication and process. The work done in its name almost always required the active participation of a receiver as well as a sender. It also presumed on the existence of noise, interference and distortion that would change messages in unpredictable ways. Fluxus also reflected a world linked by increasingly complex systems of communications and connections. The movement itself was deliberately international, involving members from the United States, Europe and Japan, and eschewing any identification with particular nations. It also demonstrated a fascination with tele-communications, through various works that referred to postal and other communications systems.

Owing to the international nature of the movement, Fluxworkers also used the postal system a great deal to exchange material and ideas. This became a process of making art in its own right. The Fluxus poet Robert Filliou invented the term 'Eternal Network' to refer to the long-term inseparableness of art and life.[11] This became synonymous with Fluxus's use of the post as a vehicle for art. Filliou, along with other Fluxus artists such as Ben Vautier, Ken Friedman, Robert Watts, Nam June Paik and Dick Higgins, used postcards and other correspondence material thus from the late '50s onwards. This kind of work was paralleled by similar projects undertaken by the artistic group, the Nouveau Réalistes in France, which had many affinities with Fluxus, and, indeed shared some members. Among those involved with *Nouveau Realisme* were Yves Klein, Daniel Spoerri, Piero Manzoni, Niki de Saint-Phalle, Christo, Arman and Jean Tinguely. Klein actually sent letters and cards franked with a plain (Klein) blue stamp. Perhaps the most complete exponent of 'mail art', as it came known, was Ray Johnson (illus. 23), a pop artist and associate of many of those who were involved in Fluxus. Johnson and his 'New York CorresponDANCE [*sic*] School' more or less defined the genre of mail, postal or correspondence art, with his sending and receiving of letters and faxes. With the comparatively recent rise of the World Wide Web and the concomitant popularization of the Internet, the telecommunication concerns of Johnson, and the Fluxus and Nouveau Realiste groups seem prescient, in that they reflect a world in which remote communication is of

23 Ray Johnson, *Untitled* (*30,000 Nuclear Bombs*), an example of Johnson's mail art, mechanical reproduction on paper.

increasing importance. Accordingly such work, until recently largely ignored by critical and art-historical fashion, has begun to be looked at as an important episode in the history of the post-war avant-garde. Many of those whose artistic practice involves digital networks have acknowledged the importance of these movements for their work. On the World Wide Web there are many sites dedicated to Fluxus, Johnson and Mail Art, which continues to thrive in electronic form as an art practice particularly suited to the Internet.

OTHER CURRENTS

Other avant-garde movements of the post-war era reflected on different aspects of the burgeoning informational culture. A particular concern with the nature of information, and the possibilities for its manipulation was to be found in French post-war practice in literature and the visual arts. Though not usually discussed in relation to the COBRA and Situationist groups it preceded, the Romanian emigré Isidore Isou's Lettriste movement presented a fascinating attempt to think about information in its most basic form. Isou's project was to deconstruct words to their constituent parts and to synthesize poetry and music, in order to produce 'a single art' with no trace of 'any original difference'. Despite Isou's megalomania, his ideas attracted, briefly, a number of adherents, including Gil Wolman and Guy Debord. As a movement Lettrisme was short-lived, but it nevertheless showed some interesting characteristics in relation to the emerging information paradigm. Isou's central theory was that the evolution of any art was characterized by alternate 'amplic' and 'chiselling' phases. The former is a period of expansion and the latter of refinement. Isou dated the amplic phase in poetry to 1857, at which point Baudelaire initiated the chiselling phase by reducing narrative to anecdote, Rimbaud reduced anecdote to lines and words, Mallarmé reduced words to space and sound and Dada destroyed words completely.[12] Lettrisme was intended to create visual works using the letter as the basic form, thus to initiate a new amplic phase. Lettriste productions consisted of paintings using graphic elements such as alphabets, Morse code and so on, to substantiate Isou's claims to have resystemized all the sciences of language and signification into a new discipline named 'hypergraphology'.[13] Whatever the merits of Isou's theories and claims and of the work produced in their name, Lettrisme reflected the emerging dominance of signs and information in the post-war period. It is unlikely that Isou would have seen the potential of computers for his practice at the time. Nevertheless his concern with codes and systems of signification, as well as his attempt to dismantle the distinction between visual and literary production, and his concern with scientific systemization, anticipate many of the concerns and methods of those now working with digital media. Given the obscurity in which his work has languished it is hard to claim that Isou has had much direct influence on such work. The most that can be said is that his ideas lived on, albeit in attenuated form, in the work of the more famous Situationist group, some of whose members were originally Lettristes. Perhaps more to the point, Isou was part of a more general French interest in signs and systems, which manifested itself in intellectual movements such as Structuralism. The Lettriste concentration on the letter also anticipated the post-structuralist and deconstructionist focus on the materiality of the sign, as articulated by Roland Barthes, Jacques Lacan and Jacques Derrida, which itself can be understood, in part at least, as a response to the dramatic developments in information and communication technologies. Perhaps Isou can be seen as somebody whose ideas were developed too soon, before either the technologies or culture existed with which to understand or legitimate them. In the light of his prescience it is time that Isou's work was reassessed.

Isou's work is as much about the visual as the literary, and as such anticipates many issues concerning digital media. Along with that of Fluxworkers such as Ben Vautier, the *Spatialisme* of the French poet Pierre Garnier, the *Konkrete Poesie* of the Swiss Eugen Gomringer and the work of Dom Sylvester Houédard, Ian Hamilton Finlay and Bob Cobbing among others, such work has sometimes been considered under the general term 'Concrete Poetry'. This denotes a shared interest in the graphic and visual potential of letters, words and texts. More recently work by Tom Phillips, Jake Tilson, Jenny Holzer and others have continued this interest, albeit in very different ways. Similar ideas were explored by the *Ouvrior pour Littérature Potentielle* or the 'Workshop for Potential Literature', otherwise known as OuLiPo, founded in 1960 the ex-Surrealist Raymond Queneau and François le Lionnais. Many of those at the original meeting of the group were already members of the College of Pataphysics, a group founded in 1949, inspired by the work of Alfred Jarry to develop a 'science of exceptions, of imaginary solutions, equivalence, and imperturbality'.[14] The aim of OuLiPo was to develop methods of applying constraints to the production of literature, partly as a reaction to the open-ended freedom of Surrealist literary methodologies. Queneau was particularly interested in the work of the mathematical research collective Bourbaki. Most the methods developed involved different kinds of word play, such as anagrams, lipograms (in which one or more letters of the alphabet are excluded from a text), transpositions, and palindromes. One of the most famous Oulipian works was Raymond Queneau's *Cent mille milliards de poèmes* (100, 000, 000, 000, 000 Poems),[15] a book physically designed so that different lines can be combined to make up the eponymous number.

Members of OuLiPo included Marcel Duchamp, Harry Mathews, Italo Calvino and Georges Perec. The last two in particular gained international recognition for their literary work, much of which employed Oulipian methodologies. Calvino employed the combinatorial narrative possibilities suggested by tarot cards in his book *The Castle of Crossed Destinies*,[16] while Perec produced an extraordinary book, *La disparition*, which in true lipogrammatic style, did not use the letter E (and which, perhaps even more extraordinarily, has been translated, without Es, into English by Gilbert Adair, as *A Void*).[17] The underlying strategies and theories of OuLiPo can be seen as a response to the combinatorial and algorithmic possibilities suggested by the computer, and to the more general information culture emerging in the '60s and '70s. Before becoming famous, and thus able to write full time, Perec worked in a laboratory run by the CNRS, the French scientific research funding council, as an assistant dedicated to organizing the information in the research library. To this end he worked on a series of extraordinary paper databases, the complexity and subtlety of which anticipated future digital developments.[18] The digital nature of Oulipian ideas was made explicit when, in the early '80s, some members initiated a new group, 'Workshop for literature assisted by mathematics and computers', '*Atelier de Littérature Assistée par la Mathématique et les Ordinateurs*' or ALAMO for short, devoted specifically to research into computer-aided methods of Oulipian literary production. But the important issue here is less that members of OuLiPo used computers and more that their work, computer-aided or not, directly anticipated or articulated methods and practices relevant to a world increasingly mediated by information and communications technologies. Again, like many of the other movements described above, their importance is increasingly acknowledged, not least in the proliferation of Web sites dedicated to their work.

## CYBERNETICS AND ART IN EUROPE

Most of the work discussed above neither used computers (other than, at most, as a tool) nor referred explicitly to computing technology or its associated ideas. Their importance for digital culture is the degree to which the ways of thinking and doing they offered anticipated the more general issues of a culture mediated by such technologies. But, at the same time, some artists began to show an active interest in computing, Cybernetics and Information Theory, as sources of inspiration for both subject matter and method, as well as actual means. Curiously perhaps this was, at least at first, a largely European phenomenon. Jack Burnham, a critic and curator with a particular interest in the relationship between art, science and technology, suggested in 1968 that Europe was a decade ahead of the United States in its appreciation of the implications of Cybernetics for art.[19] In Britain for example it had a marked effect. In the 1950s the Independent Group, whose members included Eduardo Paolozzi, Richard Hamilton, Nigel Henderson, William Turnbull and Alison and Peter Smithson, looked to the United States for alternatives to the combination of English parochialism and European avant-garde seriousness that prevailed in the arts at that time. America offered glamorous images of prosperity, as well as of the benefits of advanced technology and science that contrasted starkly with the austerities of a post-war Britain. Cybernetics and

Information Theory were among the ideas the Independent Group imported from across the Atlantic, along with American sociology and Non-Aristotelian logic,[20] which enabled them to develop a new critical approach to culture. Throughout the Group's history such ideas were discussed both informally and formally in the context of public seminars at the Institute of Contemporary Arts in London, with which they had formed a close relationship.

A little later, in the early '60s, the artist Roy Ascott (illus. 24) wholeheartedly embraced the possibilities of Cybernetics, which he encountered through the work of Norbert Wiener and others, and which he pursued through paintings, such as his *Change Paintings* of 1960; manifestoes, such as *Behaviourables and Futuribles* of 1967 and many other manifestations, all emphasizing the importance of interaction and participation between artist, artwork and audience,

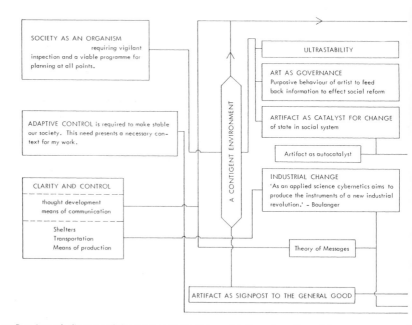

24 Roy Ascott's diagram of the cybernetic processes of culture, from the catalogue for his show *Diagram Boxes & Analogue Structures* at the Molton Gallery, London, in 1963.

as well as of process, behaviour and system.[21] As important as Ascott's own work was his role as head of Foundation at Ealing College of Art in London, a post for which he was recommended by his mentor, the abstract artist Victor Pasmore, and where he worked alongside artists such as Ron Kitaj and Bernard Cohen. There he was able to put many of his cybernetic ideas into practice in a pedagogical context. These included games in which students were encouraged to think about and to examine the processes governing their relationships with others and with their own preconceptions about themselves. Among those who came into contact with Ascott's teaching were the artist Steven Willats, who continues to this day to pursue the application of systems and Cybernetics to art in his own work. Also at Ealing Ascott taught the rock musician Pete Townshend, who was inspired by his contact with the artist and

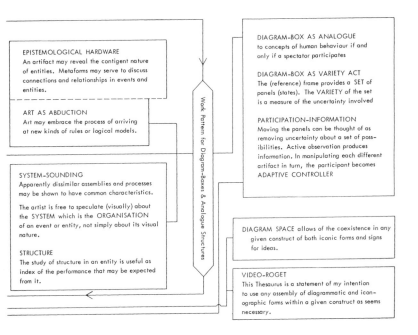

doyen of destruction in art Gustav Metzger, a guest lecturer on the Ealing course, to make the destruction of their instruments a key part of his rock band The Who's act. While at Ipswich School of Art in the mid-'60s Ascott taught Brian Eno, who, having become famous as a rock star with Roxy Music and through collaboration with David Bowie, has continually produced innovative and experimental music, in which Ascott's cybernetic legacy can be detected. Ascott has continued to explore the possibilities of Cybernetics, telecommunications and interactive media, and in particular what he describes as 'telematics' and 'technoetics', the latter concerning 'the practice and theory of emerging from the convergence of art, technology and consciousness research'. He has been largely ignored by the British art establishment. The Tate Gallery, whose collections encompass both modern and British art, does not own any of his work. He has, however, achieved international recognition for his interactive work, and his teaching.

Other important British contributions to the field of Cybernetics and art were made by the Filipino-born but London-based artist David Medalla, the polymath Edward Ihnatowicz and the cybernetician and theatre director Gordon Pask. In the 1960s Medalla built a number of cybernetic art pieces, involving mud, bubbles or sand. In 1967 he founded what he called the Exploding Galaxy which he described as 'a kinetic confluence of transmedia explorers', and which aimed to encourage participation and interaction between people and with nature. Medalla continues to produce artworks of various sorts, some of which involve cybernetic ideas. Ihnatowicz, a wartime refugee from Poland, built a number of extraordinary cybernetic sculptures, including SAM (*Sound Activated Mobile*) and *Senster*, commissioned by Phillips. Pask, who originally studied medicine at Cambridge, became interested in the work of Wiener and others in the 1950s. In 1953 he founded System Research, a nonprofit research organization, with his colleague Robin McKinnon-Wood, which carried out research on skill acquisition, styles and strategies of learning, knowledge and task analysis, design processes and other systemic issues, and which attracted funding from, among others, the Ministry of Defence, the Ministry of Employment and the United States Air Force. At the same time he worked as a theatrical producer and built a number of special purpose, electro-mechanical, chemical and biological computers, including 'Musicolour', which drove an array of different coloured lights that were lit in accordance to a musician's performance, and the 'Self-Adaptive Keyboard Instructor' or SAKI, an adaptive teaching tool for typing. His chemical computers from 1958 were self-organizing systems that grew their own sensors. Later in 1970 he built a cybernetic sculpture, *Colloquy of Mobiles* (illus. 25), in which automata 'conversed' and which allowed a human spectator to join in. This was followed by the *Course Assembly System and Tutorial Environment* or *CASTE* (1972), which enabled the user to work through complex bodies of information, and the *Thoughtsticker*, which mapped the user's ideas and suggested novel combinations.

25 Gordon Pask, *Colloquy of Mobiles*, as installed at 'Cybernetic Serendipity' at the ICA, 1968; note the computer in the background.

The Digital Avant-garde 99

Pask and Medalla's interest in the practical and technological applications of Cybernetics was shared by a number of practitioners from mainland Europe, where the possibilities of applying cybernetic theories to aesthetics were also being explored. By the end of the '50s and beginning of the '60s a number of European treatises on that subject had appeared, including Abraham Moles's *Theorie de l'information et perception esthétique*[22] and Max Bense's *Programmierung des Schönen*[23] while even earlier, in the mid-1950s the Hungarian/French sculptor Nicolas Schöffer had produced the explicitly 'cybernetic' sculpture, starting with his sound equipped art structure built in 1954 for the Phillips Corporation, and followed by his two dynamic responsive works *CYSP I* (illus. 26) and *CYSP II* (both 1956). Schöffer's work, as well as invoking the theories of Cybernetics, also harked back to an older legacy, that of Kinetic Art, which went back to the work of Marcel Duchamp, Naum Gabo, Laszlo Moholy Nagy and others concerned with producing dynamic, moving sculpture. Schöffer's sculptures went beyond these in that they were capable of autonomous and complex movements, apparently of their own volition. Schöffer's interest in kinetic and

26 Nicolas Schoffer, *CYSP I*, 1956, mixed media.

cybernetic art was shared by a number of artists, many of whom were connected with the various groups corralled under the banner of the 'New Tendency', which included the original participants who exhibited at the 'Nove Tendenije' show in Zagreb in 1961, Group Zero in Germany and the Groupe de Recherche d'Art Visuel (GRAV) from France, among whose members was Jean Tinguely. Uniting these groups was an interest in making objective, rational and scientific art, which eschewed lyricism and subjectivity. Cybernetics was important in these endeavours as both the basis for practical work, and as the basis for a scientific theory of aesthetics.

## TECHNOLOGY AND THE AVANT-GARDE

At the same time as artists were beginning to experiment with the possibilities of technology, writers such as Marshall McLuhan were considering its effects and possibilities. In particular McLuhan looked at the transformative power of media technologies. Through a number of books, most notably *The Gutenberg Galaxy*,[24] *Understanding Media*,[25] and *The Medium is the Message*,[26] he explored how the development of successive media alters human relations with the world. McLuhan was interested in the developments in media technology that altered the human relationship with the environment, regardless of the message any medium might convey, or, as he most famously put it, 'the medium is the message.' He was interested in the changing distributions in the ratio of the human senses, as in, for example, the shift from an aural to a visual culture that was concomitant with writing and, more emphatically, with printing. With the coming of electronic media such as television he saw a return to an oral paradigm and the emergence of what he famously called the 'global village', a world linked by electronic communications. An important influence on McLuhan, a devout Catholic convert, was the work of Pierre Teilhard de Chardin, the French philosopher–theologian. Teilhard's ideas were informed by scientific evolutionary theory, out of which he constructed a theological framework of progressive developments, involving successive complexifications of matter-energy in the universe. With humanity he argued the earth had entered a new stage in this progress from the biosphere, the layer of living things on the earth's surface, to the 'noosphere', a layer of mind covering the earth.[27]

The ideas of theorists such as McLuhan and the work of artists involved with the New Tendency, and that of Ascott and Pask and others, demonstrated the potential of using new technologies in art. This had been anticipated by Cage, who in the 1930s and '40s had been one of the first composers to incorporate gramophones and radios into his compositions, and earlier by Futurist composers such as Luigi Russolo. By the late '50s and early '60s artists involved with Performance and Installation were incorporating technology into their work, in particular Fluxus members Wolf Vostell and Nam June Paik. Vostell had first used TV monitors in his work in the late 1950s, and continued to do so through the 1960s. Paik had started to incorporate them in the 1960s. In 1966 Paik bought one of the first Sony Portapak video cameras, and used it to video the Pope's visit to New York, which he showed in the evening at the *Café à Go Go*, a well-known venue for art events, thus possibly being responsible for the first piece of video art. Paik's work was one of a number of attempts to exploit this new medium, which was both resonant, in that it invoked the increasingly pervasive electronic mass media, and convenient, in that it could be used by individuals. This coalesced into the set of practices known as video art, to which many of those involved in performance and related activities were attracted. Video Art thrived in the late '60s and '70s with the work of Paik, Bruce Nauman, Vito Acconci, Chris Burden, Bill Viola and Gary Hill, and continues to be a vital aspect of contemporary art practice.

By the late 1960s computers were also being used in avant-garde art practice. The possibilities of the computer as a medium for art were demonstrated by defense-funded research into the possibilities of real-time computing which led to the first uses of the computer as a visual medium. Projects such as SAGE necessitated the development of graphical interfaces, and by the late 1950s the possibilities of the computer as a visual medium was beginning to be exploited in disparate areas. In 1957 the first image-processed photo was produced at the National Bureau of Standards, and in 1958 John Whitney Sr started to use an analog computer to make animations. In the late 1950s and early '60s at Bell Labs Edward Zajac was experimenting with computer-generated film to visualize data and A. Michael Noll was starting to produce computer-generated Mondrians (see illus. 27) and his *Gaussian Quadratic* series of artworks, which used algorithmic methods to produce images. Meanwhile elsewhere, Charles Csuri was making his first computer-generated artworks, using similar techniques.

Over the next few years computer art flourished. At the end of the 1950s Ivan Sutherland produced his Sketchpad software. In 1960 William Fetter of Boeing invented the term 'computer graphics' for his human factors cockpit drawings. In the early '60s, *Spacewar*, the first video game, was being developed by Steve Russell and others, at MIT. The aeronautics and car industries quickly saw the potential of computers as design tools. In 1963 DAC-1 the first commercial

27 *Composition with Lines*, 1917 (Piet Mondrian), and *Computer Composition with Lines*, 1965 (A. Michael Noll, in association with an IBM 7094 digital computer and General Dynamics SC-4020 microfilm plotter).

28 George Nees, *Corridor*, early 1960s, computer-generated image.

CAD (computer aided design) system, built for General Motors by IBM, was shown publicly. In the same year Lockheed Georgia started using computer graphics. This was also the year of the first computer art competition, sponsored by the trade periodical *Computers and Automation*. Both first and second place in the first competition were won by entrants from the US Army Ballistic Missile Research Laboratories. The first computer art exhibition was held in 1965, at Technische Hochschule in Stuttgart, organized by A. Michael Noll, Frieder Nake and George Nees (illus. 28), while in the same year another similar exhibition was held at the Howard Wise Gallery in New York. The year afterwards, an *annus mirabilis* of computer art, two scientists at Bell Labs, Ken Knowlton and Leon Harmon produced their *Studies in Perception* (illus. 29), which greatly furthered the burgeoning field of computer imaging, IBM awarded the newly created post of Artist-in-Residence to John Whitney Sr, while Charles Csuri's *Hummingbird* (illus. 30) was purchased by the Museum of Modern Art in New York for its permanent collection.

In 1967, a movement, *Experiments in Art and Technology* (EAT) was started in New York by the artist Robert Rauschenberg, a friend of John Cage, and the engineer Billy Klüver, who had assisted Jean

Tinguely in the construction of his machines. EAT was concerned
with technology not so much as a medium than as a subject, as in
Ed Kienholz's construction *The Friendly Grey Computer*, or Lowell
Nesbitt's paintings of computers and computer peripherals (illus.
31). In Britain Eduardo Paolozzi was expressing a similar fascination with computers through the medium of screenprinting, with
his *Universal Electronic Vacuum* series and others. In 1968 a number
of artists, including Paolozzi, Hans Haacke, and Victor Vasarely,
a founder member of GRAV, were commissioned by Maurice
Tuchman, curator of modern art at the Los Angeles County Museum

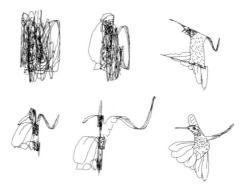

30 Charles Csuri,
*Hummingbird*, 1968,
computer-generated image.

31 Lowell Nesbitt, *IBM 1440*, 1965, oil on canvas.

of Art, to produce works as part of his Art and Technology programme. Many of the artists, including those named above, proposed projects involving computers. None except that of the poet and Fluxus associate Jackson Mac Low were successfully achieved, showing perhaps that the computer is, perhaps, a linguistic rather than an visual medium, whether language is used as a medium or for control. More successful were *Cybernetic Serendipity: The Computer and the Arts* (illus. 32 and 33) curated by Jasia Reichardt at the Institute of Contemporary Arts in London, and *The Machine as Seen at the End of the Mechanical Age* at the Museum of Modern Art in New York. *Cybernetic Serendipity* might be considered the apogee of computer-aided art, considered as a mainstream art form. It consisted of all forms of computer-influenced and aided art, including work in music, interactivity, cybernetic art, computer-generated film and computer graphics, and involved an eclectic mixture of contributors, including Cage and many others mentioned above, and scientists from university laboratories, and was highly successful.

## THE BEGINNING OF THE END OF EARLY COMPUTER ART

The late 1960s were both the apogee and the beginning of the end for both the widespread application of Cybernetics in contemporary art, and for attempts to use the computer as an artistic medium, at least

32 Franciszka Themerson's cover for the 'Cybernetic Serendipity' special issue of *Studio International*, 1968.

33 Installation shot of the 'Cybernetic Serendipity' exhibition at the ICA, London, 1968.

until the 1990s, when the Internet and the World Wide Web offered new possibilities for digital art. This is not, of course, to suggest that art influenced by Cybernetics or using computers ceased to be made. On the contrary throughout the 1970s and '80s a number of artists continued to work on those lines. Some artists involved with video also experimented with the possibilities of digital manipulation, while the arrival, in the '80s, of sophisticated equipment for such manipulation caused a brief flurry of interest from artists normally associated with more traditional media. But, on the whole, cybernetic and computer art was, rightly or wrongly, regarded as marginal in relation to both the traditional art establishment or to avant-garde art practice. To some extent this was a result of the more general decline in Cybernetics' fortunes, which, in turn reflected the sense that it was more problematic than useful as a science. An attempt to address the issues raised by this perception resulted in the development of 'second-order Cybernetics' and Autopoeisis in the late 1960s and '70s, which offered comparatively little purchase for art practice. It also reflected, possibly, a more critical response to the ideas of control and feedback that animated both cybernetic and computer-based art. In light of both the use of Cybernetics and information technology for military strategy and the increasing computerization of society for the purposes of capital, the utopian belief in their potential was hard for many to sustain.

Perhaps the main issue was that cybernetic systems and technologies were part of the means by which language was used 'operationally' in Herbert Marcuse's terms, to achieve results, regardless of truth or belief. As such they exemplified the spirit of instrumental rationality that, according to Marcuse, characterized modern scientific thought, and thereby the logic of domination which acted against the achievement of personal and political freedom.[28] Some artists started to explore the relation between power and such systems of domination, including language. One such was Hans Haacke, whose work in the '60s (see illus. 34) concerned living systems and their relationship with the environment. In his 1968 book Beyond Modern Sculpture Jack Burnham declared Haacke to be an artist engaged with what he calls an 'environmental systems philosophy'.[29] Haacke also exhibited in many of the 'New Tendency' exhibitions in the '60s and considered himself an associate of the German Zero group. For these reasons perhaps Haacke was one of those commissioned by Maurice Tuchman to produce work for the Art and Technology programme.

In the late 1960s and early '70s Haacke's work took a distinctly political turn. He began to investigate human social systems, with a particular concern for questions of power and property. In 1971 a proposed retrospective exhibition of his work at the Soloman R Guggenheim Museum in New York was cancelled because of a work he proposed exhibiting which showed the real estate holdings of the trustees of the museum. Haacke's new direction was part of a larger movement, which saw artists exploring the use of language to ask questions about the nature of art, of communication, and of power.

34 Hans Haacke, *Condensation Cube*, 1963/65, mixed-media installation.

This became known as Conceptual Art, though, as so often, the use of such a label suggests a simpler and more unified phenomenon than is actually the case. As a term Conceptual Art is used to refer to the disparate activities of numerous individuals and groups from all over the world, many of which could as well be, and often are, corralled under other labels, such as Minimalism, Land Art, Arte Povera, and Performance Art etc. Nevertheless the period around the end of the '60s did see many artists turning to language for the basis of their practice and away from a concern with the materiality of the artwork. The inspiration for this linguistic turn came from a number of sources, including Marcel Duchamp's *Readymades*, the later philosophy of Ludwig Wittgenstein, and some of the post-war avant-garde artists and movements discussed above, such as John Cage, Fluxus and the Situationists.

The pretensions of Cybernetics to enable an ordering and understanding of the world were specifically addressed by a number of artists involved with Conceptual Art. As described above, Hans Haacke applied the systemic methodologies that he had previously used for natural phenomena to the complex arrangements of power and property. In the early 1960s Robert Morris had produced works which, deliberately or not, parodied the self-reflexive nature of cybernetic thinking. These included *Box with the Sound of Its Own Making* (1962), a square box which contained a tape recorder playing a tape of its being made, and *Card File* (1962), which is a card file listing on the plastic index tabs the operations involved in its construction (the latter work is considered by some to be the first piece of Conceptual Art). Later in the '60s Sol LeWitt began to produce works whose primary existence was simply a set of instructions to be carried out by somebody else, for example, *Ten thousand random straight lines drawn by one draughtsman, 1,000 lines a day, for ten days, within a 120" square* (the title being the instructions that constitute the work itself). This can be seen as, among other things, a parodic invocation of the algorithmic means by which computers are programmed. Perhaps the most explicit critique of Cybernetics was produced by members of the English Conceptual Art collective, Art & Language (though such work constituted a small part of their output and represented concerns that were marginal to their main interests).[30] Harold Hurrell, a founder member, constructed an interactive work *The Cybernetic Art Work that Nobody Broke* (1969), for example, which precisely parodied the kind of cybernetic systems produced in the '60s by Pask and others. It allowed the user to input choices but refused all but 1 and 0. Any other choice produced aggressive messages from the system. In a different vein, Terry Atkinson and Michael Baldwin's *Key to 22 Predicates: The French Army* (1967), was apparently a kind of systematization of the French Army, which proposed absurd abbreviations, for the French Army (FA), the Collection of Men and Machines (CMM), and the Group of Regiments (GR), and then used them in series of absurd and meaningless systemizations, as in this example: 'The

FA is regarded as the same CMM as the GR and the GR is the same CMM as (e.g.) "a new order" FA (e.g. morphologically a member of another class of objects): by transitivity the FA is the same CMM as the "new shape/order one".

At first it was a little difficult to distinguish between Conceptual Art and Cybernetic Art, as was demonstrated by the inclusion of examples of both in the 1970 show 'Software, Information Technology: Its New Meaning for Art', held at the Jewish Museum in New York. The show was curated by Jack Burnham, whose book *The End of Sculpture* was, and indeed remains, a key text for those interested in the coming together of art and technology. The show featured work by Haacke and Joseph Kosuth, who would both be regarded as leading conceptual artists, as well as by Ted Nelson and Nicholas Negroponte, who are now thought of as pioneers of multimedia computing. Negroponte's contribution, *Seek* (illus. 35), was a paradigmatic cybernetic artwork in which gerbils were placed in a box filled with metal cubes. A robotic arm attempted to rearrange the cubes as quickly as the gerbils disrupted the arrangement.

35 Nicholas Negroponte/Architecture Machine Group, *Seek*, 1970, mixed-media environment.

Negroponte, then working with the Architecture Machine Group at MIT, was later to become head of the Media Lab, and is now one of the most vocal advocates of the positive aspects of new technology, through his own publications and the pages of magazines such as *Wired*. Nelson, whose contribution was a prototype hypertext system, was already known as one of the most enthusiastic proponents of the potential of computers as systems for arranging and giving access to large amounts of knowledge.

By contrast the works by Kosuth and Haacke were far more critical of technology. Haacke made two works for the show, *Visitor's Profile* and *News*. One was a parodic computerized questionnaire system, which tabulated the responses of visitors to the show to questions such as 'Should the use of Marijuana be legalized, lightly or severely punished?' The other consisted of teletype machines that spewed out continuous reels of information about local, national and international news. Kosuth did not use technology as such in his contribution (a wise decision considering that many works there, including *Visitor's Profile*, did not actually work, owing to technical difficulties, which was a contributing factor in Haacke giving up the use of technology in his work). Instead *The Seventh Investigation (Art as Idea as Idea) Proposition One* explored how language changes in different contexts by placing the same text, consisting of six propositions, into a variety of situations. Edward Shanken suggests that, though Kosuth eschewed the use of technology, his work does explore the issues of art as software and thus the correlations between art and technology intended by Burnham as the theme of the show.[31] Be that as it may, the 'Software' exhibition represented the point of departure between Cybernetics and Conceptual Art. Later in the same year the Museum of Modern Art in New York put on a large show of Conceptual Art, curated by Kynaston McShine, featuring 70 artists. The works by Kosuth and Haacke were all featured. Work by Nelson and Negroponte or that of other cybernetic or technologically oriented artists was not. The show, which was a great success, attracting nearly 300,000 visitors during the six weeks it was open, was called 'Information'. At one level this would seem to be consonant with show titles such as 'Software' and 'Cybernetic Serendipity' in alluding to technology and its possibilities. But the absence of cybernetic or systems work suggested that, for the mainstream art world at least, the cybernetic era was over. Through the 1970s and '80s, out of those practices that combined art and technology, only video art continued to sustain interest from the art world. Kinetic, robotic, cybernetic and computer art practices were largely marginalized and ignored. With the odd exception, such as Harold Cohen's show of paintings made by 'Aaron', an artificial intelligence program, at the Tate in 1984, no major art gallery in Britain or the United States held a show of such art for the last 30 years of the twentieth century.

## THE RETURN OF COMPUTER AND DIGITAL ART

The marginalization of work of this sort can be seen as a response to some of the problematic issues discussed above. But it can also be seen as a reaction to the success of the thinking behind such work. As the 1970s and '80s progressed extraordinary advances were made in extending the capabilities of digital technology. The technical developments necessitated by the Cold War were harnessed for the reconstruction of capitalism into a more flexible and responsive mode. In that period networking, interactivity, multimedia and miniaturization were all developed to a high degree. Much of this work was directly influenced by artistic practice. By these means the cybernetic thinking and practice described in this chapter entered the mainstream, and became part of everyday life, through video games, computer multimedia, the Internet, and, eventually the World Wide Web. As such it offered little for those who required that art remain in its own autonomous sphere, and not be subsumed by the mass media. Video art managed to remain autonomous by developing practices such as site-specific installation, which kept it from being consumed by television, and thus retained the critic's and curator's interest.

But this does not mean that other kinds of art involving technology did not continue to be practised. Artists such as Roy Ascott, David Medalla, Robert Adrian X, Stelarc, Lilian Schwartz and Harold Cohen continued to experiment with various technologies, and to find venues and funding from disparate sources. Many of those involved with Performance Art became involved with new media technologies, especially as Performance's momentum slowed during the 1970s. This reflects both the particular resonance between Performance Art and the new media, discussed above, and Performance's concern for engaging with its audience outside of the traditional gallery space. A useful index of this is the number of performance artists and video artists who have been shown or involved with the influential Ars Electronica Festival, which has been held in Linz in Austria since 1979. These include Nam June Paik and his long-time collaborator Charlotte Moorman, Valie Export, Dan Graham, Woody and Steina Vasulka, Diamanda Galas, Glenn Branca, Cabaret Voltaire, John Sanborn and Peter Weibel. Indeed Weibel, well known in the 1960s for his performances and interventions, was festival director from 1986 to 1995, and is now director of the Zentrum für Kunst und Medientechnologie (ZKM), in Karlsruhe, which is a highly funded research centre and museum dedicated to new media arts.

The German government's decision, taken during the 1980s, to fund ZKM was timely. The development of the World Wide Web in the 1990s has led to an efflorescence of art using and engaging with new media and technology. The ease with which Web sites can be constructed combined with the enormous reach of the Web has made it extraordinarily attractive for artists. Though art on the Web can be traced back to precedents such as work done using bulletin board systems in the 1980s and early '90s, as well as earlier work with free radio, it really took off in the mid 1990s when new browsers made the Web easier to use. One of the most influential movements working with such technology is the 'net.art', which emerged out of the nettime discussion list. Those involved make art that can only work on the Web. Among them are artists such as Vuk Cosic, Olia Lialina, Jodi, Alexei Shulgin, Heath Bunting, Rachel Baker and the Irational [sic] Organization and many others. Though much of this work is innovative, especially in exploring the possibilities of a new medium, it is also oddly familiar. Practically every trope or strategy of the post-war avant-garde has found new expression through net.art, including Lettriste-style hypergraphology, involving the representation of codes and signs, Oulipian combinatorial and algorithmic games, Situationist pranks, Fluxian or Johnsonian postal strategies, stages technological breakdowns such as previously rehearsed in video art, virtual cybernetic and robotic systems, parodies and political interventions.

There are a number of reasons for this fast-forward reprise of the post-war avant-garde. The nature of the Web as a medium makes it easy to run through different possibilities. Furthermore the particular concerns of the post-war avant-garde, in particular in relation to language, codes, signification and gesture, and the deliberate economy of means by which many practitioners achieved their aims, made such work an appropriate model for work on the computer. It also constituted an acknowledgment of the degree to which such work not only anticipated but also helped determine the form that interactive digital media would take. But the work that was most prescient about the future shape of digital media is Cage's $4'33''$. Cage intended this silent piece, with its allusion to the blank screens of Rauschenberg's white canvasses, to be a space in which anything and everything could happen. This is perhaps the perfect model for modern electronic media, from television to multimedia through to the Internet and the World Wide Web.

# 4. The Digital Counter-culture

Marshall McLuhan once suggested that 'art was a distant early warning system that can always tell the old culture what is beginning to happen to it'.[1] The work of Cage and others involved with the post-war avant-garde would seem to confirm McLuhan's theory in their prefiguring of the interactive and multimedia technologies which have come to dominate our lives. This was a less a case of prescience and more a grasp of emerging technological possibilities. Cage and the others offered a framework in which the technologies of Cold War paranoia could be translated into tools for realizing utopian ideals of interconnectivity and self-realization. The use of computers by artists also reflected the growing importance of such technologies as part of the so-called 'post-industrial society'. This was most famously advocated by the American sociologist Daniel Bell in his 1973 book *The Coming of the Post-Industrial Society*,[2] but was anticipated as early on as the 1950s in work by Bell himself, as well by Ralph Dahrendorf, Fritz Machlup, Marshall McLuhan, Jacques Ellul and others. The general thrust of such ideas was that the United States and other developed countries are in the process of developing new forms of social organization that will supersede the prevailing industrial model. Taking their cue from statistics concerning employment, they proposed that as automated industry required fewer and fewer workers, more people would be employed in the service sectors. The result of this is a society in which information and knowledge would be the dominant focus of production, the progress towards which Bell saw in evolutionary terms. At the same time Bell foresaw an increase in the number of people involved in working with 'theoretical knowledge', as opposed to the kinds of empirical investigations more typical of an industrialized society.

With hindsight Bell's ideas have been shown to be inadequate to the realities of contemporary information society, and he himself has repudiated some of his earlier claims. In particular his assumption of a technological determinism, however nuanced, has been the cause of criticism. Nevertheless the idea of the post-industrial society is still widely invoked as a kind of master explanation for present social and cultural realities. Such invocations are, as Frank Webster points out, often heavily stamped with the imprimatur of Bell's name and his rank as a Harvard professor.[3] But the diffusion of the post-industrial society as a concept probably owed more to the apocalyptic and populist writings of Alvin Toffler, who first made his name in 1970 with his book *Future Shock*,[4] which proclaimed the need to understand the future as much as the past and predicted that culture would be increasingly mediated by technology. A decade later he wrote *The Third Wave*,[5] which celebrated the on-coming Knowledge Age in which computers and communications technology would play crucial roles. Toffler advanced a number of strategies for avoiding 'future shock' and preparing the way for the imminent radical social and cultural changes, including 'anticipatory democracy' and 'flexible planning'.

Between the late 1960s and mid '70s the technological means to realize the post-industrial information society were developed, firstly with the simultaneous appearance of the minicomputer and of networked computing, then with the development of the personal computer. The last, in particular, became the technology that, simultaneously, enabled the development of a paradigm of computing congenial to a new generation of users with new needs and cultural perceptions, but also fit for the new realities of a restructured capitalism. But this was not simply a technological development, in which a need was perceived and the solution to its fulfilment supplied. Instead it was the result of the coming together of a number of elements, both cultural and technological. These included an understanding of the possibilities of digital technology arising out of military-funded research, including real-time, graphical computing and networking, as well as the tendency, inspired also by military needs, towards miniaturization, which in turn enabled the development of cheaper, smaller computers. The problem was that such developments were firmly embedded in the technocratic, cybernetic context of Cold War computing, which, in the light of the use of computers in the Vietnam War, was a target of opprobrium for many of those opposing the status quo. An effective shift in the paradigm through which computers were perceived required cultural transformations as much as technological ones.

This shift was accomplished through a number of different, though connected, developments. One was the set of adjustments and changes in the information discourses that had emerged after the War, which re-oriented them in directions appropriate for new ways of thinking. These included the emergence of 'second order' Cybernetics and of the beginnings of new discourses such as Complexity and Artificial Life in the late 1960s. At the same time new and positive conceptions of technology were being articulated, by, among others, those involved in the avant-garde, as well as the media theorist Marshall McLuhan, and the architect and visionary Buckminster Fuller. Finally there were the circumstances that brought these disparate elements together, in particular the coincidental proximity of one of the centres of the micro-electronics industry, Silicon Valley in Northern California, to San Francisco, a little further to the north, which had itself become, by the late 1960s, a centre of the counter-culture.

In the 1950s Bell Labs engineer William Shockley returned to his hometown of Palo Alto to set up a company to exploit the invention of transistors. Invented soon after the War, the transistor did the electronic switching work of the valve far more efficiently, as well as being far smaller and consuming far less electricity. It was almost immediately adopted by producers of consumer electronics, such as televisions and radios, and by the late 1950s was starting to be used in computers. Shockley sited his firm on the West Coast not just out of sentiment. By the 1950s, partly because of the presence of Stanford University, the area just south of San Francisco was already starting to become a centre for the microelectronics industry. Unfortunately for Shockley his management skills were unequal to his engineering brilliance, and within three years eight of his most important engineers, including his most gifted employee, Robert Noyce, had left to start their own company, Fairchild Semiconductors. While they concentrated on producing transistors to make money, Fairchild also put a lot of research into trying to solve the problems inherent in the technology. Though an advance over valves, transistors still presented many problems, especially in relation to military uses. Some of the systems used for guidance in military planes had up to 20,000 transistors, and, with the kinds of usage associated with such systems, the connections between transistors often came loose. Furthermore, the more complex machines became and the more wiring they involved the slower they became. The solution to these problems became a priority of military computing research.

Simultaneously with another company, Texas Instruments, they hit on the means to solve these problems. Both the engineers at Fairchild and Jack Kilby at Texas Instruments realized that the solution was to make the entire circuit out of one block of a semi-conducting material, such as silicon or germanium, preferably all at once. This idea, coupled with the notion of making the circuits flat, led to the invention, in 1959, of the integrated circuit, or IC. (In fact, G. W. Dummer, an engineer and radar expert with Britain's Royal Radar Establishment, had proposed this in 1952. He suggested that the solution might be to produce electronic circuitry in solid blocks. Dummer's prototype failed and he received little support for his idea in Britain. Nevertheless he had hit upon the solution that would eventually be developed independently in the United States.)

Unfortunately integrated circuits were expensive to produce, and thus uneconomical for most computing purposes. But they did turn out to be the ideal solution for the American Space Programme of the 1960s, which culminated in sending men to the moon, as well as for the development of new guided weapons systems such as the Minuteman II missiles. Both required far smaller and more reliable computer systems than were possible with transistors. Thus, with NASA and military funding, the continued development of ICs was made possible. In particular improvements in manufacturing processes meant that the price of individual ICs soon dropped dramatically, from over a thousand dollars in 1959 to less than ten in 1965. The success of ICs, which were soon being incorporated in consumer electronics items such as microwaves, meant that the area in which Fairchild Semiconductors and Shockley Semiconductors had sited themselves attracted large numbers of small semiconductor companies, so much so that it became known as Silicon Valley. In 1968 Robert Noyce and his colleague Gordon Moore left Fairchild to start another company, Intel. In 1969 an Intel engineer Ted Hoff was asked to design a set of twelve ICs for a Japanese calculator. He reasoned that rather than design different sets of chips for different purposes, why not design one set of chips which could be programmed to do any task, much like a computer. This idea, which was dubbed the 'microprocessor', made technically possible the idea of the computer as an affordable consumer item, but it did not lead inevitably to its development.

At about the same time as engineers in Silicon Valley were developing the technology that would miniaturize, and thereby revolutionize, computing, San Francisco, roughly 80 kilometres to the north, was becoming a centre of the so-called counter-culture. This was one of a number of reactions to the sweeping economic and social changes whose impact had been felt at a global level, particularly in the United States, France, Italy and Britain. The combination of high employment resulting from post-war economic prosperity, and the coming of age of the 'baby boom' generation born in the 1940s and 1950s, meant that young people wielded an unprecedented degree of economic and, by extension, cultural power. The late '50s and early '60s had seen the rise of 'youth culture', to begin with a largely manufactured phenomenon, designed to capitalize on the burgeoning economic power of the young through encouraging the consumption of pop music, fashion and other desirable items. But as the '50s and '60s progressed, youth culture had invested some, at least, with a broader sense of the kinds of power and influence young people might wield. This coincided with the increasing visibility of problems and antagonisms that had been largely occluded by the consensual nature of post-war society, but which could now no longer be ignored or contained, such as atomic and nuclear weaponry, the United States' military adventurism in Vietnam, the continuing issue of race and racial discrimination in developed countries, and the growing understanding of the disastrous ecological effects of industry and technology. A dominant perception was that such issues were the result of the mismanagement of previous generations.

Thus the late 1960s saw the development of movements opposed to the previous generation's ways of thinking and acting. These took a number of different forms. In France, for example, the Spring of 1968 saw wholesale political turmoil, as students and others declared a revolution against General de Gaulle's government. In the same year, Italy came near to social collapse in the so-called 'Hot Autumn' of industrial- and student-inspired confrontation, which was to continue throughout the 1970s. In the United States the non-violent tactics of the Civil Rights Movement was superseded by militant activism on the part of groups such as the Black Panthers. Also in the States, militant groups, often, but not always, student-based, were formed in active opposition to the status quo. Other groups also contested their subaltern status. Issues concerning the imbalance of power in relation to gender were articulated through the Feminist movement, for example. Alongside these militant and antagonistic movements, more conciliatory ideas also flourished. Most notably, the concept of a counter-culture, an alternative society based on values other than those supposed to be dominant at that time, found expression in various ways and places. Broadly speaking the counter-culture could be defined as a largely white phenomenon, among whose most notable characteristics were an interest in self-realization, often involving the use of drugs, LSD or 'acid' in particular, a devotion to rock music and performance. It flourished in a number of locations, but found a niche in Northern California, and especially in San Francisco, which had become a magnet for those wishing to experiment with alternative lifestyles and ways of acting and thinking. There were a number of possible reasons for this, including the role in the American imagination of California as the final frontier; San Francisco's small-scale charm; its traditional tolerance, as a port town, for forms of deviance and unorthodoxy; and its adoption by the proto-hippy 'Beat' group of writers and artists. The area where Haight Street and Ashbury Street intersect became a favourite point of meeting for those who wished to embrace the extremes of the counter-culture. On one level, the close proximity of Haight Ashbury and Silicon Valley was simply a co-incidence. The kinds of machines that needed micro-electronics, at least up to the '60s, were exemplary of the technocratic rationality that was opposed by the counter-culture, not least because of their use in Cold War strategy and tactics. One aspect of counter-cultural thinking was also resolutely anti-technological, advocating instead prelapsarian back-to-basics lifestyles. But, on another level, the counter-culture and technological-oriented entrepreneurial capitalism represented different inflections of the frontier spirit that had enabled Leland Stanford to make the fortune that founded Stanford University. This fortuitous proximity of acid and silicon brought together new technology and counter-cultural thinking and created the circumstances that produced the Personal Computer and by extension much of current digital culture.

Exemplary of the ethos of the West Coast counter-culture was the Whole Earth project, founded by Steward Brand and funded by the Portola Institute, a non-profit alternative education organization, which had been started by Bob Albrecht, who had originally worked for the Control Data Corporation. It was a venture aimed at giving people access, through regular 'catalogs', to the tools and ideas with which to lead counter-cultural or alternative lifestyles, and as such was a great success. In 1971, after three years of existence, those involved decided to publish one last catalogue and then dissolve the venture. *The Last Whole Earth Catalog*[6] was duly published that year, and was a far greater success than expected. It sold well enough to require Brand and others to set up the means to distribute the profits usefully and equitably. In 1974 *The Whole Earth Epilog*[7] was published which continued in the same vein, followed in 1982 by an update, *The Next Whole Earth Catalog*.[8] *The Whole Earth Review*, a quarterly journal, was also produced. It too engendered imitations, such as the English *An Index of Possibilities*,[9] published in the mid-'70s. *The Last Whole Earth Catalog* was more than simply a catalogue. It presents a valuable insight into the broad and heterogeneous sources of alternative thinking. As well as sources for agricultural implements, building and craft tools, musical instruments, aids to physical and mental self-help, and for the care of animals, it also contains a great deal of philosophy of various sorts. Much of this is what one might reasonably expect: Jung; Eastern religion; Native American thought and myth and so on. But sitting quite comfortably among these ideas is a great deal of Cybernetics of one sort or another. A number of books about Cybernetics and systems theory are recommended, including works by Norbert Wiener and W. Ross Ashby, as well as works on Artificial Intelligence and connectionism. One of the reasons that Cybernetics was so attractive to those involved with the 'Whole Earth' project was that it used 'whole systems thinking' as a framework in which to think about issues of ecology. Each of the Whole Earth catalogues started with a section called 'Understanding Whole Systems' which enframed the issues of ecology, biosystems and the economy in cybernetic terms. In the original catalogue the presiding genius who is used to introduce the ideas in this section is R(ichard) Buckminster Fuller, the maverick engineer, architect and theorist. Buckminster Fuller, who was notable for the development of the geodesic dome, a structure composed of geometric elements that can be built to any size, was also a poet and philosopher, whose unorthodox ideas about global issues, in particular his concept of 'Spaceship Earth',[10] were appealing to a generation becoming aware of ecological depredation. Fuller emphasized the importance of information as a negatively entropic source of wealth, that increases through research and the development of technology.

In the *Epilog* Fuller's place was taken by Gregory Bateson. Bateson was the son of William Bateson, who was among those who revived and championed the work of Gregor Mendel in genetics and evolutionary biology. He was trained as an anthropologist, and worked in New Guinea and in Bali with anthropologist Margaret Mead, who was also his first wife, but was involved in a number of different fields, including psychiatry and communications. He did valuable research after the War in the study of alcoholism and of schizophrenia, as well as in non-human communication. He was also an important contributor to the Macy Conferences on Cybernetics, described in chapter two. His work in Cybernetics during and after the War led him to develop theories of whole systems, mind–body interaction and co-evolution. Indeed it was through Bateson's influence that Cybernetics, whose influence had declined since its heyday in the 1950s, enjoyed a revival in the late 1960s and early '70s. In 1968 Bateson organized a conference, which built upon the legacy of the Macy Conferences, but brought questions regarding the observer and reflexivity to bear upon the points the conferences had raised, and which drew upon the work of cybernetic researchers such as Humberto Maturana and Francisco Varela.

## SECOND-ORDER CYBERNETICS

One of the problems was that the Cybernetics that emerged out of the Macy Conferences and elsewhere in the 1940s and '50s was typical of its period. It was largely based on engineering paradigms, and was interested in idealized systems of homeostasis and feedback. It adhered to the traditional scientific view of the observer as standing outside of the system being observed. It could thus be considered paradigmatic of the Cold War era, in which the main issues were that of effective and efficient control and communication. Throughout the period of the Macy Conferences the question of reflexivity and the role of the observer was not discussed or problematized. Cybernetics by its very nature could not entirely ignore the role of the observer. But in the event, only the psychoanalyst Lawrence Kubie attempted to bring such questions into the discussions during the original conferences. Kubie's combative style of argumentation apparently did not help his cause and his ideas failed to become part of the cybernetic paradigm.[11]

Out of their experiences as part of a team studying a frog's perception processes, Maturana and Varela had determined that for any organism reality comes into existence through interactive processes determined by its own organization. Out of these observations they developed the idea of 'autopoiesis'. An autopoietic system is one that is organized so that the components from which it is composed work towards maintaining its composition. Such systems produce the components by which they are defined and then recursively regenerate these components in order to maintain their identity.[12] Autopoietic systems are closed inasmuch as any response to changes in their medium takes place solely within the network of processes defining them as entities. The identity of such systems is defined through its organization, rather than through its material structure.

Like Maturana and Varela, Bateson understood that the world is constructed by our sensory perceptions, rather than being available in the plenitude of its reality. He explored these ideas in a number of works, which were later published in book form as *Steps to an Ecology of Mind*,[13] *A Sacred Unity: Further Steps to an Ecology of Mind*[14] and *Mind and Nature: A Necessary Unity*.[15] Owing perhaps to the approachability of his style or his wide range of interests and invocation of esoteric concepts, Bateson achieved cult status within the counter-culture. In particular his work, and that of Maturana and Varela and von Bertalanffy, founder of General Systems Theory, was of great importance to the burgeoning ecology movement. Their emphasis on the interconnected nature of phenomena and the relation between living entities and the ecosystem presented a framework through which the troubling issues surrounding the human depredation of the environment could be discussed and criticized.

At the same time the greater availability and increased processing power of computers was offering new insights into the complex ways in which systems were organized and how that organization might arise. In the mid-1960s Edward Lorenz, a meteorologist at MIT, while doing experiments with computers to model atmospheric conditions, realized that very small variations in the data used could lead to massive changes in the end result. Lorenz, with some poetic license, encapsulated the basic idea with the image of a butterfly, which, by flapping its wings in South America could, eventually, lead to tornadoes in the United States.[16] His work led to research into the long-term behaviour of systems that exhibited unpredictable and chaotic behaviour. In 1970 John Conway, a mathematician at Cambridge, England, developed what he called the 'Game of Life'. This was a rule-based cellular automaton, which, through the application of a number of simple but subtle rules, could generate complex and fascinating states over time. This seemed to demonstrate that complexity and order could be generated out of sets of simple rules. Similar conclusions could be drawn from the work of mathematician Benoit Mandelbrot, which led to his concept of fractal geometry. This term was first proposed by Mandelbrot when working at IBM. In a paper entitled 'How Long is the Coast of Britain?'[17] he showed that the answer depends on the scale of measurement used and that, in theory, it could be infinite in length. Mandelbrot's research led him to develop ideas about geometry based on work by earlier mathematicians such as Helge von Koch, Waclaw Sierpinski, Pierre Fatou and Gaston Julia, each of whom had proposed mathematically generated figures of great complexity, which they had been unable to represent visually. Using the then newly available power of computers to represent complex coloured images Mandelbrot produced extraordinary visual objects, such as the Mandelbrot Set (illus. 36) – a paisley-like arabesque pattern, the complexity of which remains constant at whatever scale or detail it is projected – which were generated out of simple algorithms. These various developments demonstrated the potential for computers to be far more than simply calculating machines.

The capacity to produce spontaneous order through algorithmic processes resonated within ideas gaining prominence in another field. In the section on economics in *The Last Whole Earth Catalog* an excerpt from Milton Friedman's *Capitalism and Freedom*[18] can be found. At first the presence of such a text in a counter-culture document such as the *Catalog* is surprising. Friedman was one of the principle advocates of neo-liberal economic theory, which

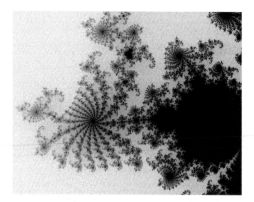

36 Visual display of a
Mandelbrot set, or fractal.

strongly advocated a free market, against the prevailing Keynesian
belief in state intervention. Advocacy of capitalism in any form
might seem hard to square with counter-cultural aspirations (especially with the hindsight of some 30 years of the application of such
ideas by Thatcher, Reagan et al). In fact the kind of radical measures
proposed by Friedman were not so far from ideas advocated by
the libertarian element within the counter-culture, especially in their
shared respect for notions of individualism. Furthermore, central
to neo-liberal economics was the conception of the market as a
spontaneously ordered institution, rather than the product of intelligent design. This was first put forward in the early '60s by Friedrich
von Hayek, who worked with, and greatly influenced, Friedman.
The beginnings of computer-oriented study of spontaneous order
in the '70s must have reinforced arguments for spontaneous order in
areas such as economics.

COMPUTING AND THE COUNTER-CULTURE

As well making Cybernetics safe for the counter-culture, *The Whole
Earth Catalog* also helped to create the context in which the personal
computer was realized, and in which interactive multimedia became
available as a consumer product. The counter-culture opened up
a space in which the personal computer could be developed. The

ideas it encouraged concerning the use of appropriate tools, self-help and empowerment made the concept of building and owning a computer a plausible reality. In particular the counter-culture was instrumental in creating the context in which the real-time interactive technologies developed by the military, or through military funding in the context of the Cold War, could be stripped of their militaristic, technocratic aura, repainted with a gloss of cybernetic idealism, taken in part from the post-war avant-garde, and repurposed as gentler, kinder tools for a new generation. Though interactive and multimedia technology was developed in the labs of the Cold War, the ability to conceive it as peaceful and progressive was nurtured at least in part by the counter-culture and the avant-garde ideas about intermedia, multimedia and performance that it inherited.

In a 1972 article in *Rolling Stone* magazine on *Spacewar*, the original computer game built by hackers at MIT, *Whole Earth* founder Stewart Brand proclaimed that 'computers were coming to the people'. Brand described this as 'good news, maybe the best since psychedelics'.[19] He was also reputedly the first to use the term 'personal computer' in print, in his 1974 book *Two Cybernetic Frontiers*. Though he credits the coining of the term to computer scientist Alan Kay, by 1975 he was also using it regularly in his journal *Co-Evolution Quarterly*, before such devices properly existed. Bob Albrecht had reputedly left the Control Data Corporation to start the Portola Institute, funders of the *Whole Earth* enterprise, because of their reluctance to consider developing a personal computer. At the same time as funding the Whole Earth project, Albrecht was also publishing a tabloid paper called the *People's Computer Company*, which was intended to disseminate information about computing to the public in the Bay Area. The philosophy of enabling access to tools and knowledge exemplified in both the *Whole Earth* catalogs and the PCC inspired other projects, such as Berkeley's Community Memory, started by Lee Felsenstein in 1973, an early experiment in using the technology to encourage and facilitate ideas of community and the free exchange of ideas, through networks.

At the same time, developments in mainstream computer research were beginning to resemble counter-cultural phenomena. One such development was the Augmented Knowledge Workshop held at the 1968 Fall Joint Computer Conference in San Francisco by Douglas Engelbart and his NLS team with the help of volunteers such as Stewart Brand (illus. 37), which has now achieved legendary status in Silicon Valley. In an announcement for a conference celebrating the thirtieth anniversary of this event, the company responsible breathlessly declared that it was like a 'trippy rock concert'. In fact given the equipment assembled for the demonstration, including twelve CRT displays (illus. 38), it must have strongly suggested the multimedia performances then being pioneered by avant-garde artists and psychedelic groups such as the Velvet Underground and the Pink Floyd, as well as the light shows found in 'underground' clubs. When asked, in an interview in an on-line journal, whether he was surprised that people associated with the counter-culture suddenly got involved with computers, Engelbart remarked that he was not, because what he did 'just did not register with many people in the "ordinary culture"'.[20] Though ostensibly a conventional engineer and scientist, Engelbart had been

37 *Whole Earth* founder and personal computer advocate Stewart Brand and others backstage at the 1968 Fall Joint Computer Conference in San Francisco, CA (Brand is in the foreground with the cine-camera).

38 Screenshot of Douglas Engelbart at his now-famous multimedia presentation at the 1968 Fall Joint Computer Conference in San Francisco, CA.

proclaiming the radical potential of computers in enabling the augmentation of human intelligence. This connection was reinforced at the conference by the presence of Brand. Engelbart's project resonated with the concerns with personal development and the appropriate use of tools and technology that underpinned the *Whole Earth* philosophy. Thus it was not surprising that, through the *Whole Earth Catalog*, the *Co-Evolution Quarterly* and journalism for *Rolling Stone* magazine, Brand argued for the potential of computers. This led not just to the conditions that enabled the PC, but also presented a context in which its future development could be imagined, as a counter-cultural and even revolutionary device.

In the same year that Engelbart and his associates undertook their famous demonstration, Nicholas Negroponte founded the Architecture Machine Group at MIT. Negroponte was a graduate of MIT where he had studied computer-aided design, and where he joined the faculty in 1966. The Architecture Machine Group was intended as a combination laboratory and think tank for studying issues of human-computer interface. In 1976 the group proposed to DARPA a project called 'Augmentation of Human Resources

39 Aspen Movie Map video-disc demonstration, 1978 (1).

in Command and Control through Multiple Media Man-Machine Interaction'. This was intended as a kind of three-dimensional virtual space that a user could interact with. In 1978, the Architecture Machine Group created the Aspen Movie Map (illus. 39). This was a system that simulated driving through the city of Aspen in Colorado, via a computer screen (illus. 40). Built using videodiscs it enabled the user to navigate through the city, and even choose the season in which they are travelling. It was, and indeed remains, one of the most sophisticated systems ever built. It exemplifies the interdisciplinary approach that Negroponte encouraged and which was demonstrated in his appearance as an installation artist at Jack Burnham's 'Software' show. Between 1979 and 1980 Negroponte and ex-MIT president Jerome Weisner put together a proposal for a successor to the Architecture Machine Group, The Media Lab. This was intended to bring together the different strengths found at MIT, including computer programmers, but also psychologists, film-makers, musicians, designers, anthropologists, designers and others who could contribute to its stated aim of studying the possibilities of information and communication technologies. The Media Lab was one of the first places where ideas about multimedia, which had

40 Aspen Movie Map video-disk demonstration, 1978 (2).

developed in the context of avant-garde art practice and counter cultural performance, were first applied to computers.[21]

*The Whole Earth Catalog* inspired maverick Theodor Holm (Ted) Nelson to proclaim a vision of the expanded possibilities of computers in his book *Computer Lib /Machine Dreams*.[22] Nelson was a philosophy graduate who had come into contact with computers while studying for a sociology masters degree at Harvard in 1960. His remarkably prescient, and at the time, eccentric, perception of their possibilities, led him to try to build a word-processing system before either the name or the concept existed. In 1965 he gave a paper at the conference of the Association of Computing Machinery (ACM), in which he laid out his vision for what he called 'hypertext', by which he referred to non-linear, linked texts. Nelson attempted to realize his ideas by developing 'Xanadu'. This was a software framework, greatly influenced by Vannevar Bush's 1945 article 'As We May Think' (which also inspired Engelbart) that would enable access to all the world's textual information, and make it possible to link and examine texts in parallel and to produce new versions. Xanadu's arrival has been imminent since the mid-1960s, but much of what it promises has been realized by the World Wide Web. Thus Nelson's influence has been felt more at the conceptual than the practical level.

One of the great beneficiaries of the turmoil of the late 1960s and early '70s, of which the counter-culture was part, was the research centre set up by the photocopier firm Xerox, XeroxPARC (Xerox Palo Alto Research Centre). The United States's disastrous and highly controversial involvement in the Vietnam War had many repercussions, including that of inciting a generation of objectors and draft refusees to acts of civil disobedience, confrontation and violence. It also brought into question the role of military funding in university research, which many felt to be a threat to academic independence. Thus, in 1970, in an amendment to the Military Procurement Authorization Bill, a committee headed by Senator Mike Mansfield proposed that 'none of the funds authorized . . . may be used to carry out any research project or study unless such a study has a direct and apparent relationship to a specific military function or operation'.[23] The Mansfield Amendment particularly affected those working in the kinds of computer research which had been largely funded by ARPA and had benefited from ARPA's open-ended remit. The National Science Foundation, which might have taken up the slack, was not given sufficient funds. At the same time Xerox was becoming alarmed at the idea of the 'paperless office', the revolution in business life that computers were, apparently, about to bring about. To meet this challenge Xerox decided to become part of the computer revolution itself. To this end it set up XeroxPARC on the West Coast of the United States. The choice of Palo Alto, rather than New Haven, the preference of Jacob Goldman, head of corporate research at Xerox, was fortuitous. Not only was Silicon Valley just beginning to become the centre of micro-electronics, but it was also near the epicentre of alternative counter-cultural thinking. All in all it was an ideal situation to attract young and unconventional computer scientists and researchers.

The first head of XeroxPARC was Bob Taylor, J.C.R. Licklider's successor at IPTO, ARPA's computing research arm. One of the first acts Taylor undertook was to buy a number of blue corduroy beanbags for the Center, which helped to create a laid-back campus atmosphere undoubtedly congenial to the kinds of researcher they wished to employ. The work being done there also attracted the ubiquitous Stewart Brand, who came to hang out, and to write about what he saw there for his prescient 1972 *Rolling Stone* article, which predicted the advent of the personal computer. In return Brand's approach informed the work at PARC. In an article about Brand in *Fortune* magazine, Alan Kay remarked that *The Whole Earth Catalog* was the first book PARC owned and that it was a symbol of what they were trying to achieve. This, combined with the Mansfield Amendment and the presence of Taylor at XeroxPARC, meant that many talented computer scientists and researchers who had been ARPA-funded were now drawn to the Centre. Among them was Kay, who had worked with Ivan Sutherland, developer of Sketchpad, at the University of Utah, and who had witnessed Douglas Engelbart's famous Augmented Knowledge Workshop in 1968. The work of Kay and others at PARC was informed by its set-up and circumstances, as well as by Seymour Papert's experiments with children and computers at MIT, which had been influenced by the structuralist cognitive psychologist Jean Piaget. In particular those at PARC developed new, intuitive methods of interacting with the computer, by conjoining Sutherland's advances in visual computing and Engelbart's developments in making the computer more 'user-friendly' with developments in areas such as bit-mapped graphics. The eventual result was the 'Alto', a new kind of computer, which, through the use of windows, a mouse, and a graphic interface, could be, at least in theory, used intuitively and easily by anyone. For a number of reasons to do with economics and perception of appropriate markets, Xerox marketed the Alto, and a later version of their ideas, the 'Star', as business machines and priced them accordingly. Though the ideas the machines manifested were greeted favourably, the inept marketing meant that they did not succeed.[24]

At the same time the computer world had developed its own kind of counter-culture, known as 'hacking'. Hacking developed in computer laboratories at MIT, then at Stanford, to which students intrigued by the possibilities of computing gravitated. Out of these environments a 'hacker' culture developed, consisting of young men dedicated to undertaking elegant 'hacks', that is, to finding out what computers were capable of, rather than criminal acts, as the term later came to mean. In exchange for more orthodox social relations they developed an almost monastic devotion to the computer. The normal rhythms of work and rest were dispensable, in exchange for long periods of engagement with complex programs. The early hackers at MIT and Stanford established one of the central archetypes of computing subculture, which continues to this day, that of the intellectually advanced but socially and sexually awkward male, who is prepared to devote most of his time to an engagement with the possibilities of digital technology, to the exclusion of almost anything else. This involved working for days and nights at a stretch, living on junk food and paying scant attention to personal hygiene and grooming.[25] Generally speaking hackers were not in any explicit sense counter-cultural, though the related activity of 'phreaking', illegally manipulating or 'hacking' the phone system, was exploited by some for its political possibilities. (The Youth International Party, or Yippie, revolutionary movement, headed by Abbie Hoffman, started *YIPL/TAP* – or Youth International Party Line/Technical Assistance Program – magazine to diffuse information about hacking the phone system. Similar information was also available in the radical underground publication *Ramparts*, which was busted in 1972 for publishing the schematics for building a blue box, a device for making free phone calls.) But some of those involved in various aspects of counter-cultural thinking perceived that the computer, despite its military and capitalist aspects, might have revolutionary potential. Others, some coming from a long American tradition of electronic hobbyists going back to the radio enthusiasts of the pre-war years, and some from the hacker community, were simply fascinated by the possibility and the technical challenge of building computers for oneself.

These different strands came together at the series of 'Homebrew' club meetings started in 1975. These were largely informal gatherings of those interested in computers in various venues around Silicon Valley, where news of emerging technologies, clever 'hacks' and gossip were all exchanged. Mostly, despite the attempts on the part of some participants to bring political issues into the discussion, these meetings concentrated on technical issues. One event in particular stimulated the founding of the Homebrew clubs. In the beginning of 1975 an electronics firm in New Mexico, MITS, offered a computer for sale on the cover of the magazine *Popular Electronics* (illus. 41). The machine in question was in kit form, was hard to assemble, and, when assembled, did more or less nothing. It could be programmed by flicking switches, but, lacking any kind of output device, the only visible evidence of operating was of a series of lights flashing on the front. Despite this almost total lack of apparent usefulness, MITS was inundated with orders for the machine, which was named 'Altair' after a planet in the TV series *Star Trek*. The idea of owning a computer, whatever it was capable of, proved extraordinarily attractive to the thousands of electronics and computer enthusiasts whose needs were not being addressed by major computer companies. The Homebrew clubs were largely devoted to ways of engaging with this simple technology, and as such appealed to 'hackers', those who enjoyed making computers do a thing for

41 The Altair microcomputer, c. 1975, reputedly the first Personal Computer.

its own sake, simply to see if it could be done. Gradually other individuals and companies produced other personal computers and peripherals that would allow more complex interactions. Many of these, such as the machine produced by the IMSAI company, have been forgotten, though they all contributed to developing the personal computer as a viable commercial proposition.

The exception to the generally ephemeral existence of these technologies and the firms who made them was a machine unveiled at a 1976 Homebrew meeting. Designed by a gifted engineer from Hewlett Packard, Steve Wozniak, and promoted by his friend Steve Jobs, this machine was the first Apple Computer, the Apple I (illus. 42). It was just a board loaded with chips. But owing to Wozniak's programming and hardware skills it was recognized as an excellent piece of hardware, which, when plugged in to a keyboard and a TV monitor could allow the user to achieve what seemed then extraordinary things, such as display graphics. The next computer, the Apple II, was far more sophisticated, incorporating a version of the BASIC programming language, and the ability to output colour graphics all housed in an elegant casing. Though it still had to be plugged into the TV, it was clearly a complete working computer. The combination of Wozniak's programming genius, and Job's

42 Apple 1, 1976.
The first computer made by Apple Computers Inc.

entrepreneurial talents meant that the Apple II was successful in ways that no other such product had been. Jobs realized that the amateurism that had characterized the personal computer industry was no longer appropriate, and employed a marketing director, Mike Markulla from Intel, and a manager, Mike Scott, from Fairchild Semiconductor. Both were older, more experienced and looked more respectable than either Wozniak or Jobs. With this Jobs turned Apple from two men in a garage into a fully-fledged company, whose turnover had, in five years, exceeded hundreds of millions of dollars. Naturally the vast amounts of money to be made in personal computing put paid to any hope of the more radical aspects that had characterized the Homebrew clubs, such as the original sense of sharing and community, continuing to have any real influence. Nonetheless Apple held, and continues to hold, onto its counter-cultural image which turned out to be advantageous for advertising and branding. The success of Apple alerted IBM to both the possibilities of the personal computer, and the threat it might pose to their own domination of the industry. By 1981 they had, with unseemly haste by IBM standards, produced their own machine, the IBM PC (illus. 43). IBM confounded many expectations by adopting some of the hacker ways of doing things, such as making available the machine's technical specifications, and encouraging others to write software for it. This was not as open-minded as it might seem, but rather a solution to the problem of developing the machine at a far greater speed than was their normal practice. This entailed using as many parts from other sources as possible, and thus opening up the market to other manufacturers. Perhaps the main beneficiary of this strategy was Microsoft. They supplied the operating system for the PC, for a flat fee, but were able to make lucrative licensing deals with producers of PC clones – machines that used the same off-the-shelf parts as the IBM but were considerably cheaper.

At the time, Apple was working on various possible successors to the Apple II, the computer that had allowed them to become

43 An IBM PC being used in an office, mid-1980s.

the world's most successful PC manufacturer. Among these were the Apple III, and Apple founder Steve Jobs' own personal project, the 'Lisa'. Jobs, who had been part of an Apple visit to PARC, decided that the innovations that PARC scientists had developed would be ideal for his ambitions for the Lisa. Realizing that Xerox itself had little intention of marketing these ideas effectively, Jobs, in a sleight of hand, negotiated a licensing agreement that allowed Apple to use the PARC interface on their computers. Lisa, the first Apple computer to incorporate the PARC-style interface (though re-engineered and developed by Apple engineers) was warmly received on its release in 1983, but was a slow and expensive machine. The next year Apple released another computer, using the PARC-style interface yet again, but both cheaper and faster. This was the Macintosh (illus. 44), developed in parallel with the Lisa, and announced in a now-legendary advertising spot during the 1984 Superbowl. The Apple Macintosh, with its bit-mapped graphics, graphical user interface, ease of interaction and stylish look defined the shape of the personal computer. Almost immediately after the release of the Macintosh, Microsoft produced a new operating system, Windows, to sit on top of MS-DOS, the Microsoft operating system which ran on most IBM and IBM-compatible personal computers, which looked and worked remarkably like the Macintosh. The potential offered by the WIMP (windows, icons, mouse, pointer) interface led to the computer's infiltration into many new or relatively under-exploited areas, including graphic design, printing and publishing, sound production, image manipulation and production, as well as extending its traditional relationship with business.[26]

It also brought multimedia and hypertext/hypermedia into the reach of commercial developers and the public. This was helped by the arrival of the compact disc, which, though originally intended for music, could equally well store other kinds of digital data. Known as the CD-Rom, the compact disc became a platform on which games and multimedia could be stored and accessed. In 1987 Apple released HyperCard, a hypermedia-programming environment intended for general use. Using the metaphor of the Rolodex card index, and integrated with a simple scripting language, HyperTalk, HyperCard enabled users to build working software, databases, hypertexts and more, as well as to integrate different forms of media and control other devices. Other multimedia authoring software was also developed to enable the production

44 Apple Macintosh model Moo1, c. 1985, with keyboard and mouse.

of CD-Roms and other interactive media and platforms. These included Macromedia Director, Asymetrix Toolbook, and Silicon Beach's SuperCard among others. This proliferation of authoring software was a response to the promise that interactivity and CD-Rom seemed to hold as a commercial product. A certain amount of hyperbole was generated about the CD-Rom in the early '90s, as, for example, the 'new papyrus'.[27] This and other such rhetorical flourishes suggested that such technology represented an advance in information technology equal to, for example, the printed book, that publishers and media companies would be foolish to ignore. Accordingly in the early '90s there was a boom of multimedia companies and multimedia departments within publishing and TV production companies. However, despite the hyperbole, the CD-Rom industry failed to take off as expected.

## THE DIGITAL COUNTER-CULTURE AND NEOLIBERALISM

As the 1980s progressed some of the more extreme elements of the Californian counter-culture embraced new technology with enthusiasm. In the late '80s, echoing Stewart Brand's earlier comment, acid guru Timothy Leary started to proclaim that personal computers were 'the LSD of the '90s';[28] bizarre publications also emerged, such as *High Frontiers*, founded in 1984, described by Mark Dery as a 'heady blend of gadget pornography, guerrilla humour, human potential pep talk, New Age transcendentalism and libertarian anarcho-capitalism'.[29] *High Frontiers* mutated into *Reality Hackers* and then *Mondo 2000*, in which form it continues as an expensive and glossy cyberculture magazine.[30] Edited by R. U. Sirius and Queen Mu, self-styled 'domineditrix', *Mondo* also has connections with even more extreme movements such as the LA-based 'Extropians', who, in a combination of Ayn Rand and Friedrich Nietzsche, proclaim the need for leaving the physical body and downloading the mind onto computers. The increasing importance of computers and their resonance with counter-cultural ideas continued to be reflected in the *Whole Earth Catalogs*. In the first catalogue computers occupied two pages. Ten years later they took up twelve. In 1988 another *Whole Earth Catalog* was produced called *Signal*[31] which was entirely devoted to information technology and philosophy. This focus reflected the sense that much of the kind of alternative thinking the Whole Earth represented was by now best realized with such technology. In *Signal* the entire gamut of complexity- and chaos-oriented theories are introduced alongside the more traditional references to Cybernetics and whole systems. This concentration on technology was accompanied by a political shift. For *Signal* Stewart Brand had relinquished the editorial role to Kevin Kelly, who, in his mid-thirties at the time, was younger than the original group of Whole Earthers. Kelly and his even younger team were far more in tune with the new technology-oriented culture of 1980s northern California. The meteoric success of Apple, a computer company started by long-haired hobbyists, encouraged the sense that personal computing was a counter-cultural production, notwithstanding the technology's development in Cold War laboratories. Apple was also felt to be a particularly Californian success, mixing entrepreneurial capitalism and counter-culture ethics without the sense of contradiction that such a combination might evoke. In this Apple was exemplary of the changed political climate in the 1980s. In response partly to the social and cultural upheavals of the '60s, and also to the failure of the Fordist-Keynesian policies pursued by many governments to cope with the complexities of contemporary globalized capitalism, many countries had experienced a dramatic shift to the right in politics. In Britain Conservative Prime Minister Margaret Thatcher had, since her election in 1979, implemented a series of radical measures intended to scale down government and to free the market from restrictions. Thatcher was highly influenced by neo-liberal economists Hayek and Friedman, the latter an erstwhile *Whole Earth* favourite. She formed a strong alliance with Ronald Reagan, who was elected President of the United States in 1980. Reagan espoused 'supply side economics', in the name of which he made dramatic cuts in taxes, and in government support of social welfare programmes, while massively increasing military expenditure.

These measures, both conservative and radical at the same time, were a response to the challenges of a society in which the post-war Fordist-Keynesian consensus no longer held. Neo-liberal economics was a kind of ideological justification for the dramatic adjustments governments perceived as necessary in the context of highly competitive globalized capitalism, and of the high social costs they incurred. It might seem at first that, both in theory and in practice, neo-liberalism would be at odds with counter-cultural thinking. But in fact, as remarked before, there is a remarkable degree of consensus. Both neo-liberalism and the counter-culture elevated the individual over the collective. Both also proclaimed the necessity of freeing the individual's capacity to act from the tyranny of organizations and bureaucracies. The hedonism that was a characteristic part of the counter-culture is not so far from the neo-liberal appeal to the self-interest of the consumer. In a curious way, the pursuit of neo-liberal policies is also the triumph of counter-cultural ideas. Another shared characteristic is a belief in the positive power of information technology. As we have seen, from the late '60s counter-culture luminaries such as Brand were extolling the potential of computers. The rhetoric of neo-liberalism also continually emphasizes the extraordinary abilities of computers and networks to enable the managing of complex interlinked markets. But the affinities between neo-liberalism and technology run deeper. Like Adam Smith's market system, described in chapter one, neo-liberal economics instantiate a kind of cybernetic fantasy of self-regulation. In his early work on theoretical psychology, Hayek acknowledged the influence of his friend Ludwig van Bertallanfy, founder of General Systems Theory, as well as of Norbert Wiener and Walter Cannon, both of who were instrumental in formulating Cybernetics. Hayek's idea of the market as a spontaneous natural phenomenon undoubtedly owed much to the influence of these ideas, as well as to Smith's theories of the 'invisible hand' and to Darwinian evolution. Accompanying these naturalizations of capitalism and technology is an active denial of the role of government. In her book *Cyberselfish* Paulina Barsook has examined the degree to which a loathing of government intervention, or indeed government altogether, combined with a belief in the capitalist entrepreneurship as the best means to encourage creativity, have become the unquestioned tenets of those working in the computer industry.[32] As she points out, such beliefs bear little or any relation to the realities of that industry and the means through which it has developed and continues to be supported. The most extreme manifestation of such libertarianism is possibly to be found in the discourse surrounding freedom of expression and privacy in relation to the Internet. In 1990 Grateful Dead lyricist and Republican John Perry Barlow, along with Lotus founder Mitch Kapor and Stewart Brand, started the Electronic Frontier Foundation, dedicated to the preservation of free speech and freedom of expression on the Internet. Invoking one of the central tropes of American history, that of the frontier, the EFF deals with all aspects of freedom of expression in the new media, including defending hackers who have run foul of the law. The EFF eschews strategies such as lobbying in Washington, and relies on support from computer professionals. One of the areas that most exercises the EFF is that of cryptography. Indeed this is one of the most difficult issues in relation to computers. The development of effectively unbreakable cryptographic techniques such as Philip Zimmerman's PGP (Pretty Good Privacy) has caused consternation in the United States' and other governments. The United States proposed various measures, known as 'Key Escrow', which would enable them to decode any encrypted communications. Particularly controversial was the NSA/FBI 'Clipper Chip', widely regarded as a form of intrusive 'digital wire-tapping'. The EFF was, and remains vigilant to the threats to free speech and the rights of privacy such proposals represent, and have been instrumental in keeping debate going on such topics. Taking a more proactive stance are the so-called 'cypherPunks' or 'crypto-anarchists', who are engaged in actively using encryption technology to undermine or subvert official channels of communication. Whether through the activities of the EFF or of such cypherPunks, the Web becomes a kind of virtual disputed territory, over which governmental forces of repression and the supporters of liberty fight for control. (Interestingly, given this aversion to government, Brand, along with Kelly and Negroponte, is also a founder of the Global Business Network, a California-based brains trust that advises multinational companies and governments, including that of the United States, about information technology and economic strategy in the post-Cold War global economy.)

By the time neo-liberal policies were being put into practice, Cybernetics and systems theories had given rise to new ways of thinking about order, organization and self-regulation. The developments in Cybernetics leading to theories about autopoiesis, work in automata, and in complex phenomena such as the weather, had given rise to new areas of scientific research, such as chaos and complexity. These had developed partly out of the work of Lorenz, Mandelbrot, Conway and others described above. Shared by these different thinkers was the idea that order could be generated out of chaos, and complexity out of simplicity. These ideas were further developed by others, including the biologist Stuart Kauffman, who had already experimented with shuffling computer-punched cards in the '60s to show, as he had expected, that the apparently random sequence settled into a 'state cycle' very quickly. Out of this he developed his theories of complexity, in which order emerges out of apparent chaos. Meanwhile Chris Langton has furthered this work by suggesting that the 'phase transitions' found in physics, in which a system moves from one state to another, from a solid to a gas for example, have their equivalents in any complex systems. He proposed that such transitions could be found in the history of complex societies. Langton, along with Thomas Ray, is also one of the main proponents of Artificial Life, which, following Conway's Game of Life, seeks to model complex, self-organising systems on the computer.

These ideas and others soon became coralled under the general term of complexity, which became recognized as an exciting, if controversial, area of research. In 1984 the Santa Fe Institute was founded as a non-profit, interdisciplinary research institution dedicated to complexity research, which attracted scientists from a diversity of disciplines, including physicist and Nobel laureate Murray Gell-Mann. The recognition of complexity as an area of research worth funding was explicitly bound up with the emergence of post-Fordist capitalism. The Santa Fe Institute itself was funded by Citibank with the expectation that its research might contribute to the bank's capacity to understand and manage the complexities of globalized capital. Much of the work done in the Institute has been and continues to be concerned with the application of complexity to economics. To some extent complexity theory represents a kind of scientific legitimation of the ideology of neo-liberalism. It enables a conflation of capitalism, nature and technology, and introduces a new version of Smith's invisible hand, one in which order emerges out of complex and apparently chaotic situations.

Whatever the no doubt eminently practical reasons for locating the Institute in Sante Fe, its position gave it an agreeably counter-cultural gloss. That particular corner of New Mexico had long attracted those in search of spiritual renewal and inspiration, including artists and writers such as D. H. Lawrence, Georgia O'Keeffe and Ansel Adams. In 1967 one of the most famous hippie communes was founded in Taos. Part of the draw was the extraordinary land-scape and the quality of the light, but added to this was the rich Native American heritage so in evidence in that part of New Mexico. This offered a set of beliefs about human relations to nature that was congenial to those critical of the depredations wrought by Western modernity and industrialization (unsurprisingly there is a good deal of Native American literature in the *Whole Earth Catalogs*). Whether intended by those researching it or not, complexity theory resonates with such holistic and mystical ideas about ecology. This found independent expression in the work of Fritjof Capra, the physicist and New Age mystic. In *The Tao of Physics*[33] he attempted to conflate developments in physics with Eastern mysticism. In *The Turning Point*[34] he proposed a shift away from Newtonian models of science towards holism and deep ecology. His 1996 book *The Web of Life*[35] drew heavily on the work of Bateson, Kauffman, Valera and Maturana and other proponents of autopoesis, systems theory and complexity, to develop similar ideas and to draw mystical conclusions. Thus the emergence of complexity theory in the late '70s and '80s brought together a number of elements that had been anticipated in earlier instantiations of the counter-culture, including neo-liberal economics, Cybernetics, ecology, mysticism and technology. It should be no surprise therefore that one of the long-term trustees of Santa Fe Institute is Stewart Brand.

Such developments enabled, through a kind of sophistry or sleight of hand, a process in which 'nature', new technology and the capitalist economy are conflated to produce a new kind of capitalist techno-nature. This derives, in part at least, from the work of economist Michael Rothschild, whose 1990 work *Bionomics: Economy as Ecosystem*[36] proposed a biological model for the understanding of economic systems. Highly congenial to neo-liberal thinking, Rothschild's ideas have been promulgated by bodies such as the Cato Institute, a libertarian Washington think tank. It has also found a ready reception in Silicon Valley and other centres of high tech production, and found its way into the writings of Kevin Kelly, Nicholas Negroponte, George Gilder and others involved with *Wired*. Gilder started out as a right-wing sociologist and political theorist, writing controversial studies of race and poverty. Later he became one of the principal advocates of supply-side economics, and was much quoted by President Reagan. More recently he has concerned himself with the possibilities of high technology. In his newsletter, the *Gilder Technology Report* he advises corporations about technological developments, while, in a series of books including *Microcosm*,[37] *Life after Television*[38] and *Telecosm*,[39] he has breathlessly proclaimed a future dominated and determined by electronic technologies. Telecosm predicts the end of the computer and the beginnings of a world dominated by wireless, broadband and network technology, with far reaching social consequences. Nicholas Negroponte, founder of the MIT Media Lab, has written a manifesto entitled *Being Digital*,[40] which looks to a brave new digital world where atoms are replaced by bits, or in other words, many of the clumsy material means of communication and representation we presently use, such as books, television videos or celluloid films, will be superseded by far more efficient and lightweight digital means. Kevin Kelly, erstwhile editor of *Wired*, has made a name for writing populist books aiming to express the technological zeitgeist, particularly inasmuch as it seems to confirm his own technological utopian and determinist neo-liberal agenda. Pre-eminent among these works is *Out of Control*,[41] in which Kelly conflates the operations of global capitalism, neo-liberal economic theory, experiments in computer-simulated 'life', the sciences of complexity and chaos, the World Wide Web and other phenomena to proclaim the advent of an 'out of control' neo-biological world.

## THE WORLD WIDE WEB

The development and reception of these ideas owed much to the increasing importance of the Internet and the emergence of the World Wide Web. In the late 1970s the Internet was beginning to emerge out of the loose conglomeration of networks that had developed around ARPANET since its founding in the late 1960s.

ARPANET had succeeded beyond its designers' expectations and in ways they had not anticipated. The development of e-mail in the 1970s, as well as other technological advances, had taken the original network far beyond its original remit. It started to become a way of communicating for people outside the computer science and military communities for whom it was originally intended. This was helped by the development of a number of 'protocols' for the transmission of data over networks, starting with 'Ethernet', in 1974, developed by Harvard student Bob Metcalfe in his PhD dissertation on 'Packet Networks'. This became a standard protocol for the linking of local networks. 'Transmission Control Protocol/Internet Protocol' (TCP/IP) developed by Bob Kahn at BBN and further developed by Bob Kahn, Vint Cerf at Stanford and others throughout the 1970s, was a protocol for remote networks, and was adopted by the Defense Department in 1980 and universally in 1983. Other important developments included 'Newsgroups', discussion groups focusing on a topic, providing a means of exchanging information throughout the world, and; 'Multi-User Domains or Dungeons' (MUDs), the first of which was created by Richard Bartle and Roy Trubshaw at the University of Essex, which allowed users to enter shared virtual spaces to communicate and role play using text. The BITNET (Because It's Time Network) connected IBM mainframes around the educational community and the world to provide mail services, beginning in 1981. Listserv software was developed for this network and later others, and gateways were developed to connect BITNET with the other networks, allowing the exchange of e-mail, particularly for e-mail discussion lists.

The increasing civilian use of the ARPANET was first acknowledged when ARPANET was split into two separate networks, ARPANET and MILNET and then, in 1989 by its dissolution. This heralded the start of the Internet as an entity in its own right, composed of many different networks, all held together by agreed transmission protocols. But though it was becoming more accessible, the Internet remained difficult to use and largely the preserve of the military, universities, and industry. Its accessibility was increased by the modem, which was originally developed in the '60s. This device is so called because it *mod*ulates and *dem*odulates between digital and analogue data, thus allowing personal computers to communicate at high speed over phone lines. In the '80s various networks and systems had developed that widened access and participation, such as Bulletin Board Services that allowed PC users to communicate widely on the Internet. Nevertheless the complexity of using such facilities largely prevented the Internet becoming widely used.

Despite these difficulties, the Internet seemed to make practically possible and, at the same time, to embody metaphorically many of the ideas that had been circulating in and around San Francisco for some time. It encompassed the theories of the Jesuit priest and palaeontologist Teilhard de Chardin about the 'noosphere', a communicative equivalent to the atmosphere, the increasing complexity of which would lead to a kind of global consciousness. It confirmed the ideas of Marshall McLuhan, such as that of the global village and the capacity of technology to expand human potential, as well as having the scope to realize utopian visions such as H. G. Wells's 'The World Brain'. Naturally those at the Whole Earth were not going to miss out on such a phenomenon. In 1985 they started the WELL or 'Whole Earth 'Lectronic Link'. This was a BBS or bulletin board service that allowed people to communicate in a variety of ways online, mainly in the form of conferences in which ideas on topics could be shared, as well as e-mail, and instant communication.[42] (It is indicative of the burgeoning relation between the counter-culture and digital technology that the WELL's existence was sustained through the patronage of 'deadheads', fanatical followers of the seminal psychedelic rock group The Grateful Dead.) Though the WELL was a remarkable success, its use was limited mostly to residents in the Bay Area and those who felt comfortable with using the computer at a fairly sophisticated level. This last was true for most of the networks that emerged in the 1970s and '80s. A few years after the WELL was founded, in the late 1980s, Tim Berners-Lee, a researcher at CERN, the European particle physics research laboratory in Switzerland, devised and implemented a method for making public scientific papers on the Internet, thus avoiding the time delays inherent in paper publishing. This became the basis of the World Wide Web (www), the method of displaying texts, images, video, animation and sound, so that they can be viewed on any computer as long as it is both connected to the Internet and has the right software. To begin with Berners-Lee's project did not achieve wide interest because of the comparative difficulty of using the software needed to access the www. This changed with the development in 1993 of a graphical browser called 'Mosaic' by Marc Andreessen and his team at the National Center For Supercomputing Applications (NCSA) at the University of Illinois at Urbana-Champaign. This made accessing the Web considerably easier, as it could run on different machines, and also opened it out to allow the incorporation of different kinds of media. Andreessen then joined up with Jim Clark, founder of Silicon Graphics to found Netscape Corporation, which produced a more sophisticated version of Mosaic also called Netscape.

At about the time the NCSA was developing Mosaic, Louis and Jane Rossetto launched a new digital technology magazine. Called *Wired*, it was edited by Kevin Kelly. Unlike other computer magazines, which were generally either dauntingly technical or, like *Mondo*, plain peculiar, *Wired* was, from the start, intended to be a mainstream publication appealing to anybody interesting in aspects of digital culture. *Wired* was, and remains, not only successful – with a circulation of nearly 450,000 – but also manages to be both mainstream and left field. It has become the most influential and powerful force for constructing and disseminating a particular ideology of technology, and granting it legitimacy. The *Wired* philosophy is a mixture of the kind of futurology touted by Alvin Toffler, George Gilder and others and embraced by Newt Gingrich and the technological determinism of Marshall McLuhan, tinged with Teilhard de Chardin's mysticism. *Wired* represents the apotheosis of the wired counter-culture, in all its technological-utopianist glory, and also its subsumption into the dominant culture. *Wired* is thus the most accessible articulation of the particular Northern Californian inflection of the counter-culture out of which has emerged a powerful and influential ideology that combines a belief in the transformative powers of technology and in the positive and self-regulatory capacities of the market. *Wired* has proclaimed the existence of the 'Digital Citizen', who is, according to Jon Katz, 'knowledgable, tolerant, civic-minded, and radically committed to change. Profoundly optimistic about the future, they're convinced that technology is a force for good and that our free-market economy functions as a powerful engine for good.'[43]

At first sight such endeavours might appear distant from the idealism of the late 1960s, concerned as it was with resisting consumer capitalism. Yet as this chapter has sought to show, there is a logical progression through which the ideals of the erstwhile counter-culture have mutated and attenuated into a whole-hearted commitment to our current technologically driven capitalism. At the heart of this utopian vision is the Internet, which embodies many of the ideals fostered and promoted by the counter-culture, and which have now become a central constituent of that capitalism. The Internet is the paradigm of the emergent, self-regulating, self-organising structures that can develop and thrive without governmental intervention. In this it is a material realization of the idea of the market as a spontaneous natural phenomenon that lies at the heart of neo-liberal economics. A model of the economy as an evolved and optimized natural system clearly resonated with the cybernetic and ecological concerns of the post-war era. It also militated against hierarchical planning and elevated the role of the individual, while still promoting the idea of the collective and the common good.

# 5. Digital Resistances

## POSTMODERNISM

The period between the early '70s and the late '80s saw the advent of the much-heralded information society. The inadequacies of Fordist-Keynesian ideas in relation to global competition and financial deregulation necessitated restructuring on the part of capitalism to more responsive, fluid models of organization. This was bound up with concurrent developments in information communications technology, which presented the technical means to realize a new flexible capitalism. At the same time those developments in ICT also led to a new range of commodities based on microelectronics, personal computers, and video games. Thus the vision of a society dominated by information and information technologies propounded by academics such as Daniel Bell or Futurologists such as Alvin Toffler would seem to have been realized. But, unlike Bell's vision of the move towards such a society as an evolutionary process, its realization was antagonistic and sometimes violent, in with traditional industries and industrial models being either radically overhauled or, effectively, dispensed with, often at great social cost. The '70s in particular saw industrial antagonism on an unprecedented scale throughout the industrialized world. In the '80s these antagonisms were 'resolved', in some countries at least, by the coming to power of right-wing governments, whose invocations of traditional values masked radical neo-liberal economic agendas.

These circumstances produced a number of aesthetic and cultural responses and sites of resistance. These were often bound up with the notion of ending and rupture, as evinced by the use of the prefix 'post', as in 'post-industrialism'. Quite early on in the 1970s commentators were declaring the supersession of modernity by 'postmodernity', and by extension, in the arts, the end of modernism and the beginning of 'postmodernism'. The repudiation of modernism's aesthetic dominance was proposed by architects Robert Venturi, Denise Scott Brown and Steven Izenour in their book *Learning from Las Vegas* (1972),[1] which celebrated the city's qualities of decorative exuberance. At the same time the literary critic Ihab Hassan wrote an influential essay declaring the advent of what he called POSTmodernISM in literature and the arts.[2] Hassan made a list of contemporary artists and writers, who, for him, either refused or problematized the paradigm of modernism, including Robert Rauschenberg, John Cage, Marshall McLuhan, and Buckminster Fuller. The Marxist critic Fredric Jameson connected postmodernism explicitly with technological change. For him it offered a framework in which to understand the cultural effects of what he called 'late capitalism'. In this he was influenced by the Marxist economist Ernest Mandel who had proposed the cyclical nature of capitalism, which, following the work of economists such as Kondratieff and Schumpeter, he analysed in terms of 'long waves', cyclical movements lasting approximately 50 years.[3] The dynamics of these movements are bound up with the use of machines, and the periodic need to reinvest in new machinery and concomitant modes of production and labour organization. According to Mandel the industrial revolution lasted from the end of the eighteenth century to 1847, and was characterized by 'the gradual spread of the handicraft-made or manufacture-made steam engine to all the most important branches of industry and industrial countries'. The first technological revolution lasted from 1847 to the beginning of the 1890s and was characterized by 'the generalization of the machine-made steam engine as the principle motive machine'.[4] The second technological revolution was from the 1890s to the Second World War, and involved the 'generalized application of electric and combustion engines in all branches of industry'.[5] The last was bound up with a 'technological' revolution, which, beginning in America in 1940 and in other imperialist countries after the War, is characterized by 'generalized control of machines by means of electronic apparatuses (as well as by the general introduction of nuclear energy)'.[6] Adopting Mandel's scheme, and his characterization of the third period of capitalism as 'late', Jameson wrote an essay entitled 'Postmodernism and Consumer Society', which was later expanded to become the opening chapter of his book, *Postmodernism: or the Cultural Logic of Late Capitalism*.[7] In it he argues that postmodernism was an acknowledgment of the triumph of capitalism, in which the last enclaves of resistance or autonomy succumbed to commodification, and that these particular conditions have produced a number of cultural symptoms, including a concentration on the autonomy and freeplay of the signifier, the use of the 'randomly heterogenous and fragmentary and the aleatory', the 'schizophrenic' experience of language and the world, and the flattening of space.[8]

It is possible to observe these cultural symptoms across a number of fields and to connect their appearance explicitly with the development of digital technology, in music, design, art and literature, as well as in philosophy. The latter included Poststructuralism, the name in Anglophone countries for the intellectual movement which developed out of structuralist thinking in France, and for which the unrest of May 1968 was catalytic. At the same time the industrial and social upheavals in Italy in the late '60s and '70s brought the development of new forms of left theory and praxis, in particular that of 'Autonomous Marxism', in which the tenets of communism were reformulated for the information society. These symptoms also encompass developments within feminist thought that emerged out of the shortcomings of the wave of Feminism that emerged in the '60s and '70s. The failure by earlier feminists to address the status of women within the technoculture of late capitalism led to the development of 'Cyborg theory' by Donna Haraway, and latterly of Cyberfeminism. In music the possibilities of digital technology combined with the legacies of art school performance-oriented rock, disco and punk, produced 'techno' and its assorted variations. Punk was also one of the inspirations, along with 'postmodern' fiction, for the science fiction genre known as 'Cyberpunk'. The technological potential unleashed by desktop publishing and graphics software, allied with the methodological potential offered by variously by Punk and French deconstructionist philosophy, produced a style of graphic design and typography known sometimes as 'deconstructionist' graphic design, and sometimes as 'The New Typography'. Though obviously coming out of different contexts and circumstances, these developments all shared a fascination with contemporary technology and in both its utopian and dystopian possibilities, as well as its glamour. They also evince similar tropes and strategies, of appropriation, juxtaposition, detournement, montage, collage, and repetition, facilitated by or reflecting upon the extraordinary capabilities of that technology.

## POSTSTRUCTURALISM

Poststructuralism emerged out of the compromised political and cultural atmosphere of France during the Fifth Republic. It was both a development of and a response to the dominance of Structuralism in French intellectual life. The mid-1960s seemed to represent the apogee of the Structuralist project in France, with even the trainer of the French football team promising to reorganize the team on structuralist principles.[9] Structuralism seemed to hold out the promise of treating the social sciences and humanities with the rigour usually found in science. Yet this promise was undermined by the logical inconsistencies in Structuralism's own programme, as in for example, its refusal to engage with the historical aspects of the phenomena it analysed. The young Bulgarian academic Julia Kristeva, arriving in Paris from Bulgaria in 1965, introduced those involved with structural semiotics to the work of the Russian literary theorist Mikhail Bakhtin.[10] Unknown in France until that point, Bakhtin's work enabled a reintroduction of the historical into the structuralist paradigm, with its insistence on the necessity of understanding of a work within its particular context. From this basis Kristeva developed the idea of intertextuality, which sought to understand how a literary work engaged with its contemporaries.

Roland Barthes was fascinated by this approach and later employed it in *S/Z*, his analysis, published in 1970, of a short story by Balzac.[11] At the same time, though starting from a different point, the Algerian-born philosopher Jacques Derrida was using ideas and methodologies developed from the work of Sigmund Freud, Friedrich Nietzsche and Martin Heidegger to engage in close readings of philosophical and literary texts, in order to reveal their inner contradictions, which he named 'Deconstruction' after the Heideggerian term 'Destruktion'. What Derrida aimed to demonstrate, among other things, was the impossibility of securing meaning in a text. For him signification is an endless play of difference without any centre that could put an end to the ever-proliferating possibilities. In 1967, when classical Structuralism was seemingly at its most powerful, Derrida published several highly influential accounts of his ideas. One was a collection of essays entitled *L'écriture et la différence*,[12] another was an extended examination of Western philosophy through the close reading of key texts, entitled *De la grammatologie*.[13] In the latter Derrida showed that Western thinking had been dominated by a 'phonocentricism' that privileged the voice, and by extension the presence of the speaker, over writing. *L'écriture et la différence* contained a paper entitled 'Structure, Sign and Play in the Discourse of the Human Sciences',[14] which, when presented at a conference at Johns Hopkins University, was instrumental in introducing North American literary critics to the ideas of Deconstruction. A number of critics, most prominently Paul de Man and J. Hillis Miller of the Yale School, subsequently took up Derrida's methods as a new paradigm in literary studies. It was via Ihab Hassan that postmodernism first directly encountered poststructuralism. Hassan had organized a conference in Milwaukee on the postmodern in the performing arts, at which one of the speakers was the poststructuralist French philosopher Jean-François Lyotard. A one-time member of the militant socialist organization *Socialisme ou Barbarie*, Lyotard was probably most famous at the time of the conference for his 1974 book *Economie libidinale*,[15] in which he proposed a kind of erotics of capitalism, as a way of critiquing the dogmatism of Marx. From his encounter with Hassan he took the term Postmodern, which he used to define what he saw as the effects of the arrival of a society in which information had become the main economic force of production. This found expression in his short book *La condition postmoderne*.[16] In this work, which originated as a report commissioned by the university council of the government of Quebec on the state of contemporary knowledge, Lyotard proposed that under the conditions of a computerized information society the great meta-narratives by which modernity had been legitimized were no longer sustainable. They could, instead, only be considered as 'language games', a concept Lyotard borrowed from Wittgenstein, operating according to different sets of agreed rules.[17] Science in particular had lost its claim to be a meta-narrative owing to the emphasis on performativity and efficiency demanded by its increasing technification.[18] Lyotard later repudiated *La condition postmoderne*, claiming he knew little about the subject in question and had not read many of the books referred to in the text. To a large extent, the book is really a covert attack on the meta-narrative to which Lyotard was most implacably hostile, that of Marxism. Nevertheless he later evinced an interest in the ideas he rehearsed in the essay. He returned to some of its themes in his later books, *The Differend*[19] and *The Inhuman*,[20] and in 1985 organized an exhibition at the Pompidou Centre in Paris, 'Les immatériaux', which looked at questions of communication, technology and the dematerialization of the sign. In *The Inhuman* Lyotard extended his analysis of the effects of information technology in a curious direction. In what can only be seen as a meta-narrative, Lyotard proposed that the dominant information culture was part of a cosmic process by which the universal tendency towards entropy is countermanded by ongoing complexification.

Lyotard's pessimistic analysis of technology can be compared to that of Jean Baudrillard, the French theorist who more than anybody else has come to define a position of postmodern hopelessness, and with it a kind of perverse euphoria. Baudrillard was a pupil of both the Marxist Henri Lefebvre and Pierre Bourdieu, neither of whom were considered as mainstream structuralists. Lefebvre in particular repudiated Structuralism. Despite this, and despite his own Marxist beliefs, Baudrillard's early work resembled that of Barthes, in, for example, his use of semiology to analyse the consumer society in his 1968 work *Le système des objets*.[21] As his career has progressed Baudrillard has moved away from both Structuralism and Marxism, towards a position owing more to Marshall McLuhan, which proclaims the total dominance of the sign, and of code as the primary organising principle of the social entity. This and his other key concepts, such as hyper-reality, simulation and simulacra, presented a seductive if despairing vision of a world of unlimited semiosis in which meaning is destroyed by the act of communication, the 'social' no longer exists, and from which there is no possibility of liberation or escape. Such ideas were, and indeed remain, controversial, and have been much criticized from all corners. The height of Baudrillard's capacity to incite was probably round the period of the Gulf War, about which he wrote in a series of articles for the newspaper *Libération*. Before the outbreak of hostilities he predicted that the War would not take place. Afterwards he proclaimed that, indeed it had not done so. This was, not unexpectedly, seized upon by some as an example of the poverty and bankruptcy of Baudrillard's world.[22]

A more positive view of the possibilities of digital technology can be found in the work of Gilles Deleuze and Félix Guattari. Deleuze was a philosopher, whose early work had consisted of a number of elegant studies in the history of philosophy, which though conventional enough in their form, concentrated on the work of those outside of the mainstream, including Lucretius, Spinoza, Hume, Nietzsche and Bergson. Guattari was a psychoanalyst and life-long political radical, who had been a member first of the French Communist Party, then of the *Opposition de Gauche*, a non-party far-left organization. Since the 1950s he had worked in the Clinique de la Borde, a well-known centre of what would be known in the UK as anti-psychiatry, which questioned the structures and functions of traditional psychiatric institutions and attempted to institute more humane and less hierarchical arrangements. Guattari had also undergone psychoanalytical training with Jacques Lacan, and had, in 1969, joined Lacan's Ecole Freudienne de Paris as an analyst member.

The events of 1968 brought Deleuze and Guattari together. They shared an interest in the failure of the revolution to take place, and the subsequent return to the *status quo ante* of a repressive social order. In particular they were concerned with what they perceived as people's desire for their own repression. To analyse this they wrote the first of their four collaborative works, *L'anti-oedipe: capitalisme et schizophrenie*.[23] This dense and often difficult work combined Marx, Freud, Nietszche and Lacan, among others, in an astonishing analysis of the relationship between desire and capitalism. *Mille plateaux*, the second part of *Capitalisme et schizophrenie*,[24] was published in 1980. This extended and expanded upon many of the ideas in the first part, as well as extending the range of their analyses to questions of language, literature and music. The complexities already evident in *L'anti-oedipe* are compounded by Deleuze and Guattari's deliberate refusal to propose a central narrative or theme for the book. They refer to the sections in *Mille plateaux* as 'plateaus', a term they derived from the anthropological work of Gregory Bateson. Bateson had used the term to describe the libidinal economy he found in Bali, which differed from that in the West, with its emphasis on climax. Deleuze and Guattari intended that the sections of their book should not reproduce the climactic and dissipative character of Western discourse, as manifested in the traditional book format with its culminations and terminations. They hoped rather that each plateau would operate as part of an assemblage of connecting parts to be approached by the reader in whichever order they chose. As this might suggest *Mille plateaux* is a complex and difficult book, though, at the same time, extraordinarily compelling, which is also a fair estimation of Deleuze and Guattari's philosophy.

The complexity of Deleuze and Guattari's thought, especially as demonstrated in *Mille plateaux*, makes any kind of précis almost impossible. But it is possible to pick out some of the ideas that have most obviously influenced those involved with new technologies and information discourses (though this runs the risk of simplifying and distorting these ideas). Three of their concepts in particular have become part of the discourse of digital culture: machines, assemblages and rhizomes. The first of these terms is introduced at the beginning of *L'anti-oedipe*, where Deleuze and Guattari remark that 'everywhere it is machines'.[25] Thus they describe throughout the book the actions of social machines, territorial machines, desiring machines, producing machines, and even technical machines.[26] Each of these delineates the actions, couplings and connections of different elements, such as that of the breast machine with the mouth machine. (This use of the term machine is, as they are careful to point out, not a metaphor, but meant literally.[27]) In *Mille plateaux*

Deleuze and Guattari's concept of machines is broadened out and developed as part of a more general discussion of what they call 'assemblages'– by which they mean combinations of heterogenous elements, composed of both matter and bodies – and enunciation or utterance.[28] What also defines assemblages are the nature of movements governing their operation, which involves both moves towards territorialization and to deterritorialization and 'lines of flight' through which the assemblage becomes something else. Deleuze and Guattari distinguish between two different kinds of assemblage, both of which are 'multiplicities', another key Deleuzoguattarian term.[29] Deleuze defines multiplicities as either numerical or qualitative. The former, for which the term 'molar' is also used, are divisible, unifiable, totalizable, and organizable, while the latter, to which the term 'molecular' is applied, are intensive and cannot change their dimensions or magnitudes without changing their nature.[30] The distinction between the two kinds of assemblage is exemplified in Deleuze and Guattari's description of the arboreal and the rhizomatic in the introduction to *Mille plateaux*. Arborescent systems, trees and such, are unifiable objects, with clearly defined boundaries. By contrast rhizomatic systems, which in biology are typified by tubers, grass or weeds, lack these qualities of definition and unity and are by contrast fuzzy, indeterminate, and connect to other multiplicities, and change in nature.[31] The rhizome, more than any other figure in Deleuze and Guattari's rich vocabulary, has been co-opted into the discourse of our current technoculture. Though Deleuze and Guattari are careful not to ascribe any superior virtue to the rhizome it clearly resonates with contemporary concerns with networks and numerous commentators have unequivocally described the Internet as rhizomatic.

For some the work of Deleuze and Guattari offered new ways of thinking about class struggle and revolutionary praxis that were appropriate to the contemporary context of a postmodern capitalism dominated by information communication technologies. This was particularly true of so-called 'Autonomous Marxism', which originated in Italy in the 1970s. This in turn developed out of *Operaismo*, 'Workerism', which articulated its ideas through the journal *Quaderni Rossi*. Among the editorial group in the early '60s was a young professor of State Theory at the University of Padua, Antonio (Toni) Negri. *Operaismo* developed several theoretical tenets, including an interest in the 'refusal of work' in the context of capitalist relations of production, and in the possibilities of autonomy for the working class away from the traditional representative structures, such as unions. The *Operaisti* noticed how young workers of the time were not adhering to the older generation's work ethic and discipline and were engaging instead in insubordination, sabotage, confrontation and the use of specialized tactics to slow down or even stop the processes of production. Out of these observations the *Operaisti* developed a theory of the dialectical relation between class struggle and capitalist development, in which the continual confrontation between capital and living labour was the cause of all technological development and structural change.[32] This differs from Mandel, for example, who, as we have seen, proposed an economic explanation for capitalism's need to further technological development. It also presented the basis for later evaluations of the capacity of the working class to resist the demands of capital through control of the means of production. In 1973 *Potere Operaia* disbanded and Negri and others joined a new group *Autonomia Organizzata* or *Autonomia Operaia*, a loose network of collectives that was intended to avoid the issues of centralized command by which, supposedly, party power repressed proletarian power.

Antonio Negri developed the connections between the ideas of *Operaismo* and *Autonomia* and those of Deleuze and Guattari while in exile in France in the late 1970s and 1980s, after his arrest for his alleged involvement in the murder of Aldo Moro by the Red Brigade. Forbidden by the conditions of his residency to engage in politics, he nevertheless involved himself in intellectual activities, including teaching at the Université de Paris VIII and the College International de Philosophie, and helping to found a journal, *Futur Antérieur*, which developed autonomist theory and other radical ideas. In *Futur Antérieur* Deleuze and he interviewed each other, and, at around the same time he collaborated with Guattari on a short book, *Nouveaux alliances de liberté*,[33] which proclaimed the need for a revivified communism, appropriate for the realities of post-Fordist capitalism. To some degree Negri's work had already opened up these questions and laid the groundwork for such a project. Seen from his vantage point, the industrial antagonisms that swept through the developed world necessitated the kind of technological and managerial innovations in the operations of capitalism described by the *Operaisti*. In this case the so-called 'third industrial revolution' enabled capital to supersede the Fordist-Taylorist paradigm, and, exploiting developments in computing and telecommunication, turned information into the most important productive force. As we have seen, for some this was the realization of a 'post-industrial' society, in which the antagonisms of industrial capitalism were supplanted under the benign auspices of information. In the absence of the traditional groupings through which class antagonism could be expressed such an idea seemed convincing and continues to underpin the neo-liberal ideology described in the last chapter. But for others, such as Negri, capitalist society continued to involve class struggle, exploitation, alienation and commodification much as before.[34] All that had changed was the location where these took place. In developed countries at least, the factory worker had become, in many instances, a controller of the complex cybernetic processes of automated manufacture (though of course it must be pointed out that traditional manual labour and assembly-line work still took place, though largely in the developing world). For many others labour had become 'immaterial', involving producing the 'cultural content' of the commodity.[35]

It is in this new definition of the composition of the working class that Autonomists found the possibility of new forms of revolutionary praxis. They found inspiration in the *Grundrisse*, the notes Karl Marx wrote between 1857 and 1858 in which he grappled with many of the themes for which he would later become famous on the publication of *Das Kapital*. Split between the sixth and seventh of these notebooks is a consideration of the effects of the application of machines to the processes of production. In a now famous passage, known as 'The Fragment on Machines' Marx suggested that the general social knowledge or collective intelligence of a society, or what he describes as the 'general intellect', of a given period can be embodied in machines as well as humans, and with the burgeoning development of automation, is likely to be so.[36] Marx, optimistically, saw the increasing embodiment of intelligence in fixed capital, machines, as likely to bring about a fatal contradiction in capitalism that would inevitably usher in an era of communism.[37] Autonomist theorists chose to interpret the concept of the 'General Intellect' as the diffusion of intellectual knowledge through society as a whole and as a necessary aspect of technological development in relation to the restructuring of capital.[38] Autonomists began to talk of the 'mass intellectual' or 'diffused intellectual' in order to discuss the proliferation of new subjectivities. 'Mass intellectuals' are those whose living labour consists in 'creativity' and 'social communication', also sometimes known as 'immaterial labour'.[39] The term covers many different kind of workers other than the traditional factory worker, including, for example, computer programmers, advertising copywriters, graphic designers, workers in roboticized factories, art workers and so on. Out of this situation Toni Negri developed an analysis of what he called the 'prerequisites of communism' immanent to post-Fordist capitalism.[40] By this term Negri referred to those institutions and arrangements that emerge out of struggles and antagonism and continue to be developed by workers' antagonism in the face of exploitation. For Negri and others the most important 'prerequisite' of communism is the fact that capitalist production is necessarily a collective endeavour and requires social co-operation. Thus they consider the rise of immaterial labour and the 'social worker' brings about the conditions for communism, largely because such 'social work' requires communication that comes before entrepreneurship. All that capitalism can hope to do is stimulate the creativity and communication required for immaterial labour and to control and exploit it from outside. Negri has continued to produce powerful exegeses of such ideas, while remaining in prison in Italy. Most recently he has collaborated with Michael Hardt to write *Empire*,[41] which has become an important text for the Anti-capitalist Movement.

In the early to mid-1980s, while Negri was collaborating with Guattari, new conceptions of the machinic and possible new relations with technology began to be articulated within feminist discourse. In the late '80s a number of feminist writers and thinkers began to question the relationship between women and such technology, and to propose new forms of possible engagement. The sociologist Sherry Turkle undertook an important study of computer culture and its relation to perceptions of selfhood, which was published in 1988 as *The Second Self: Computers and the Human Spirit*.[42] At around the same time Constance Penley, who had already developed a reputation in film studies, began to look at science fiction and at the culture of technology. This resulted, in the first case, in the special edition of the feminist film journal *Camera Obscura*, which was later published as a book, co-edited with Elisabeth Lyon and Lynne Spigel, entitled *Close Encounters: Film, Feminism and Science Fiction*,[43] and in the second in a book, co-edited with Andrew Ross, called *Technoculture*.[44] Penley and other feminists' interest in science fiction reflected, in part at least, the degree to which Feminism had empowered women to make their mark in a previously male-dominated genre. The '70s saw a generation of female SF writers come to prominence, including Ursula K. LeGuin, Anne McCaffrey, Joanna Russ, Kate Wilhelm, C. J. Cherryh, and Joan Vinge, many of who used the SF form to consider questions of gender and identity. (By comparison there were comparatively few female contributors to the SF genre known as Cyberpunk, which emerged in the mid-'80s, the notable exception being Pat Cadigan. This is perhaps not surprising, given Cyberpunk's fascination with hardware and the film noir form, with its solitary male hero.)

Feminist science fiction, like that described above, was one of the inspirations for philosopher of science Donna Haraway's polemical paper 'A Manifesto for Cyborgs',[45] first published in 1985, which intended to present positive ways for feminism to engage with technology. It is an attempt to present a socialist-feminist analysis of 'women's situation in the advanced technological conditions of postmodern life in the First World'.[46] Haraway finds the standard tools for such an analysis, Marxism, Psychoanalysis and Feminism as it was then constituted, problematic; each relies on structures that are limiting and unhelpful, such as labour as the source of subjectivity, the centrality of the family or the idea of woman as an essential, trans-historical category. Instead, Haraway finds an alternative model for women's identity in the figure of the cyborg, or cybernetic organism. This term, originally coined by engineer Manfred Clynes in 1960 to denote the imbrication of man and machines, was derived from the work in Cybernetics of Norbert Wiener and others after the War. By acknowledging such an imbrication and its blurring of the distinction between human and machine, the notion of the cyborg not only gets away from questions of individuality and individual wholeness, but from the essentialist humanist concepts of women as childbearer and raiser, which are consonant with the heterosexual marriage and the nuclear family. It complicates the binary oppositions, which have been 'systemic to the logics and practices of domination of women, people of colour, nature, workers, animals'.[47]

As Mark Dery also points out, the manifesto is short on practical suggestions for living in an increasingly technological world, especially for women who are exploited by high-tech industries.[48]

Nevertheless cyborg theory has presented a powerful set of tools for women, and others, to engage positively with new technology without abandoning the radical promise of Feminism. The Manifesto's publication as part of Haraway's collection of essays *Simians, Cyborgs and Women: The Reinvention of Nature* in the early 1990s coincided with the emergence of a new wave of feminist thought and action, which, after a moribund period in the '80s, sought to reinvigorate the gender struggle. A catalytic series of events made clear the necessity of such reinvigoration, including the Kennedy Smith and Tyson rape trials and the congressional hearings for the accusations brought against Supreme-Court nominee Clarence Thomas by his former colleague Anita Hill. One result of the anger these events generated was the Women's Action Coalition or WAC, which developed sophisticated means for using communications technology, including telephone trees, fax machines, e-mail and exploitation of media contacts. Aside from these examples of practical use, third-wave feminism did not, at first, actively engage with new technologies. But elements of the third wave did take up questions of community and identity in ways that resonated with the cyborg ideas of Haraway, and the emerging possibilities of electronic networked communication. The idea of identity and gender as constructs was an important to poststructuralist and postmodernist thought, as well to Queer Theory and the liberal strain within Feminism.

## PUNK AND DECONSTRUCTION

The developments in theory and philosophy described above echoed developments in areas such as music, design and literature. In the mid-1970s Derrida's *De la grammatologie* was published in English in the landmark translation by Gayatri Chakravorty Spivak. Its philosophical denseness and complexity made it inaccessible to all but a few. Nevertheless its questioning of the totalizing nature of dominant forms of knowledge, and its assertion of the material basis of discourse formation resonated with other attempts to come to terms with an increasingly disorganized and complex world. In Britain, for example, the period saw increasing industrial unrest, soaring unemployment and inflation, and the seeming collapse of much of the country's social fabric, most famously the miners' strike of 1973–4, which coincided with the Arab oil embargo imposed as a result of the Arab–Israeli War. This necessitated the introduction of a three-day working week in the factories and saw a country periodically reduced to candlelight. The then prime minister, the Conservative Edward Heath, called an election in 1974, to force the issue of the unions' power, which he lost to socialist Harold Wilson. Wilson's government, and that of James Callaghan who took over the premiership two years later, though more conciliatory to the unions, fared little better than that of Heath. The discontent generated by this unhappy set of circumstances would lead eventually to a vote of no confidence in Callaghan's government, and the subsequent election of a Conservative government under the leadership of Margaret Thatcher.

It was in these circumstances that Punk emerged, bringing together a heterogenous mixture of avant-garde art practice, pop music history and proto-deconstructivist style. Punk was a fully articulated subculture, with a distinctive visual style involving a bricolage of elements such as fetish clothing, teddy boy gear, ripped and torn items and, unfortunately, Nazi uniforms (though these were eschewed fairly early on). It also developed, partly through necessity, a distinctive graphic design style, which found expression in record sleeves, publicity and in 'zines, the xeroxed and collaged publications which were one of the most distinctive developments to come out of Punk. The most famous 'zine, 'Sniffin' Glue' (illus. 45),[49] edited by Mark Perry, was exemplary in its use of roughly put together found material and hand-written/drawn graphics. Jamie Reid's graphics for the Sex Pistols' record covers and publicity material employed similar techniques to great effect.[50] His

45 Cover of *Sniffin' Glue* 4
(October 1976).

famous collage of the Queen with a safety pin through her nose for the cover of the Pistols' controversial single 'God Save the Queen' is now recognized as a design classic. His motif for a later release, 'Pretty Vacant', is an American school bus, with the word 'Boredom' where the destination should be displayed (illus. 46). This clearly refers, ironically, to the iconic hippy vehicle, Ken Kesey and the Merry Pranksters Magic Bus, which had the word 'Furthur' [*sic*] as its destination, and whose passengers included Stewart Brand, demiurge of the personal computer revolution.

Reid's appropriation and detournement of the mythic bus is a critique of the counter-cultural fantasies of self-realization and progress towards a better society. His bus has only boredom for its destination and there is no better future to which it might travel.

46 Jamie Reid, 'Boredom' graphic, as used on the back cover of the Sex Pistols 1976 7" single *Pretty Vacant*.

The negativity and even nihilism that Punk expressed was in direct contrast to the optimism of the counter-culture, and was far more believable for those for whom the present consisted of limited possibilities and the future possibly worse. Punk was an aesthetic response to the political and social disasters of the 1970s. It reflected a world of industrial and social antagonism, urban decay and hope-lessness, not just through the use of specific imagery, but through the very methods of cut-up, montage and appropriation it em-ployed, which visually articulated the dislocations in the coming of post-industrial society. But Punk can be seen as not just a response to the dislocations of its period, but also as an anticipa-tion of the possibilities of technology then just emerging. Though graphical computing, multimedia, hypertext and so on were not yet widely available, they existed and their future ubiquity was already being predicted. Furthermore the shift towards a post-industrial society was predicated on the application of 'real-time' computer systems and networks, which employed such technologies and ideas. The Punk style, with its disruptions and disjunctures, its emphasis on texts and its use of iconic graphics anticipates the coming world of ubiquitous graphic computing. As shown above, the Punk strategy of do-it-yourself graphics and music was later echoed in the use of desktop publishing and graphics software by graphic designers in the 1980s. This is not to suggest that Punk had any influence on the development of these technologies, but it did create a framework in which they could be understood and used.

Meanwhile, those involved with more mainstream graphic design were beginning to come to terms with both the possibilities of new technology and the liberatory messages of Punk and Deconstruction. In 1978 the influential typography journal *Visible Language* published an edition devoted to 'French Currents of the Letter'.[51] This issue looked at how French philosophy and literature was enabling new approaches to writing. Among those discussed were many connected with what later became known as Poststructuralism, including Jacques Derrida, Roland Barthes, Julia Kristeva and Michel Serres. This issue of *Visible Language* was designed by students from the Cranbrook Academy of Art, which, under the aegis of co-chair Katherine McCoy, was encouraging interest in the intersection between graphic design and Poststructuralism. The students involved were given a seminar in literary theory by the head of Cranbrook's architecture programme, Daniel Libeskind. What resulted was an examination and critique of the conventional relations between typographical elements and the concomitant belief in legibility and transparency. (This approach had already been anticipated by Derrida with *Glas*.)

Derrida's innovative use of typography for deconstructive purposes was to enable profound philosophical investigation and expression. As Ellen Lupton points out, the interest in Poststructuralism shown by graphic designers such as McCoy was more celebration than critique, invoking the poetic rather than the critical aspects of the important thinkers.[52] What began to develop at Cranbrook and continued elsewhere was less a profound examination of the conditions of design, and more an anarchic form of self-expression by designers liberated from the ideology of transparent communication, as legitimated by allusions to contemporary French philosophy. In some senses it was more closely related to Punk's release of energies, than to the profound and difficult project of Deconstruction. This said, Poststructuralism and Deconstruction allied with a Punk sensibility offered powerful and liberating paradigms for graphic designers. In the early '80s interest in Poststructuralist approaches to design was revived at Cranbrook, through the enthusiasm of students such as Jeffery Keedy, later head of graphics at CalArts. This coincided with the development of the Apple Macintosh, which offered designers unprecedented power and potential. The Macintosh had been designed with visual computing in mind, and enabled the development of much visual and graphic design software. Though the Macintosh did not determine the rise of deconstructionist graphic design, which, as we have seen, preceded it by some years, it did greatly enable it, and assured its rapid success as a style.

In 1984 publisher/editor/art director Rudy VanderLans and typographer Zuzana Licko started a graphic-design magazine called *Emigré*, taking advantage of the ease of production offered by the Macintosh. *Emigré* rapidly gained a reputation for innovative and radical design. In particular it investigated the possibilities of type design using font design software. The experimentation exemplified by *Emigré* was paralleled by developments elsewhere. The Netherlands Studio Dumbar, founded in 1977, undertook similar experiments, which its founder, Gert Dumbar, continued in his position as head of graphic design at the Royal College of Art in London in the 1980s. Also in the UK, both *The Face* magazine and its designer Neville Brody gained a reputation for innovation and playfulness in design, as did groups such as Why Not Associates, 8VO, and designers such as RCA graduate Jonathan Barnbrook. Perhaps the most spectacular and difficult example of such design was that produced by David Carson, first for the short-lived surfing magazine *Beach Culture*, and then for the more mainstream (or at least more widely distributed) *Raygun* magazine in the early '90s (illus. 47). The latter took illegibility and challenging graphic design to new heights, or extremes, depending on your point of view, and may have represented the apogee and possible end of a particular approach. Since then this style of complex, computer-aided graphic design has become part of the mainstream visual culture, used in mass market magazines, such as *Wired*, on CD covers and publicity for mainstream music acts, as well as influencing the non-linear multi-layered graphics widely employed on music television.

Punk may have anticipated advanced technological developments but in practical musical terms it was resolutely low-tech, eschewing the complex technologies beloved by other '70s musicians. But Punk demonstrated a fascination with technology and machines, not so much as musical tools, but as symbols both of the passing industrial era and of the coming information age. Part of the bricolage of Punk style involved industrial and utilitarian imagery and clothes, such as boiler suits and workers' boots, as well as the use of stencilled graphics and industrial-style icons. This element was drawn out in

47 Cover of *Raygun*, 1994.

one of the first 'Post-Punk' movements, known later as 'Industrial Rock'. Among the early exponents of this genre was Throbbing Gristle, the band that emerged out of the art collective Coum Transmissions, which had gained notoriety with their 1976 show at the ICA, 'Prostitution'. Throbbing Gristle's musical strategies owed more to the pioneering work of John Cage than to conventional pop music and involved the use of both conventional instruments and custom-made electronic devices to produce barrages of sound. In 1978 Throbbing Gristle started their own record company, Industrial Records, in order to release their own records and those of like-minded artists. The name of their company, and that of their head-quarters in Hackney, The Death Factory, signalled their interest in producing 'industrial music for industrial people'. As Simon Ford points out in his history of Throbbing Gristle/Coum Transmissions, they were making this industrial music at exactly the moment when Britain was ceasing to be a leading industrial nation, and was becoming instead a post-industrial economy.[53]

Throbbing Gristle's industrial interests were also evident in other bands such as Cabaret Voltaire, Joy Division and The Human League, who all also employed electronic means for making music. This produced a style of music with a distinctive machine aesthetic, like that found, for example, in the collaborations between David Bowie and Brian Eno, in particular *Low* and *Heroes*, in which more-or-less conventional pop songs are juxtaposed with electronic mood pieces. *Heroes*, the most artistically successful of these collaborations, was recorded in Germany, and deliberately evoked a Germanic aura through songs such as 'V2 Schneider'. Imagery from the Nazi era and the Second World War was often employed by those involved with Punk and Post-Punk music. The early Punks in particularly had engaged in provocative gestures, such as wearing Nazi uniforms. At one level this could be read simply as a, rather clumsy, attempt to *épater les bourgeois*, using one of the few remaining effective taboos. This provoked a backlash, which was channelled into effective action by the Rock Against Racism movement, which positioned Punk away from its flirtation with fascist imagery, not least by emphasizing its connection with Reggae. Throbbing Gristle also played with imagery from the Nazi era, in particular in their fascination with death camps such as Auschwitz, while Joy Division was named after the Nazi label for the groups of prostitutes culled from the inmates of such camps. Apart from its capacity to provoke and to excite adolescent fantasies, this use of fascist imagery can also be read as anticipating, and even welcoming, the coming shift to the right in Britain and the United States and elsewhere. Germany was also of interest to English and American new wave and Punk musicians because of the experimental and avant-garde nature of its home-grown music scene. Since the late '60s there had been a deliberate attempt by some musicians in Germany to create a distinctly German pop music, as a counter to pop and rock's traditional Anglo-American hegemony. This involved performing songs in German and looking for sources of influence outside the blues and folk traditions. Among such sources were John Cage and LaMonte Young as well as the German avant-garde composer Karlheinz Stockhausen, who had been experimenting with different techniques to create music since the 1950s, including the use of tape and other electronic methods. One of Stockhausen's former students, Holger Czukay, was sufficiently impressed by developments in rock music in the late '60s to start a group with one of his own students, Michael Karoli, and a friend, Irmin Schmidt. The group were known as The Can, and later just Can. At the same time a number of other German bands were looking to create an authentically German psychedelic sound, including Tangerine Dream, Psy Free and Amon Düül I and Amon Düül II (the last two were the result of a split in the original Amon Düül, a politico/musical commune and band). Later they were joined by others such as Popol Vuh and Faust. This mixture of counter-cultural politics, psychedelia, technology and Stockhausen, became known as *Kosmische Musik* in Germany and was rechristened *Krautrock* in the UK.[54] Perhaps the most famous and successful of these groups was Kraftwerk, started in 1971 by Ralph Hutter and Florian Schneider. Kraftwerk, which means both 'men at work' and 'power station', was influenced by Stockhausen and Fluxus artists such as LaMonte Young, who was a frequent visitor to Germany at that time. Throughout the '70s Kraftwerk produced a number of extraordinary productions, particularly after taking control of every aspect of their music-making and image after 1973, when they built their own Düsseldorf studio, Kling Klang. It was at this time they started to employ a Moog synthesizer and exploit the potential of drum machines. Out of this came 'Autobahn', a 22-minute single, which evoked a motorway journey with machinic precision. This was followed by a number of other singles and albums, in which electronic means were used to evoke a world dominated by technology. Though formed before the Punk explosion, Kraftwerk's bleak urban imagery, robotic sound and distinctive style made them a paradigmatic new wave band, and ideal for the music culture of the late 1970s.

Kraftwerk's most pervasive and long-lasting influence was, surprisingly perhaps, in the area of black dance music. They influenced Giorgio Moroder's productions for Donna Summer, as well as the late 1970s productions of Sylvester. Through this and other routes, black DJs in industrial cities such as New York, Detroit and Chicago exploited Kraftwerk's machinic sound. Its evocation of alienation through technology was ideal to express the industrial decay of such cities, Detroit in particular. The kind of music produced in these conditions became known as Detroit Techno, Chicago House and New York Garage. What distinguished these different genres from previous dance music styles, apart from their mode of production, was their deep engagement with technology. In this Techno was far more than simply a musical genre. Like Punk it was a symptom of social and cultural change. If Punk reflected the disjunctures and ruptures endured by a society making the painful transition from a manufacturing to a post-industrial, post-Fordist economy, then Techno reflected the achievement of that transition, though not uncritically. The name 'Techno' itself was taken from Alvin Toffler's techno-libertarian book *The Third Wave*[55] in which he talked about the importance of the 'Techno Rebels' to the coming eponymous wave of technologically determined change. Toffler, along with Kraftwerk and the Black Futurism manifested by groups such as Parliament, all influenced Juan Atkins and Richard Davies (a.k.a. 3070), the original Techno progenitors, to produce a music that celebrated the romance of new technology while at the same time reflecting the damage that the shift away from traditional industrial manufacturing had wrought on cities such as Detroit. Atkins and Davies called themselves 'Cybotron', under which name they developed an entire dictionary of techno-speak and an over-arching video game-like concept they called 'the Grid'.

Techno and other similar genres of dance music were the start of a series of extraordinary developments, which extended beyond dance music, and embraced many other aspects of culture. Coinciding with the availability of the drug MDMA otherwise known as Ecstasy or E, which promoted both well-being and copious energy, a vibrant and creative dance culture emerged in the States, the UK and on the Continent. Unlike most previous pop and rock music culture, in which the performer was separated from the audience and presented as an icon, this culture was far less concerned with such idolatry and much more with a close relation between producer and consumer. Music was produced by DJs, often through sampling, or by visually anonymous but technically competent enthusiasts, and consumed through dance rather than passive attention to somebody else's performance, with the DJ and the audience operating almost in a kind of cybernetic feedback relation. In his or her capacity to manipulate technology, and in the paradoxically solitary nature of his or her work and rejection of the traditional theatricality of rock and pop performance, the DJ resembles another cultural figure, the hacker, who also came to prominence in the mid-'80s. On the other hand, the rave culture of which Techno is a part offers a promise of community and connection outside of the constraints of capitalism and state repression. Thus it is unsurprising that Techno and allied cultural phenomena are often invoked in relation to the ideas of Gilles Deleuze and Félix Guattari, as well as those of writers such as Toffler, ostensibly on the other side of the political divide between right and left. Techno thus becomes a kind of metonym of techno-capitalism, not just in the machine aesthetic of the music itself, but in the social and cultural arrangements and possibilities it proposes.

## VIDEO GAMES

At the same time as Techno emerged in the early '80s, the increasing ubiquity and visibility of computing was beginning to be reflected in mainstream culture. Video and computer games were beginning to become popular, offering many people their first experience of the computer as a medium and as a visual experience. The idea of using digital technology to play games supposedly goes back to the late 1950s, when an engineer, Will Higinbotham, designed a tennis game to run on an oscilloscope in the Brookhaven National Laboratory. But the first recorded digital computer game was *Spacewar*, designed in the early '60s to run on the DEC PDP-1 at the Artificial Intelligence Laboratory at MIT. Though *Spacewar* was not intended to be commercial it rapidly found its way outside of MIT to other institutions and individuals who also owned PDP-1s. The engineers at DEC even used it to demonstrate the powers of the PDP-1 to potential customers. One of those exposed to *Spacewar* in the early '60s was Nolan Bushnell, an engineering student at the University of Utah. Bushnell was inspired by what he saw and, later, attempted to develop a version for arcades. In order to do so he started one of the first computer games companies, Atari. In

1966 Rudolph Baer, a defence engineer, started to investigate the possibilities of using TV as a platform for interactive games. Its first use, in 1967, was with a simple tennis game in which flat paddles knock a square shape back and forth. In 1966 a company in Japan, SEGA (short for Services and Games) released its first arcade game, called the *Periscope*. SEGA was the result of a merger in 1964 between a photo-booth company, Rosen Enterprises Ltd, started in Japan by an American ex-serviceman, and a Japanese vending machine company, Nihon Goraku Bussan. At the beginning of the 1970s a company called Magnavox purchased Baer's television technology and started to develop *Odyssey*, the first TV plug-in device to play video games. At the same time Bushnell attempted to develop *Spacewar* as an arcade game, as well as an arcade tennis game, *Pong* (illus. 48).

*Pong* is probably the first computer game to be a major commercial success. Its reception led to the development of similar games by rival companies and started the beginnings of the computer games industry. In 1974 Atari developed a home version of *Pong*, which

48 The footballer Steve Heighway playing the computer tennis game *Pong* on a Videomaster games console (the first home-video game system) in 1977.

could be played through the television. At first the game fared badly on account of the poor sale record of *Odyssey*. Then, fortunately for Atari, Sears Roebuck ordered a large number of units, assuring its success. It also led to other companies developing home video game units, some of which were cartridge-based, allowing different games to be played with the same unit. In 1977 Taito, a Japanese company started to produce arcade games using microchip technology, rather than hardwired solid-state circuits. One of their games, *Space Invaders*, when imported to Europe and the US became hugely popular and set new standards for such games. Games such as *Pong*, *Space Invaders* and those that followed in its wake, anticipated the arrival of ubiquitous cheap graphical computing by nearly a decade. For many people they would represent their first experience of digital technology as a visual and aural medium, and indeed of digital technology altogether. The microchip, which made many such games possible, would, within little more than a decade, make computing using graphical environments a commonplace of most people's lives. In the '70s, for the want of anything better, the image of the video game acted as a metonym for the burgeoning computerization of society and started to appear in mainstream media as such.

Disney, then at a low point in its fortunes as a company, was rattled by the success of video and computer games, which in turn threatened its dominance of cartoon-style entertainment. This, along with the possibilities for animated film-making offered by computing, led Disney to release *Tron* (1982), which exploited both computer graphics and the popularity of video games (illus. 49). The plot features Jeff Bridges as a games programmer who is somehow sucked into the stylized interior of a computer belonging to a corporation which has stolen some of his ideas, and which is also bent on world domination. There, under a new identity, he meets other entities in this 'space', who tell him about the Master Control Program, which he must fight in a series of video-game like encounters,

49 'Light cycles' from Steven Lisberger's 1982 film *Tron*.

in order to escape. In conventional terms *Tron* was not a great success, critically or in terms of box-office returns, and neither the plot nor the acting are of high standard, but in other terms and particularly in retrospect it is of great interest. It represents the first concerted effort to use three-dimensional computer graphics extensively in a film. It also is the first film to attempt to imagine visually a computer-generated environment, and as such is clearly prefigures ideas about cyberspace. Arguably the limitations of computer graphics at the time make the virtual landscape more compelling and convincing than what could be produced now. The stylized, angular scenes with no pretence towards photorealism are more plausible as a representation of a computer's imaginary interior, than, say, the more visually complex VR scenography of a later film such as *The Lawnmower Man* (1996). But perhaps the most interesting aspect of the film is that, for most of its duration, the action takes place in the computer. *Tron* looks forward to films such as *The Matrix* (1999), in which the world is nothing but a computer simulation. Clearly this, like the conspiracy movies of the '70s, can be read as a kind of allegory of a culture in which technologies of control and spectacle are all pervasive. In the genre of Cyberpunk, which emerged almost simultaneously with *Tron*'s release, this connection is made far more explicit.

Also of interest was the idea of the hacker as hero. The Jeff Bridges character in *Tron*, Kevin Flynn, is a hip, anti-authoritarian computer programmer, whose attitudes and beliefs put him at odds with those in authority. As such he is arguably one of the first obvious examples of a hacker as a character in a feature film. The year after *Tron* opened, 1983, saw the release of *Wargames*, in which a young hacker manages to break into a Pentagon system and, under the mistaken impression that he is merely playing a game, comes close to sparking off a nuclear holocaust. Clearly the plot of *Wargames* revives a set of anxieties previously articulated in the '60s, with films such as *Colossus – The Forbin Project* and *Dr Strangelove*, but this time with the added frisson of contemplating the potential insecurity of extended communications networks. *Tron* and *Wargames* could both be seen as largely unsuccessful attempts to articulate in a narrative form some of the new realities of a post-industrial world. The appearance of the hacker figure as a synecdoche of a whole set of contemporary attitudes and ideas signals this. But both could only grope for appropriate forms of representation. *Wargames* harked back to the simpler paranoias of the Cold War, while *Tron* seized on the video game as a visual metonym of the computer system. But new and more effective means of representing new social and technological realities were beginning to be developed.

## CYBERPUNK

The new possibilities presented by digital technology coalesced with the cultural energies released by Punk Rock in the late 1970s, which led to Techno, also inspired some young science fiction writers to develop new and contemporary directions within the genre. In 1977, the year in which Punk entered the public consciousness, the Canadian writer William Gibson published his first short story 'Fragments of a Hologram Rose',[56] while Bruce Sterling published his first novel *Involution Ocean*.[57] Four years later, in 1981, the older writer Vernor Vinge published his novella *True Names*,[58] in which the characters inhabit the computer's virtual spaces. These different works began to define a way of representing the complex spaces and experiences of a new post-industrial, post-modern world. As such they were the first examples of the as-yet-unnamed genre of Cyberpunk. Also at this time, the French comic strip artist Möbius was producing extraordinary strips portraying dystopian visions of future urban decay.

Cyberpunk had a number of antecedents in both science fiction writing and experimental fiction. The science fiction writer Philip K. Dick wrote a number of brilliant visions of worlds in which reality and identity are fundamentally unstable, often in the context of a commodity-saturated hypercapitalist society. His most well known stories are the novels *Do Androids Dream of Electric Sheep*[59] and *Martian Time Slip* and the short story 'We Can Remember It For You Wholesale',[60] filmed by Paul Verhoeven as *Total Recall* (1984).[61] Unlike almost any other science fiction writer of the period (with the possible exception of J. G. Ballard) Dick deals with difficult issues in a media- and technology-saturated world in ways that acknowledge the fundamental instabilities of knowledge and reality. As such he anticipates many of the concerns of postmodernism, and his work constitutes one of the principle influences on the later genre of Cyberpunk. Dick's work transcends the limitations of the science fiction genre, not least because of his willingness to experiment with language.

At the same time as Dick was exploring such issues within the genre of science fiction, William Burroughs was developing radical new means of expression in more experimental forms of literature. Burroughs, probably more effectively than any of his contemporaries, used the means of literary experimentation to represent a world increasingly dominated by information and information technology. Fittingly he came from a family whose wealth was founded on adding and calculating machines. Burroughs was a descendent of the founder of Burroughs Adding Machine Company and inventor of the eponymous machine, one of the major nineteenth-century precursors of the computer as a business tool. (Originally a company producing mechanical calculating devices, Burroughs Adding Machine Company became one of the early computing companies, whose work included building the memory unit for ENIAC in the early '50s, and whose engagement in banking computing enabled it to be a competitor of sorts to IBM. In the '80s it merged with the Sperry Corporation to become Unisys, under which name it continues to be a presence in computing.) The wealth that Burroughs's invention brought allowed the inventor's grandson to enjoy many of the privileges of an American upper-middle-class upbringing, including a sizable allowance, and an expensive private education culminating at Harvard. Despite these early advantages Burroughs was attracted to other, less orthodox life choices. He was openly homosexual at a time, in the 1940s and '50s, when such an orientation was still stigmatized. He also became a heroin addict at that period, and, in 1951 managed to shoot his common-law wife, Joan Vollmer, in the head while supposedly emulating William Tell. At the same time he was involved with a group of writers, including Allen Ginsberg and Jack Kerouac, who were to become known as the Beat Generation.

Burroughs published his first novel, *Junky*,[62] in 1953 when he was 39, followed by *The Naked Lunch* in 1959.[63] In these books he started to develop his extraordinary literary technique. *Junky* does not merely describe the lifestyle of the heroin addict, it actively mimics it. *The Naked Lunch* is set in a version of Tangier, where Burroughs spent much time, called Interzone, and deals again with addiction and the kind of life it imposes, but in a remarkable, disjointed fashion that defies easy understanding or précis. These techniques were further developed in the collaboration between Burroughs and the poet Brion Gysin in the '60s. Gysin was a British-born artist who shared many of Burroughs's arcane interests, including the Persian sect the Assassins, magic and misogyny. Together Burroughs and Gysin developed the cut-up technique of randomly assembling sentences. This was widely employed in the trilogy of novels starting with *The Soft Machine* [64] of 1961, and followed by *The Ticket That Exploded* [65] of 1962 and *Nova Express* [66] of 1964. These books are possibly some of the most cogent expressions of a world saturated with media and information. In these works, and for Burroughs in general, language is a virus that perpetuates itself through the mass media, a situation he both articulates and resists through the use of technologies such as tape recording and techniques such as the cut-up. Burroughs has been hailed as prefiguring many postmodernist literary concerns, in particular his focus on language and indeterminacy and his refusal of the traditional role of author, as well as producing Cyberpunk novels, *avant la lettre*.

If Burroughs's work prefigures the postmodern narrative then that of Thomas Pynchon exemplifies it. Pynchon is in a sense the archetypal American postmodern novelist. His novels are vast, hermetic texts, dense and difficult to read and full of hidden references, heterogeneous modes of writing and an almost total absence of stable meaning. Even Pynchon's famous invisibility, equalled only by that of J. D. Salinger, adds to his impeccable postmodern credentials. He has been hailed by a number of critics as a writer deeply engaged with questions of Cybernetics, systems and information. [67] The two books that best exemplify Pynchon's concerns in this area are *The Crying of Lot 49* [68] and *Gravity's Rainbow*. [69] The former, mercifully short by Pynchon's standards, concerns the attempts of the main character Oedipa Maas to make sense of the real-estate holdings of her ex-lover Pierce Inverarity. In her journey to discover the truth about his business affairs she undergoes a number of strange adventures, and uncovers bizarre underground conspiracies, including the existence of an alternative postal system, which has operated against the state monopolies throughout history. It is through this device and others, such as Oedipa's identification of the town of San Narciso, home of the mysterious Yoyodyne Corporation, as a kind of printed circuit, that, according to Fredric

Jameson, Pynchon allegorizes the effect of contemporary media and technology on the modern world.[70]

Pynchon's next book, the ambitious and brilliant *Gravity's Rainbow*, published in 1973, took the theme of the technologizing of the modern world to extremes. A summary of its impossibly complex plot is impossible. (Indeed the only adequate summary could only be the text of the book itself, similar to Borges's map at the same scale of the territory it represents.) Set in 1944, and revolving around the final stages of the War in Europe the book concerns the V-2 rocket programme. The rainbow of the title alludes both to the arc that describes the novel's elliptic set of connections as well as the trajectory, literal and historical, of the V-2 rockets. It revolves around a bewildering number of characters, including American lieutenant Tyrone Slothrop, whose peripatetic sex life exactly predicts the location of V-2 targets in London; the Pavlovian Edward Pointsman who obsessively captures stray dogs for his experiments; the 'antipointsman' statistician Roger Mexico, whose love for Jessica Swanlake offers a salve against the terror of the War; the beautiful spy Katje Borgesius, lover of both Slothrop and Blicero, a.k.a. Weissman, the V-2 commander, who engages in orgies based on the story of Hansel and Gretel with Katje and Gottfried; and so on. It incorporates mysterious wartime organizations such as PISCES and 'The White Visitation', the latter dedicated to psychic research. According to John Johnston, Pynchon's intention, in this extraordinary and confusing melée of characters and episodes, is to trace the 'birth of a "rocket-state" that will unify as a "meta-cartel" an international network of new industries – plastics, electronics, aviation – growing out of the ruins of World War II. In a tentacular expansion, this network will soon provide the material basis for a technopolitical world order.'[71]

Johnston suggests *Gravity's Rainbow* 'maps or projects a set of concerns, in fact a whole sensibility conspicuous in America in the late 1960s, onto events in Europe at the end of World War II'.[72] The period in which Pynchon was writing saw, among other things, widespread discontent in many countries with the dominant political order, particularly in relation to interventions such as those by the United States in Vietnam, as well as a series of economic crises which necessitated a radical restructuring of capitalism. Bound up with the latter was the accelerated development of computing technology and its increasing employment in the civilian sphere. Though the action of the book precedes the widespread use of computing technology, it 'assumes that the integration of America's military-industrial complex and the networks of global capitalism depended upon – indeed was one with – the digitalization of information'.[73]

Many of the elements of Cyberpunk came together in 1982 when Ridley Scott filmed Philip K. Dick's novel *Do Androids Dream of Electric Sheep*, retitled as *Blade Runner*. Scott turned Dick's story into a futuristic film noir set in a rain-drenched, orientalized Los Angeles. The book's main character, Deckard, a 'blade runner' dedicated to searching out and liquidating androids, apparently indistinguishable from 'natural' humans, has been turned from one of Dick's typical everyman naïfs into a world-weary figure closer to one of Chandler's private detective characters. However it was not so much the plot or the typical Dickian concerns about identity and subjectivity that made *Blade Runner* so compelling, as the look of the film. Influenced by Möbius, Scott's vision of a near-future cityscape presented the most perfectly realized backdrop for articulating contemporary concerns and fears about a society dominated by global corporations and information technology. From the pyramidical building housing the Tyrrel Corporation (the manufacturers of the androids Deckard is hunting), which dominates the landscape, its sides incised with patterns so as to resemble the surface of a microchip, to the street-level prosthetics laboratories, the film presents a visual allegory of a society dominated by techno-science and information technology. The pervasive darkness and continuous rain obliquely suggests that such a domination comes with a price in relation at least to the environment. The presence throughout the film of floating advertisements extolling the virtues of off-world colonization suggests a world that is no longer a desirable place to live.

*Blade Runner* came out at a time when new technology was becoming far more visible in mainstream culture. The early '80s saw the development of the Apple Macintosh, the machine that made computing 'friendly' and accessible (and for the launch of which Ridley Scott directed an advertisement of record breaking expense in *Blade Runner* style); the emergence of Techno music, the paradigmatic dance noise of the post-industrial urban landscape, and the beginnings of 'deconstructionist' graphic design. William Gibson's science fiction novel *Neuromancer* [74] resonated perfectly with these elements of the *zeitgeist*. Though not responsible either for originating the term, or for the ideas it came to embody, Gibson's book is the paradigmatic work of 'Cyberpunk'. In it he 'coalesced an eclectic range of generic protocols, contemporary idiolects, and a pervasive technological eroticism combined with a future-shocking ambivalence'.[75] An eclectic set of influences, including Raymond Chandler, Burroughs and Michael Herr, author of Vietnam reportage classic, *Dispatches*,[76] are combined to produce a dystopian vision of the near future, in which the nation state is of negligible importance and the world is dominated by high-tech corporations, or as Gibson calls them as part of an insistent orientialism, *zaibatsu*. Everywhere vast conurbations have spread, such as Chiba City in Japan or the Sprawl on the Eastern Seaboard of the United States. The most important space in *Neuromancer* is the non-space of the computer networks, or, in Gibson's by now famous term, 'cyberspace'. Gibson's vision of a three-dimensional realization of networked computer data is by now both famous and influential. This description he gives in *Neuromancer* has become canonical.

> Cyberspace. A consensual hallucination, experienced by billions of legitimate operators, in every nation by children being taught mathematical concepts ... A graphic representation of data abstracted from the banks of every computer in the human system. Unthinkable complexity. Lines of light ranged in the nonspace of the mind, clusters of constellations of data. Like city lights, receding ...[77]

Part of Gibson's brilliance is the reticence with which he articulates such concepts. In this he lets his ignorance of computing work to his advantage. *Neuromancer* was famously written on a manual typewriter, and it is clear that Gibson is uninterested in the practicalities of what might actually be possible. Despite this, the concept of cyberspace in the terms articulated by Gibson became, and to some extent remains, a legitimate and fashionable area of concern, responsible for example for a number of academic conferences. Through his notion of cyberspace Gibson also managed to find a more exciting way to represent hackers and hacking. In his future vision hackers have become 'console cowboys' (thus invoking the frontier mythology that has animated much discussion of networks and hacking). Such cowboys 'jack in' to cyberspace, which effectively means being able to move virtually through cyberspace in order to access data.

Gibson followed *Neuromancer* with two more books set in the same future, *Count Zero*[78] and *Mona Lisa Overdrive*,[79] and has since developed similar ideas in a number of novels and stories. Though Gibson is not the originator of the term Cyberpunk or of the ideas it embodies, he is possibly the most interesting and gifted exponent of the genre. This is, perhaps, because of his adventurous and sophisticated use of language, which far exceeds that of other Cyberpunk writers, and his refusal to try to present convincing future technological scenarios. In this he is closer to experimental writers such as Burroughs or Pynchon than to most of his peers working in the science fiction genre. That said, the emergence of Cyberpunk as a distinctive subgenre within science fiction produced a number of exciting and innovative fictions, including those of Rudy Rucker, Pat Cadigan, Neal Stephenson, Bruce Sterling, and, in the UK, Jeff Noon. Sterling, as well as writing a number of books with near-future scenarios, collaborated with Gibson on *The Difference Engine*,[80] an amusing 'Steampunk' novel set in an alternative Victorian past in which Babbage's protocomputers have been successfully built and have thus initiated an early version of the information age.[81]

Stimulated perhaps by the increasing media presence of hackers and hacker culture, or the increasing popularity of technologically-oriented music and literature, Hollywood soon began to explore the possibilities of Cyberpunk. In the 1990s a number of attempts were made to translate the genre into film. *Johnny Mnemonic* (1995) is set in the early twenty-first century and features Keanu Reeves as the eponymous hero, a courier who stores data in his brain. The plot centres on his need to get rid of some particularly sensitive medical data while being chased by, among others, the Yakuza. *Johnny Mnemonic* received a lukewarm reception, both critically and commercially, and is possibly most noteworthy for being directed by Robert Longo, better known in the '80s as an artist in the heroic mould of Julian Schnabel, and for featuring Reeves in the first of his Cyberpunk roles. Reeves also featured in Kathryn Bigelow's *Point Break*, a wonderful, trashy film about bank heists, Buddhism and surfing. For her excursion in the Cyberpunk genre, *Strange Days* (1995), she turned instead to Ralph Fiennes, who, though clearly a better actor, was perhaps less able to embody the digital zeitgeist as effectively as Reeves's blank and awkward handsomeness. Set in the days before the new millennium at the end of the twentieth century, Strange Days features Fiennes as Lenny Nero, an ex-cop turned hustler, who deals with tapes that can record people's memories. In the course of his work he comes across the future equivalent of a snuff movie, which plunges him into a conspiracy involving police and others in authority. David Cronenberg's *eXistenZ* (1999) features Jennifer Jason Leigh as a virtual reality games designer who, in fleeing pursuers intent on taking her life, enters the world of her latest game, the eponymous eXistenZ.

Despite having reputable directors and scriptwriters these films were on the whole unsatisfactory, not least in their attempts to portray the effects and possibilities of new technology. In each case, as with more egregious productions such as *The Lawnmower Man* (1996), the technologies themselves are supposed to suggest brave new worlds mediated to unprecedented degrees by media and information technology. Yet in the main they come across as no more than unconvincing gimmicks. By having to give the technology substance in order to make it visible and filmic, the sense of its ubiquity and power is lost. These problems were overcome in the Wachowski Brothers' film *The Matrix* (1999) by a simple, yet brilliant sleight of hand. The film is set in what appears to be an American city in 1999, in which the central character Thomas Anderson (Keanu Reeves again) is a computer programmer by day and a hacker at night, known to others as Neo. Neo is plagued by a nagging sense that all is not as it seems in the world. This is confirmed when he meets a young women and fellow hacker calling herself Trinity. Trinity takes Neo to meet Morpheus, who is a kind of hacker guru figure, and who reveals to Neo the reasons behind his unease. It is not the end of the twentieth century, Morpheus tells Neo, but sometime in the twenty-second. The world, everything that surrounds them, is no more than a computer simulation, engineered by intelligent machines who have taken over the world and, in effect, farm human beings cocooned in pods in order to feed on the energy they generate. While in their pods humans are given the illusion that they are in the world of 1999. Morpheus, Trinity and others have liberated themselves and are now actually in a space ship, evading the attentions of the machines, while trying to find ways of liberating other humans. Morpheus is convinced that Neo is 'the one', who has special powers to defeat the machines. Morpheus, Trinity and the others on the ship can enter the computer simulation and interact with the world in special ways, though they have to be careful to avoid the attentions of certain men in black who also have special powers, and who are, in fact, a kind of machinic secret police force.

## HACKING CULTURE

Cyberpunk, Techno and deconstructionist graphic design represented consonant reactions across different genres to the emergent technoculture. Cyberpunk's juxtaposed ideolects, Techno's use of repetition and sampling and eschewal of the artist's presence, deconstructionist graphic design's use of layers and experimentation with typography, all reflected a world of diffused and distributed communication mediated through networks of powerful information technology. It is in the same context that the figure of the hacker emerged and was defined in its modern sense. Though, as we have seen, hacking already existed both as a name and a concept, it referred largely to the obsessive interest in the possibilities of computing evinced by Computer Science and Artificial Intelligence students at places like MIT and Stanford. It was not until the 1980s that hacking as a criminal/outlaw activity became widespread. Much to the disgust of the original hackers, the name became used to describe those who used computer networks to gain access to other people's computers. In 1982 the FBI arrested a group of hackers in Milwaukee calling themselves the 414s (after the local area code), after members were accused of 60 computer break-ins perpetrated against institutions such as Memorial Sloan-Kettering Cancer Center and the Los Alamos National Laboratory. At the same time the Comprehensive Crime Control Act gave the Secret Service legal jurisdiction over credit card and computer fraud. Hacker groups started to proliferate in the '80s, including the aforementioned 414s and the Legion of Doom in the United States and the Chaos Computer Club in Germany. At the same time publications such as 2600: were founded to share tips on phone and computer hacking. The US government responded by passing a series of laws designed to crack down in hacking, such as The Computer Fraud and Abuse Act of 1986 and The Electronic Communications Privacy Act of the same year. Various agencies were formed in the late '80s to combat computer crime including the Computer Emergency Response Team, a US defense agency whose mission was and continues to be to investigate the growing numbers of attacks on computer networks.

The late 1980s and '90s saw a kind of running battle between hackers and the authorities, in the form of the government and other frustrated institutions, such as universities. In the United States massive police operations, such as Operation Sundevil in 1990 have been mounted against hacking. Notorious hackers such as Kevin Mitnick, and others with handles such as Phiber Optik, Dark Dante, Data Stream, Eric Bloodaxe, and Knight Lightning all succumbed to arrest in this period, though hacking continues as frenetically as before. Despite this and in spite of the possible damage done by hackers or the dangers their activities represent, hacks are, by and large, simply pranks. That is to say that they are undertaken usually as a kind of game the aim of which is to outwit the authorities. There is little sense of sophisticated political intention in the acts or their descriptions by the hackers. Even the ludicrous names adopted by hackers suggest a fervid imagination, rather than anything more sinister. Indeed the names hackers adopt suggest that much of the hacker imaginary has come to be informed by Cyberpunk. The hacker is a creation of the culture in which he is simultaneously condemned and fetishized.

But, the apparent playfulness of most hacking apart, as a form of resistance it resonated with other ideas and movements. Though demonized by the mass media and criminalized by the state, the hacker has entered, through means such as Cyberpunk and Techno music, the cultural mainstream as a model of more general engagement with a world dominated by computing technology. Artists engage in 'reality hacking', critics of 'hacking culture' or even of 'hacking texts'. Different kinds of hacker culture have emerged across the globe, from Northern and Eastern Europe to Japan. The hacker has become a recognizable, and self-explanatory staple figure in film, TV and other mass media. Hacking and the models of practice it offers connects with theories such as those of Derrida, described above, as well as with other theoretical viewpoints on life in post-industrial technologized capitalism, which offer alternative possibilities for thought and action.

Hacking as a form of resistance reflected the autonomous nature of other activist phenomena of the '80s and '90s. These included the nomadic rave culture that emerged in Britain in the '80s, involving groups of DJs such as Spiral Tribe, which operated alongside ecological and other activism, often involving action against road building and other environmentally problematic activities or resistance to unpopular Government measures, such as the Poll Tax. Such popular forms of resistance were largely repressed through legal means – accompanied by heavy-handed police involvement – by the Thatcher government. Nomadism as a response to the repressive context of late capitalism was articulated in the United States by Hakim Bey, whose notion of 'Temporary Autonomous Zones' is both a highly influential, and widely criticised articulation of resistance to contemporary technoculture. Hakim Bey is the pseudonym of Peter Lamborn Wilson, who spent a decade travelling around the Islamic world, in particular Iran, studying the mystical side of Islam, in particular Sufism. He published a number of works about Sufi mysticism, translations of Persian poetry, and an account of eighteenth century pirates' utopias. He is also on the board of Autonomedia, a small alternative publishing company responsible for cheap editions of alternative theory and literature. In 1985, as

Hakim Bey, he published *T.A.Z. The Temporary Autonomous Zone, Ontological Anarchy, Poetic Terrorism.*[82] In this work he proclaimed the existence and necessity of temporary nomadic zones, which act as enclaves against the powers that be, and are dissolved before they can be repressed or co-opted. Bey/Wilson took his inspiration from Deleuze and Guattari and from his knowledge of early-modern pirate utopias, and from cyberpunk science fiction, in particular the work of Bruce Sterling, and his notion of 'Islands in the Net'. The concept of the TAZ has been invoked in the many kinds of alternative spaces that emerged in the 1980s and '90s, such as raves, festivals, and interventions such as those practised by Reclaim the Streets. It has also been seen as a strategy for using the Internet and the Web, which for some acts, oxymoronically, as a kind of permanent TAZ. Yet it has also incited a large amount of hostile comment from others on the left who might be expected to be sympathetic. Venerable anarchism commentator Murray Bookchin dismisses Bey's ideas as 'lifestyle anarchism', while autonomist activists in Italy have gone so far as to publish a book of fake Hakim Bey essays as a form of critique.

Hacking as a form of symbolic and aesthetic resistance found another kind of expression in the '90s when artists started to exploit computer networks as the locus of new forms of avant-garde art practice and political activism. As the World Wide Web came to notice in the early to mid-'90s, it foregrounded the potential of electronic networks as public spaces in which identity and gender can remain fluid and indeterminate. One recent result of this was the emergence of so-called 'Cyberfeminism', the name under which the work of a number of critical theorists and practitioners was corralled, and which denoted a shared concern with the utopian possibilities of new electronic media in relation to gender. Like Feminism, Cyberfeminism evades easy definition. It takes a number of different forms and encompasses disparate points of view. It is possible, however, to discern three distinct areas of cyberfeminist activity. One is theory, exemplified by the work of Sadie Plant[83] and Rosi Braidotti,[84] and in a different inflexion by Allucquère Rosanne Stone.[85] Another is in particular kind of art practice, as, for example, that of VNS Matrix or Linda Dement. The third is in developing new modes of behaviour and understanding for women in relation to digital technology and the Internet. This is exemplified by the 'Grrrl' phenomenon, which proposes a utopian model of free and liberating identity for women on the Net. Its variations include 'webgrrls', 'riotgrrls', 'guerrilla grrls' and so on. A fourth is the creation of on-line (and off-line) collectives or organizations, such as the Old Boy Network, FACES or Femail.

The possibilities of the Web also inspired the work of the Critical Art Ensemble, that of the Italian Luther Blissett Project, the Mongrel Collective in Britain, as well as artists involved with 'net.art', described in chapter three, including Vuk Cosic, I/O/D, Jodi, Olia Lialina, Heath Bunting, Rachel Baker and the Irational Organization [sic], who have explored the possibilities of the net as a medium, rather than simply a means of representation. The Critical Art Ensemble was started in 1987, in Tallahassee, Florida by Steve Kurtz and Steve Barnes, as a collective project involving performance, theory, video, slide shows, painting and guerrilla-style intervention. As they developed their practice further it involved greater degrees of theory, as did their output. In 1994 they published a manifesto of resistance to the new realities of post-Fordist capitalism, *The Electronic Disturbance*,[86] followed two years later by *Electronic Civil Disobedience*,[87] in which Marxism, Poststructuralism, Situationism and Anarchism were combined to produce a rough-and-ready set of tactics and responses. Both books invoke the idea of the nomadic as a strategy by which the highly fluid and responsive nature of contemporary capital can be resisted and even overturned. Rejecting the idea of a collective will of organized proletarians so beloved of Marxists, the CAE put their faith in a 'technocratic avant-garde' who can disrupt capitalism's operations through decentralized and technologically informed means. In the Netherlands the 'Foundation for the Advancement of Illegal Knowledge' disseminated ideas garnered from squatting, free radio and media activism, as did the online journal *Crash Media*, and the print magazine *Adbusters* in the United States.

The most famous and perhaps most romanticized example of hacking as a form of resistance is probably that of the Zapatistas. On 1 January 1994, the day the North American Free Trade Agreement (NAFTA) came into being, guaranteeing free trade between the United States and other countries in America, the 'Ejercito Zapatista de Liberacion Nacional', a guerrilla group consisting of some 3,000 women and men, took over most of the southern Mexican state of Chiapas. Most of the Zapatistas, as the group is more popularly known, are Indians from the Chiapas area, though many of their leaders, including their spokesperson, Subcomandante Marcos, are middle-class intellectuals. The Zapatistas' aim is to resist the encroachment of neoliberalism on the peasant communities of Chiapas and elsewhere, and on Mexico as a whole. The crucial aspect of their strategy has been inspired use of media, in particular the Internet. They are thus what Manuel Castells describes as the 'first informational guerrilla movement'.[88] Whether the Zapatistas can, in the end, prevail is doubtful. But they do point to possible forms of resistance to the otherwise overwhelming dominance of neoliberalism, using the very tools by which the latter seeks hegemony. The Zapatistas have brilliantly adopted a number of hacking techniques as well as other forms of electronic disturbance to spread their message.

For many digital networks seem to offer the means to realize Walter Benjamin's demand, described in his essay 'Art in the Age of Mechanical Reproduction', for an aestheticized politics to combat the fascist politicization of aesthetics. Benjamin proposed that mechanical reproducibility liberated works of art from their unique and authentic existence in time and place, and, thereby, their parasitic dependence on ritual.[89] Benjamin's polemical essay in which these ideas were expressed was written as a response to the dangers of Fascism and Nazism, and indeed capitalism, and to their subjugation of the masses by the ritual and spectacular use of mass media. To some extent those dangers remain with us, despite the defeat of Fascism and other forms of overt totalitarianism. The hacker, in turn, invokes another idea of Benjamin's. In his 'Theses on the Philosophy of History' he tells a story of how, during the French Revolution, on the first evening of fighting, clocks in towers were simultaneously fired upon, so as to stop the day, and symbolize the revolutionary exploding of the continuum of history.[90] In this he differentiates between two different kinds of time, clock time, which for him is also the empty homogenous time of catastrophic progress, with revolutionary time, 'charged with the time of the now'.[91] It is through the optic of Benjamin's thought that the work of those resisting the apparently inevitable progress of wired capitalism can be understood. Clocks, such as those in Benjamin's story, are not just symbols of the concept of progressive time he abhorred, but the means by which the organization of time necessary to the operations of capitalism has been realized. In place of such clocks, we have computers organising not just working time, but every aspect of life under late capitalism. The hacker who, for whatever reason, disrupts the operation of a computer system or network is a modern counterpart to Benjamin's sniper. What may at first seem to be a pointless act of sabotage is in fact a profoundly utopian gesture. It proposes the possibility of alternative ways of organizing time and space and other kinds of community than that relentlessly imposed upon the world by technologized capital.

# 6. Digital Nature

In the last chapter it was suggested that *The Matrix*'s most brilliant conceit is to make the technology by which its paranoid vision is sustained invisible. By making the world a computer simulation the Wachowski Brothers have understood that the machinery that characterizes and dominates late modernity cannot be adequately represented in physical terms. This is not simply because computers are not exciting to look at, or because they do not evince the same dynamism as machines of previous eras. It is because computers themselves are not the machinery in question. They are merely points at which the vast, complex and largely invisible assemblage of information and communication systems through which late modernity operates, are made visible and accessible. *The Matrix*, whether deliberately or not on the part of its makers, realizes one of the main aspects of technology in this late part of late modernity. In a world dominated by computing technology the computer is no longer simply without 'emblematic or visual power', as Fredric Jameson puts it, but actually disappearing, becoming invisible.

In this it reveals, in metaphoric form, a central aspect of our lives. In the developed world at least, we live in a society supersaturated by digital technology. This was made vividly clear by the furore over the so-called Millennium Bug, which showed that that technology is present in almost every aspect of our lives. To some degree at least we are beginning to cease to notice its presence and how it affects us, or at least take these aspects for granted. We sit in front of our computers at work, surf the net, send e-mails, play games on consoles, watch television that is both produced and, increasingly, distributed digitally, read magazines and books all of which have been produced on computers, travel with our laptops, enter information into palmtops, talk on our digital mobile phones, listen to CDs or MP3s, watch films that have been post-processed digitally, drive cars embedded with microchips, wash our clothes in digitally programmable machines, pay for our shopping by debit cards connected to digital networks, and allow the supermarkets to know our shopping habits through loyalty cards using the same networks, withdraw cash from automatic telling machines, and so on.

Digital technology's ubiquity and its increasing invisibility have the effect of making it appear almost natural. The tendency to take it for granted can easily attenuate into a sense that it has evolved into its present form naturally, by way of a kind of digital nature. This naturalization is problematic, in that it has distinct political repercussions. Like conservative fantasies about the countryside, it ignores the complex human forces that determined its development and present importance. Despite the sentimental rhetoric it inspires, the English countryside is an entirely artificial creation and takes its present form as the result of human needs, labour and social antagonism. So too our new digital nature, which, as I hope this book has shown, is the creation of different, sometimes antagonistic forces and needs. This book can be understood as a kind of cultural archaeology, digging under the surface of our contemporary digital landscape in order to reveal the underlying structures that gave it its present shape. It is these structures rather than any natural tendencies within the technology that have determined how and when we use it.

Thus our current digital landscape has been broadly shaped by the informational needs of capitalism and its drive to abstraction, and more specifically by the calculative and cryptological needs of the Second World War and the security concerns of the Cold War. To some extent all the digital technologies we use were developed in these contexts, as was much of the intellectual means we employ to understand the effects of those technologies. When, as recently happened, a hapless stocktrader allowed stocks to be sold at ten times their value through hitting the wrong key, he was the beneficiary of hair-trigger technology developed for the defence needs of the Cold War. The interactive trading system he was using is a direct descendent of interactive early warning systems such as SAGE. Similarly when someone uses the Web or sends an e-mail or uses a digital paint, graphics or modelling program such as Photoshop or Autocad they are taking advantage of other Cold War technologies. All the above were developed out of research originating with the Advanced Research Projects Agency (ARPA), which was funded by the United States Defense Department to research into the possibilities of technology. That so much of the technology we now take for granted was developed in the context of the Cold War raises some interesting questions. Underpinning the way we do business, produce media, entertain ourselves and communicate are technologies that bear all the trademarks of the Cold War paranoia that produced them.

And yet other forces have acted upon how we understand and use such technologies, and have opened up possibilities within them other than the purely instrumental. Out of the post-war avant-garde, for example, the very questions of interaction, attention and communication that animated Cold War planners found different meanings and purposes. The work of Cage and others in the 1950s, responding to the same Cold War issues in a very different manner, developed a framework for thinking about the use of interactive and multimedia technology beyond its military applications. In the 1960s artists and others involved with media began to realize such ideas in technological form, in video, computers and multimedia.

Out of this developed much of the current way we understand and use digital media. Though emerging out of similar concerns and in a similar context to the Cold War technological developments described above, the avant-garde re-oriented interactive and multimedia in a more utopian direction. These two strands were brought together under the aegis of the West Coast counter-culture. It presented the ideal context for Cold War technology and avant-garde practice to coalesce as a utopian project. In particular the philosophy of enlightened tool use promulgated by publications such as *The Whole Earth Catalog* along with its interests in self-realization and self-expression and the more general multimedial psychedelic culture, presented the conditions for the development of the computer as a personal tool and a medium. These conditions were instrumental in the development of the Personal Computer, as well as in research into the possibilities of multimedia and inter-activity. Computing has not only developed ideas about how to do things from the counter-culture but also a more general utopian vision of technology as socially progressive and capable of expanding human potential. Though most people's experience of computing is fairly mundane, it retains a counter-cultural aura as a liberatory technology, the use of which will advance humanity, much as LSD was supposed to in the 1960s. This idea is still exploited by computer companies such as Apple and Microsoft as part of their publicity, with slogans such as 'Think Different' [*sic*] and 'Where Shall We Go Today'. Paradoxically the counter-cultural legacy of technological utopianism has found new expression as part of a more general ideology of neo-liberal, libertarian, high-tech capitalism, whose most cogent expression is found in the magazine *Wired*.

Opposing the hegemony of techno-utopian capitalism has been the development of subcultural styles in literature, music and design, through which questions of alternatives and modes of resistance could be rehearsed. These have interacted and combined with theoretical developments such as French philosophers Gilles

Deleuze and Félix Guattari's concepts of assemblages, rhizomes and nomads; Jacques Derrida's analysis of thinking as writing; the Autonomist Marxist's ideas about the General Intellect and Immaterial Labour; Donna Haraway's conception of the cyborg as a model for thinking about gender and identity in a high-tech world, and Hakim Bey's concept of 'Temporary Autonomous Zones', which act as enclaves against the powers that be, and are dissolved before they can be repressed or co-opted. Punk in the late '70s, itself a response to the dislocations of capitalism as it shifted to an informational mode, inspired many of these developments, including the sci-fi genre Cyberpunk, musical styles such as Industrial Rock and Techno and other electronic genres, as well as deconstructionist graphic design and fashion. Out of these different elements there has emerged a distinctive digital style in which the extraordinary social and cultural developments of the last twenty years have been reflected. This style has entered the mainstream of contemporary culture, finding expression in film, television, book and magazine design.

These are, then, some of the main elements out of which our current digital culture has been assembled: Cold War defence technologies; avant-garde art practice; counter-cultural techno-utopianism; postmodernist critical theory; new wave subcultural style. Though, as time goes on, their presence becomes harder to detect. Each of these elements is immanent within the technologies we use and the means we use to understand them. To acknowledge the heterogeneous nature of digital culture is increasingly necessary, as the technology through which it is perpetuated becomes both more ubiquitous and more invisible. The less aware we are of the social and cultural forces out of which our current situation has been constructed the less able we are to resist and question the relations of power and force it embodies. If, on the other hand, we can see that these forces are culturally contingent and in no sense natural and inevitable then we have the basis for asking questions.

Moreover we are able to see that concealed within our current digital culture are already models for such questioning. This is becoming increasingly important in the light of current technological developments. The implementation of technologies such as broadband digital content distribution and digital wireless networks will massively increase the degree to which digital technology is imbricated with our everyday existence. At the same time the power and reach of digital surveillance is increasing with great rapidity. Soon no aspect of our lives will remain untouched by these ubiquitous invisible forces. Neo's revelation in *The Matrix* of a world constructed out of data becomes oddly plausible.

# 7. Digital Culture in the Twenty-first Century

Despite all the predictions about the so-called 'Y2K bug', the new millennium did not see the breakdown of banking computer systems, or the collapse of the systems governing the distribution of welfare provision, or even the operational failure of medical equipment, air conditioning systems, elevators, electricity grids, traffic or air-traffic control systems or any other system that uses digital technology, let alone the accidental launching of nuclear missiles. Yet, the new century had barely begun when another apocalyptic event took place that, though not directly caused by or linked to digital technology, revealed the precariously inter-linked nature of the emerging digital culture.

On 6 September 2001 an exhibition by the artist Wolfgang Staehle called '2001' opened at the Postmasters Gallery in New York. Staehle was already recognized as a pioneer of art involving the Internet. In 1991 he had founded THE THING, a bulletin board that became one of the first and most influential forums for the discussion of new media art and theory. By the time of his Postmasters show Staehle had developed a distinctive practice involving the projection of high-resolution digital images onto gallery walls. What made these images unusual was that they were coming from a real-time live feed, refreshed every few seconds. In effect the spectator was seeing the view represented more or less as it actually was at the

50 Still from a series of continuously refreshed images of Lower Manhattan shown at Wolfgang Staehle's '2001' exhibition.

moment of viewing. For this exhibition Staehle had projected three such real-time images: one of the Fernsehturm, the distinctive and recognizable television tower in Berlin; one of Comburg, a monastery near Stuttgart; and a view of Lower Manhattan from a camera positioned in Brooklyn (illus. 50). Seen in normal circumstances, Staehle's images convey an experience of stillness, despite being more or less live, and brilliantly bring into question the difference between live and still imagery, and the broader issues of time and representation.

In the case of the image of Lower Manhattan, this stillness was shattered five days later in a most extraordinary and unpredictable fashion, when the World Trade Center, which dominated the projected view, was attacked and destroyed by two hijacked aircraft. Staehle himself was not particularly pleased by the unanticipated and uncalled-for fame and even notoriety that the terrorist event brought to this particular exhibition. Nevertheless it helped delineate an important connection between the real-time technology used by Staehle and the context in which the attacks took place and were received. He was taking advantage of the extraordinary capacity of new digital networks and new technologies to make information and representations immediately available, which in turn is transforming our relation to events as they happen and also transforming the nature of those events themselves.[1]

This is nicely indicated by the title of a book about the attacks written by Middle East expert and academic Fred Halliday, *Two Hours that Shook the World*.[2] Halliday's title clearly refers to journalist John Reed's classic eyewitness account of the Bolshevik revolution of October 1917, *Ten Days that Shook the World* (1919).[3] The difference between the two titles indicates with admirable economy the increasing speed at which world-transforming events take place. This speeding up is directly related to the increasing ubiquity and availability of media, digital and otherwise, through which such events can be witnessed. News of the events during the Russian Revolution was only obtainable afterwards through print media such as newspapers. By the time of the September 11 attacks it was possible for people all over the world to watch the assaults more or less as they took place and to witness the aftermath, including the dramatic collapse of the towers themselves. Furthermore this was not just possible through mainstream media such as television but also through news websites. In fact the demand for news was so great that the Internet more or less seized up and many people abandoned it and turned to radio and television.

Nevertheless the speed at which news of the attacks went around the globe was evidence of a highly interconnected world brought together, in part at least, by new media and new technologies. Soon after, bulletin boards and chatrooms on the Web became host to an extraordinary proliferation of eye-witness accounts, images, debates, conspiracy theories and accusations about the attacks. Much of this discussion took place through Web-based phenomena such as 'blogs' (short for weblogs, regularly updated and automatically archived webpages, often though not always personal, in which opinions and ideas could be expressed and debated). Interestingly the organization supposedly responsible for the attacks, Al-Qaeda, was itself a product of the widely distributed and loosely connected, non-hierarchical structuring made possible by the Internet and the World Wide Web, as well as mobile telephony and other developments in information communication technologies. As such, and despite the apparently archaic nature of their religious beliefs, Al-Qaeda, if such a thing exists at all in any real sense, is a paradigmatic product of digital culture. In many ways it seems to embody the principle of 'rhizomatic' decentered networks that underlie the Internet itself and is also proclaimed as the basis of new forms of politics by both libertarians and those in radical opposition to capitalism.[4]

Following the attacks in 2001, the elusive nature of Al-Qaeda made it easier for the United States Government to suggest, with little or no evidence in support of such a claim, that the terrorist organization was in league with the Iraqi dictatorship. This, along with spurious claims about Iraq's supposed possession of 'weapons of mass destruction', became the basis for making the case to the United States Senate and the United Nations for an invasion of Iraq, which took place in 2003. Aware since the Vietnam War of the power of the media to make the waging of war unpopular with the electorate, the United States Government was careful to control how journalists and television crews were able to get close to any action. Nevertheless the ease of use, availability and capacity to be distributed widely that characterized new media made it possible to circumvent government control of information.

In 2004 Joseph Darby, a soldier serving in Iraq anonymously passed a CD-Rom to the Military Police that contained horrifying images of prisoners being abused in Abu Ghraib prison. Unsurprisingly, these images caused revulsion and disgust throughout the world, and also surprise, among some at least, that representatives of a supposedly civilized nation could descend to such barbarism. It was particularly noticeable that these images were not taken covertly for the purposes of revealing hidden abuses, but by the perpetrators themselves, in a celebratory and open fashion. Young soldiers, sometimes women, were photographed, smiling, with their thumbs up, standing over the stacked or chained bodies of prisoners. Such behaviour may well be far more prevalent in wartime than we might care to think. But what distinguished the events in Abu Ghraib was not that they happened, but that the means of recording these activities was so readily and shamelessly embraced by the participants themselves; thus such graphic evidence was easily obtained and distributed because of the availability of cheap digital cameras, often built into mobile phones, and the ease of burning the images taken with them onto CD-Roms or of uploading them onto the Internet.

Similarly, much of the more critical debate about Abu Ghraib and the Iraq War more generally also took place (and continues to do so) on the World Wide Web, particularly through blogs, which allow for far more unbridled comment and even news than the increasingly supine news media in the United States. Blogs entered the public consciousness in the States when they became an important component of Howard Dean's campaign to become the Democratic candidate for the 2004 Presidential election, along with internet tools for grass-roots organization of groups. Though, in the end, Dean failed in his ambitions, nobody could fail to notice the capacity for mobilizing support at a grass-roots level that such technology offered. In a recent book, media theorist Brian McNair has described the result of the emergence of the blog as 'cultural chaos'.[5] For McNair the fact that anyone, or at least anyone with access to the right technologies, can blog means the end of what he describes as the 'control paradigm', in which the media help sustain the social order through the dissemination of dominant ideas and values and at the same time serve the interest of those in control. There are now numberless blogs on the Web, not least because setting one up is both easy and often free. The very proliferation of blogs does of course militate against individual voices being heard, but nevertheless some do, and, in the light of an increasingly conformist and often cowardly news media, blogs offer at least the possibility of genuine debate (as well as a lot of highly debatable and often offensive ideas).

What makes such phenomena interesting is not so much any immediate kind of public sphere (blogosphere!) they might now make possible, but the more general long-term change they represent, in which our whole conception about how the media is structured, and who has access to it, is changed. In place of the hierarchical mass-media model of communication flowing from the centre outwards, we glimpse a more distributed flat or bottom-up paradigm. It means that media companies will be increasingly obliged to take notice of the expectations of a new kind of consumer (and perhaps even a new kind of subject); one who does not expect to be treated as an anonymous invisible passive consumer, but an active user of media, who is used to creating her own means of responding to needs and desires.

Blogs are often cited as one of the principle phenomena of the so-called 'Web 2:0', the name given to the conception of the World Wide Web as a space for collaboration and reciprocal communication. Among these developments are 'social network' software such as MySpace, Bebo, FaceBook and Second Life (which involves users interacting in a shared virtual three-dimensional space), or YouTube, Flickr and del.icio.us, which respectively allow video clips, photographs and web bookmarks to be uploaded to the Web; 'peer-to-peer' software such as Napster and BitTorrent for sharing digital music and video files; powerful search engines, most famously Google; new forms of public debate and self expression, such as blogs and podcasts; and new forms of organizing and distributing knowledge, such as Wikipedia. In particular the kinds of online communities fostered by MySpace and other similar sites, for example Bebo and Facebook, as well as link and file-sharing software such as Flickr and de.li.co.us, are encouraging a new understanding of how it is possible to make the media responsive to personal needs and niche concerns. It may be that most people do not take, at first anyway, advantage of these possibilities. Nevertheless, such possibilities will determine how the media will be structured and considered.

The transformations in the media brought about by new techno-logies are transforming how we think about ourselves. In particular we are no longer passive consumers of the media, but, increasingly, also actively producers. At the most banal this means that through technologies such as Tivo or the iPod we can programme our media content as we wish, rather than in the way it is presented to us by television or record companies. In one sense this is neither new nor, strictly speaking, a digital phenomenon. From the moment record-able video-cassettes and audio-cassettes were first available we no longer had to watch a programme at the moment it was broadcast, or listen to the contents of a record in the sequence it was put together. Banal as this might seem, it was transformative for how we related to media products, such as television and music. The period in which video- and audio-recording technologies became widely available also saw the beginnings of sampling and mixing in popular music, in which found material was reused to make new tracks, which can be seen as a prefiguring of our current shift from passive consumption to active production. But there is an important differ-ence between these earlier analogue phenomena and the new digital means of controlling how one consumes media content. The former were subordinate to the mainstream media, such as records, radio and television, which still determined in general how their content was consumed, whereas the new technologies are fundamentally altering our relation to media in a profound and radical way.

In his book *The Long Tail*,[6] the editor of *Wired*, Chris Anderson, analyses what he sees as the effects of new technologies on commerce. Anderson is much concerned with what he describes as the 'infinite shelf space' made available virtually on sites such as iTunes, which can 'stock' millions of tunes rather than the mere thousands or tens of thousands available in a traditional bricks-and-mortar shop, as well as the multifarious ways objects such as tunes can occupy dimensions and be found and, perhaps most importantly, be reappropriated. For Anderson the new economy of on-line commerce makes it possible to invert the traditional form of the market from selling large amounts of a few things, to selling small amounts of a large number of things. This is the 'long tail' of his book's title, the shape of the graph showing the distribution of sales according to popularity, which is shaped somewhat like a tick, with the vertical stroke representing the small number of items in a market that sell in great quantities, and the horizontal stroke, extending almost infinitely, the far greater number of items that sell very little and which are normally ignored by conventional forms of marketing. But with new technologies this is changing, and an almost infinite array of niche micromarkets can be catered for. Accompanying this is a far greater sense of control on the part of the consumer: Anderson quotes Rupert Murdoch as claiming that 'young people don't want to rely on a God-like figure from above to tell them what's important. They want control over their media, instead of being controlled by it'.[7]

An example of this and of how consumers are controlling their media can be found in 'peer to peer' systems such as BitTorrent, which enables large files, such as films and television programmes to be downloaded, or Napster, which allowed users to share audio files by treating each user's computer as a host. Naturally much of the use of such systems contravenes copyright law, and the maker of Napster has been famously involved in a court case on those grounds. To some extent such activities are a more technologically sophisticated and widely distributed successor to the way that audio- and video-cassettes have been used to share or illegally sell copyrighted material. It also parallels the illegal distribution of films and software on CD-Roms, characterized by those in authority as 'piracy'. This said, peer to peer file sharing is also bringing about a new paradigm of consumption, in which the consumer not only gains far more control over the range and types of music he or she consumes but is able to become part of distributed networks of like-minded individuals with similar tastes.

This has been fairly blatantly exploited by Apple Computers, who explicitly market their computers' capacity to 'rip and burn' commercial CDs, and whose iTunes software and iPod present a kind of legalized version of file sharing, as well as encouraging strange new things such as 'podcasts', mini-programmes, designed to be downloaded and listened to on an MP3 player such as an iPod. (Interestingly the reason why Sony was so slow in entering the MP3 player market, which, for the developer of the original Walkman, should have been an obvious opportunity to exploit their reputation for innovation and quality, was that they had also invested in recorded music, and the two sides of their operation were potentially faced with a conflict of interest.) In this context it is interesting to consider Google's plans to digitize millions of books and make the results available online, which will surely alter our relationship with the printed word. What is almost certain is that it will not simply be a more convenient means of using books in way that we already do, but is likely to change how we conceive of books and their contents. But not all forms of web-based cultural production are commentaries or developments of pre-existing material. The podcast offers a similar kind of access to others for anyone who can make a digital recording and find some way to post to the Net. Similarly, internet radio makes it possible to 'stream' audio content over the World Wide Web, and Web 2:0 sites such as YouTube and Flickr lets users post video or photographic imagery for anyone else to see.

These forms of new media have begun to effect older, more mainstream media. For example the experience of listening to the radio is no longer either entirely passive, or even simply an experience of listening. In the United Kingdom the BBC is the state provider of television and radio (and, increasingly, Web and digital content), paid by licence fee levied from every owner of a television, rather than by advertising. BBC Radio 1 is the popular music radio station intending to appeal to a young audience. Each programme in the Radio 1 schedule has an accompanying set of web pages on the BBC website, as do the programmes on the other BBC stations. In most cases these contain little more than information about the programme. But, in the case of Radio 1 at least, the Web pages offer much more. They are integral parts of the experience at a number of levels. Many of the programmes operate webcams that allow listeners who also have access to the Web at the time to look at live streaming video of the disc jockeys and their production teams. The Web pages have another use that is perhaps more radical in its implications for the transformations of media, even as it appears quite banal. Listeners are often encouraged to upload images of themselves onto the website, which are then visible to other listeners/ viewers. Increasingly such uploading can be achieved without access to a computer. Anybody with a 3G-enabled mobile camera phone can do so either through a multimedia message or through email (though the latter is more complicated). Mobile phones are also used by listeners to participate in other ways, for example to text in a vote whether, according to the image they have uploaded, a partic- ular listener is good looking or not. (This kind of participatory, multimedia broadcasting is a long way from the paternal vision of the BBC promulgated by its original Director General, Lord Reith.) The situation gets more complicated when one factors in the fansites that have no official connection to the shows or persona- lities with which they are concerned, but those working on the show are clearly aware of them. Of course radio of all sorts has always involved participation, in the form of listener requests, phone-ins and so on.

It would also be a mistake to suggest that increased possibilities of audience participation represent some kind of new participatory democratisation of conventional mass media, of the sort suggested by Post-Marxist theorists of the 1960s such as Hans Magnus Enzensberger, for whom any transmitter is also, in principle, a receiver. For all the appearance of encouraging audience participa- tion, radio stations such as the BBC are still organizations dedicated to conveying their messages to a large audience with real little expectation of reciprocity. This is equally true of similar phenomena in other media, such as television, where 'reality TV' shows such as *Big Brother*, for which audience participation is through websites, official or otherwise, via message texting and phoning in votes, accompanied in this case by commentary on radio stations such as those described above and in the tabloid press. But this complex set of interactions between radio, television, newspapers, computer networks and telecommunications reveals a great deal not just about the vertical integrations of mass media and communications systems in our culture, but about how media are starting to be used and thought about, and about new possibilities for reciprocity.

An example of this is *The Mongolian Cow Sour Yogurt Supergirl Concert*, a Chinese talent show similar to *Pop Idol*, which took place in 2004, and which has revealed an extraordinary transformation regarding how people think about, engage with and use media. It was watched by 400 million Chinese viewers, more than the population of Western Europe, and inevitably perhaps, comprised the largest domestic television audience ever. There are, however, a number of aspects of the show that are far more interesting than are viewing figures. One is that it did not emanate from the central state Chinese broadcasting company, but from a provincial company in rural Hunan with a satellite connection. In a society that is still both highly centralized and controlled, that such a show should become a China-wide phenomenon is in itself fairly amazing. Part of its considerable appeal was that women of any age could participate. Many of the contestants, as well as the winner, Li Yuchun, were very different from the kind of glamorous women normally seen on Chinese television. Many rather optimistic or idealistic claims have been made for the supposedly empowering, feminist values of the *Supergirl Concert*. Much more to the point and far more radical, and possibly the real reason for its success, was that the audience were allowed to vote, or rather, given the sensitivities around both the term and concept of voting in China, send 'a message of support' to their favourite performer. Given that a pilot of the official Chinese Central TV version of the programme, which presumably did not involve voting, failed, it suggests that the real empowerment related to being able to intervene with and alter mass media.

In 2006, in response to such developments, the British broadsheet newspaper *The Observer* ran an investigative article about the future of television. It started with a description of how a future sixteen-year old called Chloe will be watching television in the year 2016.[8] According to the article Chloe 'keeps up with text and video messages by unrolling a paper-thin screen from wherever she is. A tiny camera beams images from her day to a video diary on her personal website, which interacts with those of her friends.' It continues to describe how Chloe will watch television on demand in a world without CDs or DVDs, TV listings or TV schedules, but with websites geared specifically for teenage girls, with narrowcast content made by independent broadcast companies or even by other teenagers. This is already beginning to happen, with the ever-greater availability of television content on the World Wide Web, not least through the BBC's new iPlayer, which allows BBC programmes to be watched for a week afterwards, and even downloaded. It seems likely that broadcasting, as we currently understand the term, is in the process of being radically changed.

The notion that new information communications technologies offer the possibility of a kind of bottom up model of organization that can dispense, in part at least, with hierarchies of authority, is most famously embodied in Wikis and, in particular, the Wikipedia (illus. 51). Wikis are websites that can be edited by viewers, and the Wikipedia is the most famous example of a wiki, being an online encyclopaedia that anyone can add to or edit. The idea that a process of this sort should be open to all is also found in one of the most important and potentially revolutionary concepts emerging out of new media, that of 'open source'. This is largely concerned with the

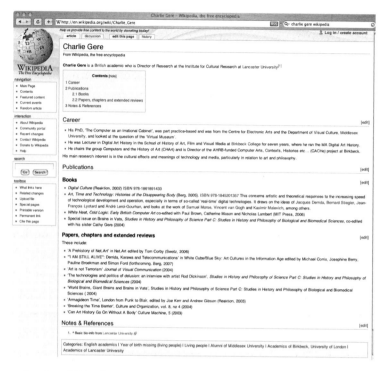

51 Page from Wikipedia.

idea that the most effective way to produce good, effective software is by making the original code available to anybody to add to, edit and distribute. The most famous examples include the Linux operating system and the Mozilla code for Netscape. The idea of open source has been extended to cover a far wider range of activities, beyond computer software and, through groups such as the Free/Libre Open Source Software (FLOSS) movement, is increasingly being applied to issues of social organization, intellectual property rights and so on. A good example of the application of open source ideas to areas beyond computing is the Creative Commons not-for-profit organization that encourages and facilitates the licensing of creative work in ways that others can develop without breaking copyright law.

Strong claims have been made for such developments in terms of their capacity to offer new forms of cultural and social organization and subjectivity. A good example of such claims can be found on the website of the P2P Foundation, founded by Michael Bauwens with the aim of 'researching, documenting and promoting peer to peer practices'.[9] It 'proposes to be a meeting place for those who can broadly agree with the certain propositions', which include the claim 'that technology reflects a change of consciousness towards participation, and in turn strengthens it'. Bauwens suggests that 'peer to peer relations . . . is a new form of political organizing and subjectivity, and an alternative for the political/economic order, which . . . points the way to a variety of dialogical and self-organizing formats' and 'ushers in a era of 'nonrepresentational democracy', where an increasing number of people are able to manage their social and productive life through the use of a variety of auto-nomous and interdependent networks and peer circles'. Bauwens also invokes the idea of an 'information commons' and the need for 'fundamental changes in the intellectual property regime', which he finds 'reflected in new forms such as the free software move-ment', whose principles provide for 'models that could be used in other areas of social and productive life'. By such means Bauwens wishes to reconnect 'with the older traditions and attempts for a more cooperative social order, but this time obviates the need for authoritarianism and centralization'. He suggest that peer to peer technology has 'the potential of showing that the new egalitarian digital culture is connected to the older traditions of cooperation among workers and peasants and to the search for an engaged and meaningful life as expressed in one's work, which becomes an expression of individual and collective creativity, rather than as a salaried means of survival'.

Whether the utopian visions of either Bauwens or those involved with Wikipedia, FLOSS and Creative Commons are widely shared by many users of new media is a moot point. For example the social network spaces MySpace or Facebook reveal something about the way in which Web 2:0 is being used. Browsing on either is a fascinating, if rather voyeuristic, experience. Individual users' webpages can be customised, and contain personal information, pictures of friends who are also on MySpace, accompanied by a message stating how many friends the user has, and displays of often rather intimate email messages from those friends. (When it first started, one of the people identified as a founder of MySpace, Tom Anderson, would be the first 'friend' each subscriber had online. By clicking on a link on each page it's possible to see pictures of and links to all of a user's friends, with Tom always among them. Thus the satirical/ self-pitying t-shirt slogan 'Tom is my only friend'. By spring 2008 Tom had 221,036,100 friends. (Following the purchase of MySpace by Rupert Murdoch's News Corporation, 'Tom' is now a corporate identity rather than a reference to a specific individual.) The customization of the page by users and presentation of personal information act as a kind of visible self creation. The messages are also links to the other users' own webpages, which means that it is possible to browse across complex webs of connections. In MySpace there are also links to music, or to videos from sites such as YouTube. Both MySpace and FaceBook offer a glimpse of a new kind of community, one no longer bound up with physical location, but created through shared interest in and self-definition by media.

As both *The Observer* article and the experience of looking at pages in MySpace or FaceBook suggests, there is a strong incitement to narcissism in much of what the new media are offering. Blogs and podcasts seem to offer a means to literally realize Andy Warhol's much quoted prediction of the coming celebrity culture, that 'in the future everybody will be famous for fifteen minutes', and in a sense this future is already with us, with developments such as YouTube and other similar websites. Never one to miss a trick, Apple Computers has released a software suite called 'iLife', which combines their iPhoto, iMovie, iWeb, iDVD and GarageBand programs and is the 'easiest way to make the most out of every bit of your digital life. Use your Mac to collect, organize and edit the various elements. Transform them into mouth-watering masterpieces with Apple-designed templates. Then share the magic moments in beautiful books, colorful calendars, dazzling DVDs, perfect podcasts, and attractive online journals. All starring you.' The last sentence in particular (which interestingly no longer features in the publicity for more recent versions of the software) indicates part of the appeal of new media in a digital culture, that they offer everybody the chance to become a star, however briefly, in a world obsessed by celebrity.

The above might suggest that with new digital media and networks we are either glimpsing the emergence of a new 'participatory culture' of greater cooperation or solidarity, or alternatively our digital culture runs the risk of producing a pandemonium of competing media noise, self-promotion and meaningless disembodied interaction, in an increasingly atomized society. But perhaps another response is possible, or even necessary, one that goes beyond such an opposition between greater cooperation and increasing atomization. We live in a world in which we are increasingly both bound together and separated by the globalized networks of information communications technologies. It is perhaps unsurprising that the concept of 'friendship' has become more visible and important as traditional forms of community are eroded, and new forms of subjectivity and connection are being developed. Yet in a situation where 'Tom' can claim to have well above 200 million friends, the very term 'friendship' needs rethinking. Thus what our increasingly networked digital culture may need is a new 'politics of friendship', new conceptions of the relation between self, and other and new understandings of community.

It may be that we will have to expand our notion of who or what might be part of any future community, especially given the increasing capacity for participation. Back in the 1950s and '60s it was seriously proposed that computers would be able to achieve some kind of intelligence, or even consciousness. Based on an out-moded modernist conception of cognition as an interior process, Artificial Intelligence, at least as it was originally understood, has been largely discredited.[10] But more recent developments, many of which came out of AI, are presenting us with objects and technologies that can act, communicate, signify and participate, even if these capacities do not seem to involve anything like human intelligence or consciousness. Examples include recent research into developing simple forms of intelligent behaviour by combining robotics with neural networks, as undertaken by computer scientist Rodney Brooks at MIT.

It is unlikely that, in the foreseeable future, even minimally intelligent robots are going to trouble our everyday lives. By contrast, far smaller and less potentially impressive developments are already provoking questions about the capacity for technology to act and participate. Recently a new buzz phrase has been coined: the 'Internet of Things' refers to the new world of networked and interconnected devices, which can communicate with each other and with other systems and entities.[11] For example, Radio Frequency Identification (RFID) is a new technology that allows data to be automatically sent from objects that contain RFID tags (illus. 52). Examples of its use include tagging of books in libraries that allow security systems to check whether books have been issued when they leave the library

52 RFID in a form of a sticker with bar code on the opposite side, security chip for a DVD.

precincts, public transport systems that enable travellers to have travel passes that are scanned automatically, passports, traffic toll systems, stock inventory, prisoner control and many other uses.

Unsurprisingly the use of RFID chips is controversial, especially in terms of the implications of their potential future applications. Recently I received an email asking me to sign a petition against the proposed tracking of road vehicles, presumably using exactly such technologies. More sinister or perhaps more comical, according to Wikipedia, at a 2003 Senate hearing, Senator Debra Bowen reportedly asked 'how would you like it if, for instance, one day you realized your underwear was reporting on your whereabouts?' They have also been described as 'spychips' by consumer privacy advocates. Among certain Christian groups RFID chips are considered another candidate, after credit cards and bar codes, for the 'Mark of the Beast' that will presage the Great Tribulation.[12]

This may seem a little far-fetched, but such eschatological anxiety does suggest something of the momentous changes taking place in our current digital culture, changes that effect every aspect of our lives, and which are increasingly hard to discern as they become increasingly easy to take for granted. In particular we are arriving at a point where digital technologies are no longer merely tools, but increasingly participants in our increasingly participatory culture, for better or worse. The need to keep questioning our situation (with which I ended the Conclusion to the first edition of this book) remains more pressing than ever, especially as the technology itself is more and more invisible as it becomes an integral part of the very fabric of our existence.

# References

## INTRODUCTION: WHAT IS DIGITAL CULTURE?

1 Raymond Williams, *Keywords: A Vocabulary of Culture and Society* (London, 1976), pp.76–82.
2 David Abrahamson, 'An Evaluative Bibiliography: Digital Culture, Information Technology, the Internet, the Web', *Journal of Magazine & New Media Research* (Hosted by Maryland College), vol. 3, no. 1, Spring 2001; http://www.bsu.edu/web/aejmcmagazine/journal/archive/Fall_2000/abrahamson3-1.html.
3 Gilles Deleuze and Claire Parnet, *Dialogues* (London, 1977), pp. 126–7.
4 Walter Benjamin, *Illuminations* (London, 1973), p. 265.
5 Ibid., p. 265.
6 Ibid.
7 Ibid., p. 266.

## 1. THE BEGINNINGS OF DIGITAL CULTURE

1 Alan M. Turing, 'On Computable Numbers with Application to the Entscheidungsproblem', *Proceedings of the London Mathematical Society*, Series 2–42 (1936), pp. 230–65.
2 For a clear and comprehensive description of Turing's machine, see Andrew Hodges' wonderful biography of Turing: Andrew Hodges, *Alan Turing: The Enigma of Intelligence* (London, 1985), pp. 96–110.
3 Ibid., pp. 14, 145, 279.
4 Hodges describes Turing's machine imagery as 'shockingly industrial' for Cambridge (p. 107).
5 Karl Marx, *Capital* (Harmondsworth, 1976), trans. Ben Fowkes, vol. 1, pp. 125–257.
6 Adam Smith, *The Wealth of Nations: Books I–III* (London, 1986), p. 110.
7 Charles Babbage, *On the Economy of Machinery and Manufactures* (London, 1832).

8 Count Luigi Federico Menebrea, *Sketch of the Analytical Engine Invented by Charles Babbage . . . with notes by the translator. Extracted from the Scientific Memoirs etc . . .* (London, 1843), p. 696. [Lovelace herself was the translator of Count Menebrea's account of Babbage's engine and the quote above is taken from her added notes.]

9 Adam Smith, *Wealth of Nations* (New York, 1909–1914), vol. IV, chap. 2, p. 9.

10 Fernand Braudel, *Civilisation and Capitalism 15th–18th Century* (London, 1982), vol. II: *The Wheels of Commerce*, p. 224.

11 Otto Mayr, *Authority, Liberty and Automatic Machinery in Early Modern Europe* (Baltimore and London, 1986), p. 199.

12 For a comprehensive account of the relation between information and entropy, see Jeremy Campbell, *Grammatical Man* (London, 1982).

13 George Boole, *The Mathematical Analysis of Logic* (Cambridge, 1847).

14 George Boole, *An Investigation of the Laws of Thought* (London, 1854).

15 Gottfried Wilhelm von Leibniz, *Dissertatio de arte combinatoria, ex arithmeticæ fundamentis complicationum ac transpositionum doctrina novis præceptis exstruitur . . . nova etiam Artis meditandi, seu Logicæ inventionis semina sparguntur. Præfixa est synopsis totius tractatus, et additamenti loco Demonstratio Existentiæ Dei ad mathematicam certitudinem exacta* (Lipsiæ, 1666).

16 Martin Van Creveld, *Command in War* (Cambridge, MA, 1991), p. 97.

17 James R. Beniger, *The Control Revolution: Technological and Economic Origins of the Information Society* (Cambridge, MA, 1986), pp. 226–37.

18 James Cary, *Communication as Culture: Essays on Media and Society* (New York and London, 1989), p. 217.

19 Ibid., p. 220.

20 Ibid.

21 Jonathan Crary, *Techniques of the Observer: On Vision and Modernity in the Nineteenth Century* (Cambridge, MA, 1990), p. 13.

22 Ibid.

23 Ibid.

24 Shawn James Rosenheim, *The Cryptographic Imagination: Secret Writing from Poe to the Internet* (Baltimore and London, 1997), pp. 1–2, pp. 61–2 and passim.

25 Michel Foucault, *Discipline and Punish* (London, 1977), p. 189.

26 Ibid.

27 Ibid., p. 190.

28 Walter Benjamin, *Illuminations* (London, 1973), pp. 219–73.

29 George Herbert Wells, *World Brain: H. G. Wells and the Future of World Education* (London, 1994).

30 Ibid., p. 20.

31 Ibid., p. 120.

32 Ibid., pp. 121–2.

33 Benjamin, *Illuminations*, p. 223.

34 Ibid., p. 244.
35 For a full account of Turing's role in the breaking of the German U-Boat codes, see Hodges, *Alan Turing*, pp. 160–255.
36 For an account of the early development of computing, see Paul E. Ceruzzi, *A History of Modern Computing* (Cambridge, MA, 1998), esp. pp. 13–46.

## 2. THE CYBERNETIC ERA

1 Claude Shannon and Warren Weaver, *Mathematical Theory of Communication* (Urbana, IL, 1949).
2 Arturo Rosenblueth, and Norbert Wiener, 'Behaviour, Purpose, and Teleology', *Philosophy of Science*, vol. 10, (1943), pp. 18–24.
3 Warren McCulloch and W. H. Pitts, 'Logical Calculus of Ideas Immanent in Nervous Activity', *Bull. Math. Biophysics*, vol. 5, (1944).
4 Pamela McCorduck, *Machines Who Think* (San Francisco, 1979) p. 66.
5 Johann von Neumann and Oskar Morgenstern, *Theory of Games and Economic Behaviour* (Princeton, 1944).
6 Norbert Wiener, *Cybernetics or Control and Communication in the Animal World* (Cambridge, MA, 1948).
7 Norbert Wiener, *The Human Use of Human Beings* (Cambridge, MA, 1950).
8 Erwin Schrödinger, *What is Life?* (Cambridge, 1992).
9 Excellent accounts of the relation between Cybernetics, Information Theory and genetic research, including Schrödinger's role, can be found in Lily E. Kay, *Who Wrote the Book of Life* (Stanford, CA, 2000) and Evelyn Fox Keller, *Refiguring Life: Metaphors of Twentieth Century Biology* (New York, 1995).
10 Alan M Turing, 'Computing Machinery and Intelligence', *Mind* (1950).
11 Donald Hebb, *The Organisation of Behaviour: A Neuropsychological Theory* (New York, 1949).
12 Ferdinand de Saussure, *Course in General Linguistics* (London, 1983), pp. 99–100.
13 Ibid., pp. 65–7.
14 Ibid., pp. 67–9.
15 Ibid., pp. 110–20.
16 Ibid., pp. 68–9.
17 Claude Levi-Strauss, *Elementary Structures of Kinship* (London, 1968).
18 Algirdas Julien Greimas, *Sémantique structurale: recherche de méthode* (Paris, 1966).
19 For an account of Jacques Lacan's relation to Cybernetics and Information Theory, see Anthony Wilden, *System and Structure: Essays in Communication and Exchange* (London, 1977).
20 Jacques Lacan, The Seminars of Jacques Lacan, vol. II: *The Ego in Freud's Theory and in the Technique of Psychoanalysis* (Cambridge, 1988).

21 Paul N. Edwards, *The Closed World: Computers and the Politics of Discourse in Cold War America* (Cambridge, MA, 1996), p. 40.
22 Ibid., pp. 1–2 and passim.
23 Ibid., p. 75.
24 Ibid., p. 110.
25 Ibid., pp. 110–11.
26 Arthur L. Norberg and Judy E. O'Neill, *Transforming Computer Technology: Information Processing and the Pentagon 1962–1986* (Baltimore and London, 1996), pp. 5–12.
27 J. C. R. Licklider, 'Man–Computer Symbiosis', *IRE Transactions on Human Factors in Electronics*, Vol. HFE-1 (1960), pp. 4–11.
28 Vannevar Bush, 'As We May Think', *The Atlantic Monthly*, vol. 176, no. 1 (July, 1945), pp. 101–8.
29 Paul Baran, 'On Distributed Communications, Rand Corporation Memorandum RM-3420-PR', August 1964. It is available on the Web at www.rand.org/publications/RM/RM3420/.
30 Paul E. Ceruzzi, *A History of Modern Computing* (Cambridge, MA and London, 1998), p. 13.
31 Kenneth Flamm, *Creating the Computer: Government, Industry, and High Technology* (Washington DC, 1988), p. 134.
32 Norberg and O'Neill, *Transforming Computer Technology*, pp. 130–1 and Edwards, *The Closed World*, pp. 137–45.

## 3. THE DIGITAL AVANT-GARDE

1 John Brockman, *The Digerati: Encounters with the Digital Elite* (San Francisco, 1996), p. xix.
2 David Revill, *The Roaring Silence* (New York, 1992), pp. 165–6.
3 Ibid., p. 164.
4 Ibid.
5 Simon Shaw Miller, '"Concerts of everyday living": Cage, Fluxus and Barthes, Interdisciplinary and Inter-media Events', *Art History*, vol. 19, no. 1 (March, 1996), pp. 4–5.
6 Umberto Eco, *The Open Work* (London, 1989), pp. 1–23.
7 Ibid., pp. 44–83.
8 Rose Lee Goldberg, *Performance Art: From Futurism to the Present* (London, 1988) pp. 126–7.
9 Gianni Vattimo, *The Transparent Society* (Cambridge, 1992), p. 1 and *passim*.
10 Elizabeth Armstrong and Joan Rothfuss, *In the Spirit of Fluxus* (Minneapolis, 1993), p. 24.
11 Robert Filliou, *Teaching and Learning as Performance Arts* (Cologne, 1970).
12 Translations by David W. Seaman of a selection from Isou's manifestos can be found in *Visible Language*, vol. XVII, no. 3 (1983).

13 Stewart Home, *The Assault on Culture: Utopian Currents from Lettrisme to Class War* (Stirling, 1991) pp. 12–16.

14 Harry Mathews and Alastair Brotchie, *OuLiPo Compendium* (London, 1998), pp. 127–9.

15 Raymond Queneau, *Cent mille milliards de poèmes* (Paris, 1961). Stanley Chapman's translation is included in Mathews and Brotchie, *OuLiPo Compendium*, pp. 15–33.

16 Italo Calvino, *The Castle of Crossed Destinies* (London, 1977).

17 Georges Perec, *A Void* (London, 1994).

18 David Bellos, *Georges Perec* (London, 1999), pp. 250–67.

19 Jack Burnham, *Beyond Modern Sculpture: The Effects of Science and Technology on the Sculpture of this Century* (London, 1968), p. 343.

20 Anne Massey, *The Independent Group: Modernism and Mass Culture in Britain 1945–59* (Manchester, 1995), p. 91.

21 Edward A. Shanken, 'From Cybernetics to Telematics: The Art, Pedagogy, and Theory of Roy Ascott', in Linda Dalrymple Henderson and Bruce Clarke, eds., *From Energy to Information* (Stanford, 2000).

22 Abraham Moles, *Information Theory and Aesthetic Perception*, translated by Joel E. Cohen (Urbana, IL and London, 1968).

23 Max Bense, *Aesthetica IV: Programmierung des Schönen. Allgemeine Texttheorie und Textästhetik* (Baden-Baden/Krefeld, 1960).

24 Marshall McLuhan, *The Gutenberg Galaxy: The Making of Typographic Man* (Toronto, 1962).

25 Marshall McLuhan, *Understanding Media: The Extensions of Man* (New York, 1964).

26 Marshall McLuhan, *The Medium is the Message* (New York, 1967).

27 Pierre Teilhard de Chardin, *The Future of Man* (New York, 1969).

28 Herbert Marcuse, *One-Dimensional Man* (London and New York, 1991), pp. 153–5.

29 Burnham, *Beyond Sculpture*, pp. 346–9.

30 The idea of a close relationship between Cybernetics and Conceptual Art has been suggested by Edward A. Shanken, in his essay 'Art in the Information Age: Technology and Conceptual Art', in Michael Corris, ed., *Invisible College: Reconsidering Conceptual Art* (Cambridge, forthcoming), though in a telephone conversation, Art & Language member and art historian Charles Harrison suggested that Shanken had overstated the relationship. I am nevertheless greatly indebted to Shanken's work in this area.

31 Edward A. Shanken, 'The House that Jack Built: Jack Burnham's Concept of "Software" as Art', in Roy Ascott, ed., *Reframing Consciousness: Art and Consciousness in the Post-Biological Era* (Exeter, 1999).

## 4. THE DIGITAL COUNTER-CULTURE

1 Marshall McLuhan, *Understanding Media: The Extensions of Man* (New York, 1964)
2 Daniel Bell, *The Coming of the Post-Industrial Society: A Venture in Social Forecasting* (New York, 1973).
3 Frank Webster, *Theories of the Information Society* (London and New York, 1995), p. 31.
4 Alvin Toffler, *Future Shock* (New York, 1970).
5 Alvin Toffler, *The Third Wave* (New York, 1980) .
6 *The Last Whole Earth Catalog* (London, 1971).
7 *The Whole Earth Epilog* (Baltimore, 1974).
8 *The Next Whole Earth Catalog* (Sausalito, CA, 1980).
9 *An Index of Possibilities* (London, 1974).
10 R. Buckminster Fuller, *Operating Manual for Spaceship Earth* (London and Amsterdam, 1969).
11 For an excellent and succinct account of the development of second order Cybernetics, see N. Katherine Hayles's book *How We Became Posthuman: Virtual Bodies in Cybernetics, Literature and Information* (Chicago and London, 1999), pp. 131–59.
12 Humberto Maturana and Francisco Varela, *Autopoesis and Cognition: The Realization of the Living* (Dordrecht and London, 1980).
13 Gregory Bateson, *Steps Towards an Ecology of Mind* (New York, 1972).
14 Gregory Bateson, *A Sacred Unity: Further Steps to an Ecology of Mind* (New York, 1991).
15 Gregory Bateson, *Mind and Nature: A Necessary Unity* (New York, 1979).
16 Lorenz first aired this idea at a talk at the December 1972 meeting of the American Association for the Advancement of Science in Washington DC.
17 Mandelbrot, Benoit, 'How Long is the Coast of Britain' in *The World Treasury of Physics, Astronomy and Mathematics*, ed. Timothy Ferris (Boston, MA, 1991), pp. 447–55.
18 Milton Friedman, *Capitalism and Freedom* (Chicago, 1962).
19 Stewart Brand, 'Spacewar: Fanatic Life and Symbolic Death Among the Computer Bums', *Rolling Stone*, 7 December 1972.
20 David S. Bennahum, 'Doug Engelbart: The Interview' in *Meme* 3.01, www.memex.org/meme3-01.html.
21 Stewart Brand, *The Media Lab: Inventing the Future at MIT* (New York, 1987).
22 Ted Nelson, *Computer Lib/Machine Dreams* (Richmond, WA, 1987).
23 Paul E. Ceruzzi, *A History of Modern Computing*, (Cambridge, MA, and London, 1998) p. 258.
24 Douglas K. Smith and Robert C. Alexander, *Fumbling the Future: How Xerox Invented, Then Ignored, the First Personal Computer* (New York, 1988).
25 For a general account of hacker manners and hygiene, see Steven Levy,

*Hackers: Heroes of the Computer Revolution* (London etc., 1984). For a more sociological view, see Sherry Turkle, *The Second Self: Computers and the Human Spirit* (London etc, 1984), pp. 201–46.

26 For a full description of the genesis of the Apple Macintosh, see Stephen Levy, *Insanely Great: The Life and Times of Macintosh, the Computer That Changed Everything* (London, 1994).

27 Steve Lambert and Suzanne Ropeiquet, *CD-Rom, the New Papyrus: The Current and Future State of the Art* (Redmond, WA, 1996).

28 Quoted in Mark Dery, *Escape Velocity: Cyberculture at the End of the Century* (London, 1996), p. 22.

29 Ibid., p. 35.

30 Vivian Sobchak, 'New Age Mutant Ninja Turtles: Reading Mondo 2000' in Mark Dery, ed., *Flame Wars*, (Durham, NC, 1993), pp. 569–84.

31 *Signal* (New York, 1988)

32 Paulina Barsook, *Cyberselfish* (London, 2000).

33 Fritjof Capra, *The Tao of Physics* (London, 1975).

34 Fritjof Capra, *The Turning Point* (New York, 1982).

35 Fritjof Capra, *The Web of Life* (New York, 1996).

36 Michael Rothschild, *Bionomics: Economy as Ecosystem* (New York, 1990).

37 George Gilder, *Microcosm* (New York, 1989).

38 George Gilder, *Life After Television* (New York, 1992).

39 George Gilder, *Telecosm* (New York, 2000).

40 Nicholas Negroponte, *Being Digital* (London, 1995).

41 Kevin Kelly, *Out of Control: The New Biology of Machines* (London, 1994).

42 Howard Rheingold, *The Virtual Community: Finding Connection in a Computerized World* (London, 1994).

43 Jon Katz, 'The Digital Citizen' in *Wired*, 5.12 (December 1997).

## 5. DIGITAL RESISTANCES

1 Robert Venturi, Denise Scott Brown and Steven Izenour, *Learning from Las Vegas* (Cambridge, MA, 1972).

2 Ihab Hassan, 'POSTmodernISM: A Paracritical Bibliography' in *The Postmodern Turn: Essays in Postmodern Theory and Culture* (Colombus, 1987).

3 Ernest Mandel, *Late Capitalism* (London, 1978), pp. 108–146.

4 Ibid., p. 120.

5 Ibid., p. 120–21.

6 Ibid., p. 121.

7 Fredric Jameson, *Postmodernism, or the Cultural Logic of Late Capitalism* (London and New York, 1991).

8 Ibid., p. 25–6.

9 François Dosse, *History of Structuralism* (Minneapolis and London, 1997), vol. I, p. 317.

10  Julia Kristeva, *Desire in Language: A Semiotic Approach to Literature and Art* (New York, 1980).
11  Roland Barthes, *S/Z* (Oxford, 1990).
12  Jacques Derrida, *Writing and Difference*, trans. Alan Bass (London, 1978).
13  Jacques Derrida, *Of Grammatology*, trans. Gayatri Chakravorty Spivak (Baltimore, 1976).
14  Derrida, *Writing and Difference* (1978).
15  Jean-François Lyotard, *The Libidinal Economy* (London, 1993).
16  Jean-François Lyotard, *The Postmodern Condition: A Report on Knowledge* (Manchester, 1984).
17  Ibid., pp. 9–11 and passim.
18  Ibid., pp. 44–7.
19  Jean-François Lyotard, *The Differend: Phrases in Dispute* (Manchester, 1988).
20  Jean-François Lyotard, *The Inhuman: Reflections on Time* (Cambridge, 1991).
21  Jean Baudrillard, *The System of Objects* (London, 1996).
22  Christopher Norris, *Uncritical Theory: Postmodern Intellectuals and the Gulf War* (London, 1992).
23  Gilles Deleuze and Félix Guattari, *The Anti-Oedipus* (London, 1984).
24  Gilles Deleuze and Félix Guattari, *A Thousand Plateaus* (London, 1988).
25  Deleuze and Guattari, *Anti-Oedipus*, p. 1.
26  Ibid., pp. 1–8, 36–50.
27  Ibid., p. 1.
28  Deleuze and Guattari, *A Thousand Plateaus*, pp. 88–89 and passim.
29  Ibid., p. 8 and passim.
30  Paul Patton, *Deleuze and the Political* (London and New York, 2000), p. 35–6.
31  Deleuze and Guattari, *A Thousand Plateaus*, pp. 6–7.
32  Mario Tronti, 'The Strategy of Refusal', in *Working Class Autonomy and the Crisis: Italian Marxist Texts of the Theory and Practice of a Class Movement: 1964–79* (London, 1979), pp. 7–21.
33  Félix Guattari and Antonio Negri, *Communists Like Us: New Lines of Alliance* (New York, 1990).
34  Antonio Negri, *Revolution Retrieved: Selected Writings on Marx, Keynes, Capitalist Crisis and New Social Subjects 1967–1983* (London, 1988).
35  Maurizio Lazzarato, 'Immaterial Labor' in Paolo Virno and Michael Hardt, *Radical Thought in Italy* (Minneapolis, 1996), pp. 133–47.
36  Karl Marx, *Grundrisse* (London, 1973), pp. 693–706.
37  Ibid., p. 700.
38  Antonio Negri, *Marx Beyond Marx* (South Hadley, MA, 1984).
39  See Lazzarato 'Immaterial Labor' (1996).
40  Antonio Negri and Michael Hardt, *The Labor of Dionysus: a critique of the state form* (Minneapolis, 1994), pp. 275–83.
41  Antonio Negri and Michael Hardt, *Empire* (Cambridge, MA and London, 1994).

42 Sherry Turkle, *The Second Self: Computers and the Human Spirit* (New York, 1984).

43 Constance Penley, Elisabeth Lyon and Lynne Spigel, *Close Encounters: Film, Feminism and Science Fiction* (Minneapolis and London, 1991).

44 Constance Penley and Andrew Ross, *Technoculture* (Minneapolis, 1991).

45 Originally published as 'Manifesto for Cyborgs: Science, Technology, and Social Feminism' in *Socialist Review* (1985), no. 80, pp. 65–108. Expanded and reprinted as 'A Cyborg Manifesto: Technology and Socialist-Feminism in the Late Twentieth Century' in Donna Haraway, *Simians, Cyborgs and Women: The Reinvention of Nature in the Late Twentieth Century* (New York, 1992).

46 Constance Penley and Andrew Ross, 'Cyborgs at Large: Interview with Donna Haraway' in Penley and Ross, *Technoculture* (1991).

47 Haraway, 'Cyborg Manifesto' (1991), p. 177.

48 Mark Dery, *Escape Velocity: Cyberculture at the End of the Century* (London, 1996), p. 246.

49 Danny Baker and Mark Perry, eds, *Sniffin' Glue: The Essential Punk Accessory* (London, 2000).

50 Jamie Reid and Jon Savage, *Up They Rise* (London, 1987).

51 'French Currents of the Letter', *Visible Language*, vol. xii, no. 3 (Summer 1979).

52 Ellen Lupton and J. Abbott Miller, *Design, Writing, Research* (New York, 1996), p. 9.

53 Simon Ford, *Wreckers of Civilisation: The story of Coum Transmissions and Throbbing Gristle* (London, 1999), 7.16.

54 Julian Cope, 'History of Krautrock Part 1' in *Wired*, 130 (December, 1994), p. 40.

55 Alvin Toffler, *The Third Wave* (New York, 1980).

56 William Gibson, 'Fragments of a Hologram Rose', in *Burning Chrome* (London, 1988).

57 Bruce Sterling, *Involution Ocean* (Sevenoaks, 1981).

58 Vernor Vinge, 'True Names' in *Binary Star* (February 1981), no. 5, pp. 133–233.

59 Philip K. Dick, *Do Androids Dream of Electric Sheep* (London, 1969).

60 Philip K. Dick, 'We Can Remember It For You Wholesale' in *The Collected Stories* (Los Angeles, 1987).

61 Philip K. Dick, *Martian Time Slip* (Sevenoaks, 1976).

62 William Burroughs, *Junky* (New York, 1953).

63 William Burroughs, *The Naked Lunch* (New York, 1959).

64 William Burroughs, *The Soft Machine* (New York, 1961).

65 William Burroughs, *The Ticket That Exploded* (New York, 1962).

66 William Burroughs, *Nova Express* (New York, 1964).

67 David Porush, for example, devotes a chapter of *The Soft Machine* (New York, London, 1985), his study of Cybernetics and literature, to Pynchon's work.

68 Thomas Pynchon, *The Crying of Lot 49* (New York, 1966).

69 Thomas Pynchon, *Gravity's Rainbow* (New York, 1973).

70 Fredric Jameson, *The Geopolitical Aesthetic: Cinema and Space in the World System* (London, 1992), pp. 16–17.

71 John Johnston, *Information Multiplicity: American Fiction in the Age of Media Saturation* (Baltimore and London, 1998), p. 62.

72 Ibid., p. 66.

73 Ibid., p. 63.

74 William Gibson, *Neuromancer* (London, 1984).

75 Scott Bukatman, *Terminal Identity: The Virtual Subject in Post-modern Science Fiction* (London and Durham, 1993), p. 146.

76 Michael Herr, *Dispatches* (London, 1978).

77 Gibson, *Neuromancer*, p. 67.

78 William Gibson, *Count Zero* (London, 1986).

79 William Gibson, *Mona Lisa Overdrive* (London, 1989).

80 William Gibson and Bruce Sterling, *The Difference Engine* (London, 1991).

81 For an excellent account of Cyberpunk as a genre, see Dani Cavallero, *Cyberpunk and Cyberculture* (London, 2000).

82 Hakim Bey, *T.A.Z. The Temporary Autonomous Zone, Ontological Anarchy, Poetic Terrorism* (New York, 1991).

83 See Sadie Plant, 'On the Matrix: Cyberfeminism Simulations' in Rob Shields, ed., *Cultures of the Internet: Virtual Spaces, Real Histories, Living Bodies* (London, 1996), pp. 170–83 and *Zeros + Ones: Digital Women + the New Technoculture* (London, 1998).

84 See Rosi Braidotti, *Nomadic Subjects: Embodiment and Sexual Difference in Contemporary Feminist Theory* (New York, 1994), as well as Rosi Braidotti and Nina Lykke, *Between Monsters, Goddesses and Cyborgs: Feminist Confrontations with Science, Medicine and Cyberspace* (London, 1996).

85 Allucquère Rosanne Stone, *The War of Desire and Technology at the Close of the Mechanical Age* (Cambridge, MA, 1995).

86 Critical Art Ensemble, *The Electronic Disturbance* (New York, 1994).

87 Critical Art Ensemble, *Electronic Civil Disobedience* (New York, 1996).

88 Manuel Castells, *The Information Age: Economy, Society and Culture, Volume II: The Power of Identity* (Oxford, 1997), p. 72.

89 Walter Benjamin, *Illuminations*, pp. 219–53.

90 Ibid., p. 264.

91 Ibid., p. 263.

## 7. DIGITAL CULTURE IN THE TWENTY-FIRST CENTURY

1 See Charlie Gere, *Art, Time and Technology* (Oxford and New York, 2006), for a discussion of the cultural effects of real-time technologies.

2 F. Halliday, *Two Hours that Shook the World. September 11, 2001: Causes and Consequences* (London, 2002).

3  J. Reed, *Ten Days That Shook the World* (New York, 1919).
4  See chapter Five, 'Digital Resistances'.
5  B. McNair, *Cultural Chaos: Journalism, News and Power in a Globalised World* (London and New York, 2006).
6  C. . Anderson, *The Long Tail: Why the Future of Business is Selling Less of More* (New York, 2006).
7  Ibid., p 37.
8  D. Smith and A. O'Keeffe, 'How Will You Watch TV', *The Observer*, 12 March 2006.
9  All quotes taken from the P2P Foundation website, 'about' page, http://blog.p2pfoundation.net/about/ (accessed 28 January 2008).
10  See chapter Two, 'The Cybernetic Era'.
11  E. Biddlecombe, 'UN predicts "internet of things"', 2005: http://news.bbc.co.uk/1/hi/technology/4440334.stm (accessed 18April, 2008).
12  Wikipedia contributors, 'Radio-frequency identification', *Wikipedia, The Free Encyclopedia*: http://en.wikipedia.org/w/index.php?title=Radio-frequency_identification&oldid=206145058 (accessed 21 April 2008).

# Acknowledgements

Thanks to numerous friends and colleagues at Birkbeck, Cambridge, Middlesex and the London College of Printing for their encouragement and support, to Cathy Gere, Bob Cooper and Nat Goodden for reading various versions, to Jasia Reichardt for advice and help with illustrations, and to Marq Smith and everybody at Reaktion for taking it seriously. Thanks also and love to my family for support and tolerance.

# Photographic Acknowledgements

The author and publishers wish to express their thanks to the following sources of illustrative material and/or permission to reproduce it:

Reproduced with the permission of Professor Roy Ascott: p. 24; Bletchley Park Trust: pp. 13, 14; reproduction courtesy of Charles Csuri: p. 30; reproduction © Disney Enterprises, Inc.: p. 49; The Earl of Lytton: p. 5; photos courtesy of the Bootstrap Institute: pp. 19, 37, 38; en.wikipedia.org/wiki/ Charlie_Gere: 51; photo courtesy Richard L. Feigen & Co.: p. 23; photo courtesy of Hans Haacke, © Hans Haacke/ DACS, 2002: p. 34; © Estate of Ray Johnson: p. 23; reproduction by permission of Kenneth Knowlton: p. 29; photo: Manchester Daily Express: p. 48; photo Midnightcomm: 52; photos courtesy of the MIT Media Lab, © MIT, 1978: pp. 39, 40; reproduction courtesy of the MIT Museum, Cambridge, MA: p. 18; photo courtesy of The MITRE Corporation: p. 17; photos courtesy of the National Archive for the History of Computing, University of Manchester: pp. 9, 10, 11, 22, 43; reproduction courtesy of Nicholas Negroponte: p. 35; reproduction by permission of A. Michael Noll: p. 27; reproduced courtesy of Postmasters Gallery, New York: 50; reproduced courtesy of RAND Corporation: p. 20; reproduction courtesy of *Raygun*/David Carson: p. 47; reproduction courtesy of Jasia Reichardt: pp. 25, 26, 27, 32, 33; © Jamie Reid, reproduction courtesy of Jamie Reid: p. 46; by permission of Elionore Schöffer: p. 26; The Science Museum/Science & Society Picture Library: pp. 1, 2, 3, 4, 5, 6, 7, 8, 12, 13, 14, 15, 16, 41, 42, 44, 48; reproduction from *Sniffin' Glue: The Essential Punk Accessory* (London, 2000), courtesy of Sanctuary Publishing: p. 45.

# Index

**adams**media

KT 2121217 1

ISBN 10: 1-4405-6084-6
ISBN 13: 978-1-4405-6084-2
eISBN 10: 1-4405-6085-4
eISBN 13: 978-1-4405-6085-9

Contains material adapted and abridged from *The Everything® Baby Sign Language Book* by Teresa R. Simpson, Technical Review by Terrell Clark, PhD, copyright © 2008 by F+W Media, Inc., ISBN 10: 1-59869-564-9, ISBN 13: 978-1-59869-564-9, and *The Everything® Sign Language Book, 2nd Edition* by Irene Duke, copyright © 2009 by F+W Media, Inc., ISBN 10: 1-59869-883-4, ISBN 13: 978-1-59869-883-1.

Photographs on pages 34, 36, 48, 50, 64, 74, 102, 150, and 156 by Joe Ciarcia / Symphony Photography. All other photographs by Notable Productions. Models: Stacey Culver, Molly Howitt, and Tiffany Nardini.

Manufactured in the United States of America.

10  9  8  7  6  5  4  3  2  1

*This book is available at quantity discounts for bulk purchases.*
*For information, please call 1-800-289-0963.*

# Contents

# Introduction

There is something magical about signing with your baby. It gives you a glimpse into the workings of his little mind and provides extra insight into his personality. It is nothing short of amazing.

Today, parents by the thousands are discovering the immense benefits of signing with their babies, and they are learning that a signing baby is a happy baby. Signing is a beautiful way to communicate with your child. It is fun and educational, and it is an excellent way to spend quality time together.

*Essential Baby Sign Language* offers you a way to start communicating with your child more quickly and efficiently than ever before. Featuring seventy-five of the most important signs babies need every day, this book helps you and your baby to start signing *now*. Through a combination of need-based and high-impact signs, you will be able to teach your baby how to express what they want and get them into the habit of signing regularly.

Now you and your baby can start signing today!

# CHAPTER 1

# Why Start Signing?

Babies communicate in a variety of ways from the moment they are born. The youngest of babies will connect with his parents both by crying and by making eye contact. This most primitive of exchanges enables a baby to express his needs or displeasure and also allows him to bond with his parents.

As a baby gets older, his methods of communication become more sophisticated. He graduates to using coos and smiles to express his contentment, and his cries become distinctive to his needs. At this time, he is probably discovering the many amazing things he can do with his hands, one of which can be to learn how to sign.

The benefits of signing with your baby are numerous. In addition to the developmental advantages it brings, parents and caregivers love being able to interact with their children. In this chapter, find out why sign language is the "new" language being spoken in playgroups, parks, and day-care centers across the country and how easy it is for you and your child to acquire.

## The Benefits of Baby Sign Language

As the parent or caregiver of a baby, you have undoubtedly spent a great deal of time in one-sided conversation. With minimal response from your little one, it can be difficult to know how much, if any, of the conversation she comprehends. On the flip side of that conundrum, it is likely that your baby has also engaged in some one-sided conversations of her own. She may coo, babble, or use baby jargon. She may be trying to express her needs or just chatting about the world around her.

Although you and your baby won't engage in fluent sign-language conversations, you will find that the level of communication sign language provides will change your life in a positive and noticeable way. The use of sign opens up a whole new expressive world for the two of you and gives you the ability to engage in far more meaningful conversation than you are otherwise able to have.

## Less Frustration for Baby

As babies become more expressive, they also become more frustrated when they are unable to convey their thoughts, wants, or needs. They are doing all they can to be clear, yet they can't seem to get anyone to understand them. This communication gap can lead to temper tantrums, crying jags, and a feeling of dissatisfaction. As your baby begins to acquire these essential signs, she will discover that signing can get a response from you that crying and "talking" doesn't always bring. This will result in a happier baby who derives a great deal of satisfaction from being understood.

## Less Frustration for You

It goes without saying that a happier baby results in a happier parent. As baby's frustration is diminished due to her newfound ability to communicate, you will find that her improved mood will greatly improve yours, as well. But the benefits don't end there. In the same way that baby gets frustrated when she can't get her point across to you, you likely feel a certain amount of frustration when you are unable to convey your message to her. As your baby begins to understand your signs, you will begin to see the communication gap narrowing. Of course, a baby understands your spoken words long before she begins to speak, but when you are able to use signs that she herself is able to use, you will know with certainty that she comprehends what you are saying to her.

### Improved Self-Expression

Another important benefit of baby sign language is that signing babies are better able to express themselves in all sorts of ways. That is, they are able to convey their thoughts and feelings in a way that nonsigning babies cannot. This ability may result in babies who are more confident and outspoken. They may come to understand the validity of their feelings earlier and understand that it is acceptable to express them.

### Instant Camaraderie

A special bond will form between you and your baby when you practice sign together. Think of it as a special language between you and your baby. It is amazing to be able to communicate with your child. With this shared language the two of you are likely to build a deeper friendship that can last a lifetime.

When your baby first begins to sign, she will likely try out her signing skills with everyone around her, and she may grow frustrated when she discovers that not everyone responds to her signs. She will soon figure out who can understand her and who can't. Those who can will enjoy sharing this special language with your child.

## Dispelling Common Myths

As with anything else in life that is misunderstood, a few myths seem to rear their ugly heads over and over in regard to baby sign language.

As a signing parent, it is important that you believe in what you are doing. This will help to keep you and your child motivated. If you find that you are having doubts about the validity or effectiveness of baby sign language, talk to other signing parents and listen to their insight and experiences.

## Myth: Slower to Talk

The idea that babies who sign are slower to talk than their nonsigning peers is one that comes from the misunderstanding that sign language actually replaces the spoken word. For babies who are able to hear, that just is not true. In fact, babies who practice sign language are often quicker to talk than their nonsigning peers. Why? Because part of using signs with babies involves saying each word out loud as you are signing. For this reason, many signing babies will learn a new spoken word and its sign at the same time.

## Myth: Pushed Too Hard

Many people who are uneducated about baby sign language feel that these babies are being pushed too hard to learn a skill that is outside of their natural ability. These naysayers liken baby sign language to things like trying to teach a baby how to play concert piano or do long division.

### Essential Tip

Although a parent who signs with her baby is not necessarily trying to create a super-baby, it is possible to subject her to undue amounts of pressure. This is true for any skill a baby is learning, such as walking, talking, or potty training. Remember to be patient with your child and let her learn at her own pace.

The truth is, babies have a natural inclination to gesture and do so on their own to express their needs. Babies will raise their arms when they want to be picked up and point to an object that they want to have. Using sign language just taps into this natural ability.

### Myth: Confusion for Baby

Subscribers to this myth believe that signing with babies will be confusing because they will not understand what you are saying. In the beginning, of course, they will not understand, just as they do not understand an unfamiliar new word the first time you speak it. However, as you continue to sign with your baby, comprehension will set in. When that happens, your baby will likely be less confused by language than her nonsigning peers.

### Myth: Babies Can't Sign

People who believe a baby can't learn to sign are people who have never witnessed it for themselves. These unbelievers may think that a baby is just making meaningless gestures or that a parent is seeing something that isn't really there. Unfortunately, these skeptics will not be convinced until they see a signing baby in action. There are thousands of signing babies and toddlers whose signing skills could easily prove that babies *can* sign. It won't be long before your baby can prove it, too!

## Enjoy the Time with Your Baby

In addition to those dispelled myths, you may also be concerned that the process will be a time-consuming chore for you and your baby. Fortunately, learning sign language does not have to be a difficult process. It is easily incorporated into everyday life and quickly becomes a habit.

In addition, most of the signs you will be practicing with your baby are basic and simple to form. Both parent and baby usually remember them easily.

Not only can signing be simple, it can (and should) be fun for everyone involved. Whenever you spend one-on-one time with your baby, you are helping to create a bond that will last a lifetime. Bonding is something that happens not in an hour or a day but rather through repeated sessions of quality time. Signing with your child is one way to add a little bonding time into your routine. It provides an opportunity to learn together and engage in conversation with one another.

# CHAPTER 2

# How to Get Started

If you are new to baby sign language, you may feel a bit overwhelmed and unsure of where to start. You may wonder if you are actually capable of signing with your baby and what to expect when and if he masters the signs. The good news is that it takes no special skills to sign with your baby, nor does a baby require great aptitude to acquire sign language. If you practice sign language frequently and consistently, you can expect your baby to experience these three basic stages of the learning process:

- First, he will begin to take notice while you sign.
- Next, he will imitate your signs.
- Finally, he will attach meaning to the signs and use them to communicate.

Imitation may be the sincerest form of flattery, but it is also an important learning tool for babies. Even very young infants will mimic mouth movements. As a baby gets older, he finds that imitating his parents usually earns him a favorable response. This fuels his fire and encourages him to continue mimicking you.

As you sign with your baby, he will be presented with many opportunities to imitate you. In fact, he may form some signs before he comprehends their meaning, simply because he wants to do what you are doing. This desire to imitate is one reason why babies tend to pick up sign language so easily.

## When Is the Right Time?

The general consensus among baby-signing experts is that six to eight months is the perfect age to begin introducing your baby to sign language. At around six months, a baby is gaining comprehension of language and probably understands a few words. At around seven months, babies have developed enough fine motor skills to form some basic signs. This physical and mental development is what makes sign language a valid form of communication for babies. In addition, most babies are alert, observant, and eager to learn during this age range.

It is important to note that regardless of the age at which you introduce sign language, it may be a few months before your baby signs back to you. Even babies who are introduced to sign language at six months most commonly make their first signs between eight and ten months of age.

Even though there are great benefits to introducing sign at this time, you can be just as successful if you begin earlier or later. If you have missed the six-to-eight-month range, start signing with your child now because it is never too late. Similarly, there is nothing wrong with demonstrating sign language to your four-, five-, or even one-month-old.

## It's Never Too Early

If you are the parent of a newborn, you may be eager to get started. In the case of a baby under six months of age, "getting started" for a parent simply means learning and practicing the signs yourself. Although your baby may find your signing to be entertaining, he will not be able to sign back at this stage, and he may not even pay attention to the signs you are making. So why start early?

There is one primary advantage to using sign language before a child is six months of age: It gets you into the practice of forming signs. If you make a habit of it early on, then signing will just come naturally to you. If you have decided you do not want to wait until your child is six months old before beginning to sign with him, here are a few tips to get you started:

- **Don't get discouraged.** Remember that because you are starting early, you will have to wait even longer to see that first sign.
- **Focus on baby's earliest needs and interests.** Choose signs that pertain to your young infant's everyday life. Good early signs include MILK, MOMMY, DADDY, and DIAPER.
- **Be consistent.** Don't change methods because you aren't seeing results. That will only set back your progress.
- **Learn all you can.** Because you will have a head start on your baby, it is a good time to learn the signs yourself.
- **Don't pressure the skeptics.** Because it will probably take months for your baby to begin signing, don't bother to push signing on the skeptics in your life until your baby is a little older or begins to sign.

It is important to understand that this early start will probably not make your baby any more proficient at sign language than his peers who begin at six months of age. Neither is your child likely to learn the signs any sooner. However, a parent who is in the habit of signing early on may be more consistent than a parent who is starting right along with her child. This, in turn, may mean that baby has an easier time learning to sign.

# Better Late Than Never

So your child is ten months, eighteen months, or even twenty-nine months old, and you've just discovered the benefits of sign. Have you missed your chance? No! Your child can still benefit from sign. Understand, of course, that the extent of these benefits depends on his age and level of development. No matter how old or how advanced he is, however, there is never any harm in teaching your child a second language. In fact, children from birth to ten years of age can typically learn a second language almost as proficiently as their native language. So it is never too late to start!

## Older Infants

Older infants usually have no trouble picking up signs. The biggest reason why it is better to introduce sign at six or seven months of age instead of eleven or twelve months is that by waiting, you miss out on some preverbal time in which your child could be signing. The other reason is that during the optimal age range, a baby is first starting to acquire language comprehension, which makes it an ideal time to begin learning a language.

**Essential Tip**

Don't be surprised if your older baby learns to say a word before he learns to sign it, particularly familiar words like "Mommy" or "bottle." This is because you will be speaking each word as you sign it, and an older baby has reached an age when he is likely trying to say his first words.

Keep in mind that a child who is nine, ten, or eleven months old is still in the early stages of language comprehension. Parents who begin using sign language during this stage usually find that their babies are quite successful. It seems that a briefly delayed start does not adversely affect a child's signing progress. The most important aspect of practicing sign language with a baby of any age is to sign frequently and consistently.

## Does Time of Day Matter?

Although it is true that there are periods throughout a baby's day in which he is more alert, signing opportunities may not always occur during those periods. It is one thing to wait for such a time before reading a book to your child or doing an activity with him, but you don't necessarily have that option with signing. Signing opportunities crop up at all sorts of times throughout the day, including mealtimes, diaper changes, outside time, and numerous other times when your baby may or may not be at his most alert. All of this is not to say that you cannot take advantage of times when your baby is most alert. On the contrary, you should watch for these moments and use them to introduce a sign for a toy, a pet, or another interesting object.

**Essential Tip**

If you are trying to determine your child's periods of alertness, there are a few times throughout the day that are often a baby's best times for learning. Although every baby is different, watch for alertness during the following times: after feedings but before naptimes, early evening before bed, and about an hour after waking up in the morning.

Your signing efforts will be most effective if you demonstrate the signs at a natural time. Signing must become a way of life for you and your baby. The best way for that to happen is to incorporate baby sign language as seamlessly as possible into daily routines.

## Choosing the Right Environment

An environment free from distractions is certainly the best environment in which to learn anything, including sign language. On the other hand, an environment with a lot of stimulation provides many things that can be labeled with signs. The key to striking the right balance is to choose an environment that is free from unnecessary distractions such as the television blaring, another child running through the room, or the incessant ringing of the telephone. Sometimes these distractions cannot be avoided, but when possible, keep them to a minimum.

### Environments for Beginning Signers

When you first introduce signs to your child, any distraction can be problematic. At this stage in your signing adventures, you are introducing your baby to more than just the signs themselves. You are demonstrating the concept of signing. He is learning that signing is a form of communication and that he can use it to express himself. If your baby has his mind on something else, he is less likely to pick up the sign or to make the connection between the sign and communication.

For example, imagine that you are feeding your baby a bottle before naptime. You know that he routinely falls asleep during this feeding, so you have gotten into the habit of turning on the television. Unbeknownst to you, however, your baby is watching or listening to the television, too. If that's the case, he is unlikely to get much out of your sign demonstrations. In addition, if you are engrossed in something else, you may even forget to sign for your baby.

## Delayed Gratification

No matter when you start signing with your baby, the reality is that it will take a while to see results. Some babies start signing in just a few short weeks. Others may take several months. So what would cause one baby to sign early and another to sign later? There are several factors to consider, including the age of the baby, the frequency and consistency of the signs he is exposed to, and even his temperament. A stubborn baby may resist signing, whereas a curious baby may be intrigued by it. A baby who loves to perform may be eager to sign, whereas a passive baby may be oblivious to your efforts. It all boils down to the fact that every baby is a unique individual and as such, each will develop various skills (including signing) at his own pace. Although you do not have any control over your child's personality or stage of development, you can encourage his signing endeavors by being consistent and offering abundant praise.

### Just Keep Signing!

In the film *Finding Nemo*, one character, Dory, has a personal mantra: "Just keep swimming . . ." This philosophy keeps her going strong, even when things aren't going as well as she might like. In the same way, "Just keep signing!" should be the signing parent's mantra. That persistence and determination is *the* key to using sign language with your baby.

---

**Essential Tip**

Although it is necessary to sign repeatedly to your child, be careful not to overload him with too many different signs in the beginning. This could result in confusion. Once he begins to sign on his own, feel free to add as many signs as you want.

---

As a signing parent, you will soon find that "Just keep signing" proves to be the answer to almost every signing dilemma. What should you do if your baby won't sign to you? Just keep signing! What if your baby isn't forming a sign correctly? Just keep signing! What should you do if your baby forgets a sign? Just keep signing! Sounds simple, doesn't it? That's because it is.

## Why It Pays to Be Patient

At some stage in your signing journey, you may experience doubt that your baby will ever learn to sign, frustration that your efforts seem to be fruitless, or impatience with your baby's slow progress. These feelings plague many signing parents because practicing sign language with a baby can be a thankless job with little reward—at least at first. If you *just keep signing*, however, your baby will begin to understand your signs. Shortly after that, your baby will finally sign to you.

If you feel discouraged, surround yourself with signing babies in a class or a playgroup. Seeing all those signing success stories will motivate you to be patient and stick it out. Those other babies didn't learn to sign overnight. Instead, their parents spent many weeks repeating signs over and over again—just like you. If these parents have seen results, you can be sure that you will, too.

> **Essential Tip**
>
> It is helpful to see that other babies have successfully learned to sign, but remember that every baby is different and develops at his own pace. Just because it took one baby three months to form his first sign doesn't mean it will take your baby that long. Likewise, other babies may learn to sign before yours does.

For all of your efforts, there is no greater reward than to see your baby sign. That very first sign validates the weeks and months put into this endeavor and it is a unique milestone for which you and your baby should be proud. From here, your baby will seem to pick up one new sign after another, making all your patience and determination worthwhile.

# CHAPTER 3

# Strategies for Success

Even just covering the basics can be difficult, but don't get discouraged. The information in this chapter will provide you with advice to get you going, pitfalls to watch out for, and encouragement to keep you motivated. So get to it and happy signing!

## Choosing Your Starter Words

Your baby's first experiences with sign will lay the foundation for all her future signing endeavors. By carefully choosing fun and simple starter signs, you will provide her with a pleasurable signing experience that will motivate her to sign further. Some parents choose to start out with one or two signs; others introduce four or five all at once. It is best to stay in the range of one to five signs to avoid overloading your baby with too much information too soon. Also remember that you will have to learn just as many signs as your baby, and you do not want to overload yourself, either.

**Essential Tip**

Several American Sign Language signs incorporate a letter from the manual alphabet in their formation. For example, the sign for AUNT starts out with the letter A. For this reason, you may want to familiarize yourself with the ASL manual alphabet (see the Appendix) during the early stages of signing.

It is important to choose words that your baby will have an interest in signing. Initially, this interest will keep her riveted while you demonstrate the signs. As she begins to understand what the signs represent, her interest will prompt her to imitate the signs. When she sees that signing brings a response, she will eagerly form the signs again and again.

## Need-Based Signs

An infant's needs are pretty basic. In fact, other than a whole lot of love, your baby probably requires little more than milk, clean diapers, and sleep. That may seem simple enough, but deciphering her cries can be quite a challenge. If only she could tell you exactly what she wants. By introducing need-based signs to your baby, you will be providing her with a vocabulary that will allow her to ask for the things that are most important to her. Examples of need-based signs include the following:

- DIAPER
- DRINK
- EAT
- MILK
- BED

Need-based signs represent things your baby is already very familiar with and things she desperately wants to communicate. As she begins to comprehend that signing will enable her to communicate, she will eagerly attempt to form these signs.

## High-Impact Signs

Because of their own unique personalities, babies are fascinated and stimulated by different things. Perhaps your baby is excited by the family cat. Perhaps she is overjoyed by the sight of her blanket. Using the signs for things that interest your baby is a great way to motivate her as she begins her signing journey.

> **Essential Tip**
>
> Most babies have relatively short attention spans. The things that excite them this week may be perfectly mundane by the next. Be cautious when choosing high-impact signs, and try to stick to the ones that seem to have more staying power so that your baby doesn't lose interest in the sign.

Choosing high-impact signs for your baby's starter words is also a good way to encourage her exploration of the topics that interest her. If your baby is particularly excited by birds, for instance, then introducing the sign for BIRD is a good way to expose her not only to the word, but to examples of it. As you model the sign, you will likely be showing her actual birds, photos of birds, toy birds, and more. Because of her curiosity about the subject, she will be more likely to respond to the signing.

## Introducing the Signs

Even after you have chosen the type of sign you are going to start with, you will still have to choose that very first sign. This may seem daunting, but there are really only two "rules" to keep in mind: Choose a sign that is easy for baby to form and one that you will have many opportunities to demonstrate.

For example, perhaps you have chosen MILK as the first sign you are going to introduce to your baby. This is a great first sign because it is easy to form and it can be used over and over every day. Introducing it is very easy. After your baby gets settled into your arms and begins to nurse or take a bottle, demonstrate the sign for MILK in her line of vision. Make the sign two or three times while also orally speaking the word each time. It is not necessary to repeat the motion throughout the entire feeding (your hand would surely grow weary). It is most important to demonstrate the sign at the beginning of the feeding. If she is not overtired or distracted by something else, she will likely watch your hand movement intently. If your baby looks away during the feeding and then looks back at you, you can certainly take the opportunity to demonstrate the sign again.

### Essential Tip

Sometimes it may seem as if your baby just won't pay attention to a sign. Babies are easily distracted and will frequently look away. Your baby will not acquire a sign the first time (or even the tenth time) you model it for her, so don't worry if she looks away sometimes. Keep repeating the sign and she will eventually pick up on it.

The key to signing with your baby is repetition. Every single time you feed her, you should form the sign for MILK. Likewise, if someone else feeds her, that person should demonstrate it as well. Another learning opportunity for your baby is while another child is drinking from a bottle or nursing. If you see that your baby notices the other child, speak the word "milk" out loud and then form the sign. The more often your baby is exposed to it and the more diligent you are, the faster she will learn the sign.

Now that you have introduced your baby's first signs, you are going to be eagerly waiting for her to sign back. Unfortunately, this stage of the game requires a lot of patience on your part. Depending on when you begin using sign language with your baby, you may have weeks or months to wait before you see results. This delay can result in frustration for you and increased skepticism from others. If you feel yourself growing discouraged, just remember that babies everywhere are learning to sign. Your baby can, too. Don't give up. When your baby finally does sign back to you, it will have been worth the wait.

## Take It Slow

Eventually, the magical day will come when your baby makes her first sign. It may be unsteady, but she will do it. You, of course, will be thrilled. Finally seeing results after weeks of waiting can give you a renewed sense of purpose. Now that you know your baby can and will sign, you may be tempted to demonstrate signs for everything you can think of. But doing this could actually hurt your child's progress instead of helping it. Too many signs at once (especially in the beginning) can result in your child getting her signs confused, feeling overwhelmed, or not comprehending the meanings of the signs.

Like any new skill, your baby will learn sign language one step at a time. It is best to introduce her to one or two signs, and when she has mastered those to introduce her to a couple more. Just don't forget to keep using the old signs after the new ones have been introduced. It is worth noting that after she has acquired the first few signs, the rest will probably come more quickly and easily. This is because your baby now comprehends the fact that signing is a way for her to communicate.

If your baby begins to show indications of confusion after using several signs, it may be time to slow down your signing. Do not add any more signs for a while, and continue to use the ones you have already been using with her. When she seems to have them down without any confusion, it will then be appropriate to introduce new signs again.

You may also notice that your baby seems to drop a sign now and then. One day she will be using a particular sign, and then suddenly it seems to be gone from her repertoire. Generally, this is because your baby is so busy demonstrating new signs that she can't be bothered with the old ones. Continue to model the sign in front of her, even when she isn't using it herself. This will help her to retain its meaning until she is ready to use it again.

## Positive Reinforcement

As with almost everything your baby does, she will be looking to you to gauge your reaction when she first begins to sign. Your response can make all the difference in the world to her signing progress. When you react to your baby's accomplishment with excitement and pride, she is likely to want to repeat it.

---

**Essential Tip**

Positive reinforcement works because children want the approval of their parents. Giving your child a lot of praise for a job well done also helps to instill in her a sense of pride. This pride in her own efforts and approval from you will encourage her to continue to sign.

---

When your baby learns a new sign, you may not recognize it at first. Therefore, be on the lookout for any gesture that at all resembles a sign you have been using with her. If you suspect she might have signed, react! It is better to react to nothing than to miss a chance at acknowledging her accomplishment.

Most importantly, never demand perfection from your child's signs or force her to sign in order to get what she wants. This will only frustrate her and cause her to want to give up. With patience and encouragement, your child *will* learn to sign.

### Pile on the Praise

Praising your child for making a sign will probably come naturally to you. In fact, the first few times she signs, you will probably have a hard time containing your glee. Some great ways to praise your baby include clapping, telling her what a great job she did, offering a big smile or laugh, or hugging her. She will take great pride in herself when she sees that you are getting excited about something she has done. This praise will encourage her to sign over and over again.

It is also a good idea to involve others in the praise. If both Mommy and Daddy are in the room, then they should both praise baby for a job well done.

## Reactions Speak Louder Than Words

As important as praise is, the way you respond to your child's sign is even more important. Because every sign represents a word or an action, the best way to reinforce that comprehension is by reacting appropriately every time your child signs. When she forms the sign for EAT, feed her. When she makes the sign for DIAPER, change her. If you respond to her request quickly, she will soon learn that sign language is an effective way to get what she needs.

> **Essential Tip**
>
> During this early stage of signing, it is particularly important that everyone who plays a role in your baby's daily life is familiar with the signs you are using and knows how to react appropriately if your baby should sign. You wouldn't want your baby's first sign to go unnoticed because an unknowing caregiver missed it.

There may be times when you are unable to respond immediately to your baby's sign. For instance, if you are in the car and she makes the sign for DIAPER, you may be unable to change her right away. In a situation like that, acknowledge her request: "Oh, do you need a diaper?" Then assure her that you will change her as soon as you can stop. This will not be as effective as immediately giving her what she wants, but it will let her know that you understand and that you are acknowledging what she has said.

Your baby will soon discover that she can get what she wants—simply by signing. This dawning will be the start of her signing adventures. With this knowledge, your baby will want to learn as many signs as she can.

## Speak Up!

Although sign language is a wonderful form of communication, your baby will still someday need to learn to talk. Sign language can actually improve her language acquisition skills if you simply incorporate the spoken word with the signing one. Each time you form a sign, label it with the corresponding spoken word. Likewise, if your baby forms a sign, reiterate the spoken word as you address her request.

In addition to simply labeling the word, it is also beneficial to a baby's vocabulary and understanding of her native language to use the word in context. For example, if you are demonstrating the sign for BLANKET, you might say something like this:

"Blanket. Let's cover you up with your blanket."

Or if your baby makes the sign, you might say this:

"Blanket? Would you like to have your blanket?"

Always remember to give your child a chance to respond. Although she might not do more than coo or grunt, she is getting a feel for the rhythm of speech.

By repeating these words over and over as well as using them in context, you are actually giving your baby an advantage over many nonsigning children who are less likely to hear a word repeated as frequently. Before you know it, your child will first be signing and then speaking.

CHAPTER 4

# The Essential Signs

# I LOVE YOU

When your baby learns the sign for I LOVE YOU, you will have started a special practice that may continue indefinitely.

FIGURE 4-1: I LOVE YOU

The sign for I LOVE YOU, as shown in FIGURE 4-1, is one that is familiar to many people.

1.  Hold up your hand, palm facing outward.

2.  Extend your thumb, index, and pinkie fingers (your middle and ring fingers should remain folded down onto your palm).

This is a familiar and well-understood sign to many children and adults, however, babies and toddlers may have some difficulty forming the sign at first due to the dexterity that it requires. Just continue to model the sign when saying "I love you" and eventually, your child will acquire it.

It is also worth noting that the sign for I LOVE YOU and the sign for AIRPLANE are almost identical. So if you think your child is signing I LOVE YOU, just be on the lookout for an airplane.

# YES

The sign for YES is helpful because many babies will shake their heads for "no" much sooner than they nod for "yes." This sign gives them an alternative to nodding.

FIGURE 4-2: YES

The sign for YES can be made in tandem with a nod of the head or by itself.

**1. Make a fist with your right hand.**

**2. Flick it forward at the wrist, as if your hand is nodding.**

Although a shake of the head for "no" is more common among young babies, many also nod their heads for "yes." If your baby is already nodding, you may find that you do not need the American Sign Language sign for YES. As with "no," if you wish to use the sign anyway, start by doing both signing and nodding. Nodding is a natural gesture anyway, and there is no need to drop it in order to use the sign.

# NO

Although your baby will understand the spoken word early, using the sign for NO can help to reinforce its importance.

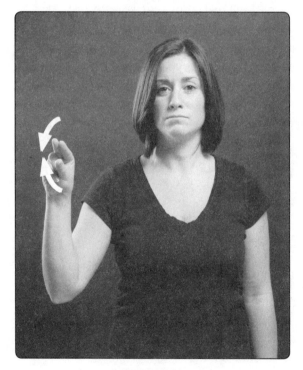

FIGURE 4-3: NO

The sign for NO is easy to form.

1.   Extend the thumb, index finger, and middle finger of your right hand.

2.   Bring the fingertips together with the fingers flattened, almost as if trying to indicate someone talking.

Most babies understand the word "no" by the time they are ten months old. This is undoubtedly due to the fact that curious babies who love to explore hear the word so often. Demonstrate the sign *while* shaking your head. This will help your baby to connect the word and the head shake with the corresponding sign.

> **Essential Tip**
>
> Most children understand "yes" and "no" very early. Nonetheless, introducing the signs for these concepts will help to reinforce their meaning, as emphasis will be placed on the words and your baby will gain added exposure to them.

# UP

Your baby will use the sign for UP to point out things of interest and to show you what she wants.

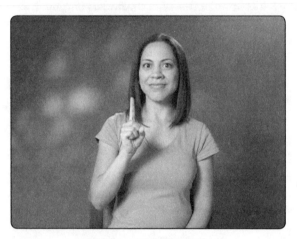

FIGURE 4-4: UP (STEP ONE)

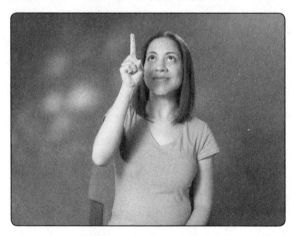

FIGURE 4-5: UP (STEP TWO)

The sign for UP is about as simple as it gets.

1. Point your index finger upward, as shown in Figure 4-4.

2. Raise your arm a few inches, as shown in Figure 4-5.

When introducing this sign and this concept, be sure to use objects with which your baby is already very familiar. You don't want her to understand the sign for UP as the sign for that object. If she already knows the sign for TOY, have someone toss a ball up in the air while you demonstrate the sign. Be sure to tell her verbally that the ball is up.

## PLEASE

It is never too early to begin teaching manners. The sign for PLEASE will help your child get into the habit of asking politely, even before he can speak the words.

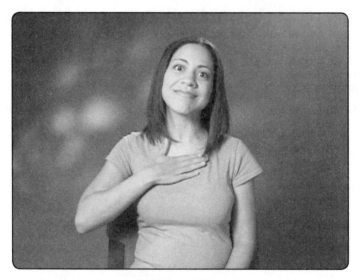

FIGURE 4-6: PLEASE

The sign for PLEASE is a simple one but is perhaps best demonstrated through example.

1.   Place your hand flat against your chest, as shown in Figure 4-6.

2.   Move your hand around in a circular motion.

The original intent of this sign was to express pleasure, as in "I am *pleased* to hear you say that." Now, though, the sign has gained widespread use in the Deaf community as a sign of politeness when making a request, as in, "Will you *please* do this for me?"

**Essential Tip**

Even if the other members of your household don't sign with your baby, try to get them on board with this sign. If your baby sees others signing PLEASE when making their requests, she will begin to understand the connection between a request and the sign. Likewise, if you ask your baby to do something or hand you something, be sure to sign PLEASE to her, as well.

# THANK YOU

Not only does it ingrain good manners, but gift givers will be thrilled when your baby is able to express her thanks.

FIGURE 4-7: THANK YOU (STEP ONE)

FIGURE 4-8: THANK YOU (STEP TWO)

The sign for THANK YOU looks as if you are blowing a kiss.

1.  Bring the tips of your fingers to your lips, as shown in Figure 4-7.

2.  Extend your palm out flat, as shown in Figure 4-8.

You'll have plenty of opportunities to model this sign. Every time your child gives you something or does something helpful, exclaim, "Thank you!" and form the sign. Then try giving something back to her and look at her expectantly, as if waiting for her to do something. If she does not form the sign, simply demonstrate it for her again. It will take time, but she will eventually understand the concept.

> **Essential Tip**
>
> Most children are unable to consistently say "please" and "thank you" until they are at least two years of age. So even after your child has learned the signs for these words, she may not use them every time. In the meantime, praise her when she does remember, and offer her a gentle reminder when she does not.

# MOMMY

This sign will likely be used time and time again. Be sure to teach it to your baby's caregivers so they can acknowledge it when he asks for Mommy.

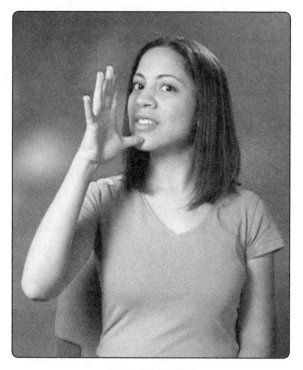

FIGURE 4-9: MOMMY

If you are a mother trying to use this sign with your child, it will be difficult to do so yourself. Your baby will likely not understand to what you are referring. Instead, someone else will have to demonstrate the sign each time your baby catches sight of you (such as when you walk into the room or when you come home from work).

1.   Spread your hand open with your thumb pointing toward you.

2.   Tap the tip of your thumb to your chin as shown in Figure 4-9.

To further emphasize the meaning of this sign, be sure to say "mommy" or "momma" every time you or someone else forms it.

# DADDY

Like the sign for MOMMY, DADDY is another sign that babies will use on a regular basis.

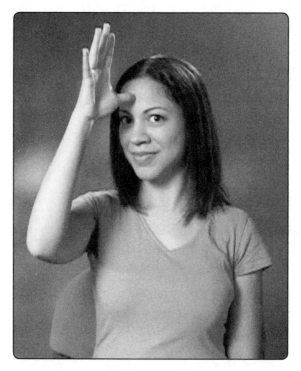

FIGURE 4-10: DADDY

The sign for DADDY, as shown in FIGURE 4-10, is very similar to the sign for MOMMY.

1.  Spread your hand open with your thumb pointing toward you.

2.  Tap your thumb to your forehead.

In the same way that it is difficult for a mother to model the sign for MOMMY to a child, it is equally difficult for a father to model the sign for DADDY. Someone else should make the sign whenever he enters the room. Again, be sure to reiterate this word verbally as you sign it.

> **Essential Tip**
>
> The sign for MOMMY and the sign for DADDY are very similar. Your baby may confuse the two quite a bit in the beginning. If you find that he signs for Mommy but really wants Daddy (or vice versa), give him to the parent he wants and then demonstrate the correct sign.

# SISTER

If your baby has a sister, use this sign because a baby will not be capable of spelling out her sister's name in sign language.

FIGURE 4-11: SISTER

The sign for SISTER is another two-handed motion that may take some practice.

1. Form the "G" hand shape with both hands.

2. Touch your cheek with your right hand.

3. Bring your right hand down and rest it upon your left hand.

Your baby will likely begin to understand its meaning long before she begins to sign it. In the meantime, your baby may simply point to or reach for her sister.

> **Essential Tip**
>
> If your baby has more than one brother or sister, a bit of creativity may be necessary to distinguish one sibling from another. If your other children have particularly short names, you may choose to spell them out. Otherwise, you might consider making the sign for BROTHER or SISTER and then adding the first initial of the child's name.

# BROTHER

The same thing goes if your baby has a brother. Using this generic sign will eliminate the need for spelling out his brother's name.

FIGURE 4-12: BROTHER

The sign for BROTHER is a two-handed motion that is fairly complex for a baby. And because the sign for BROTHER and the sign for SISTER are remarkably similar—both ending in the same way—be sure to emphasize the first part of each sign to help your baby differentiate between the two.

1. **Make the "G" hand shape with both hands.**

2. **Extend the thumb of your right hand and touch it to your forehead.**

3. **Still holding the "G" hand shape, bring your right hand down and rest it upon your left.**

As with SISTER, it may take weeks or months for your baby to begin forming this sign. Give it time, and eventually your baby will delight you by asking for his brother.

> **Essential Tip**
> Ideally, your other children will be participating in signing with the baby as well. If so, you will want someone other than the siblings themselves to demonstrate the signs to your baby. If, however, your baby's siblings are not in the habit of signing with him, then it will actually be beneficial to have them make the signs themselves. This will cause your baby to associate these signs with the siblings they represent.

# AUNT

If your baby has multiple aunts, consider attaching initials to the signs, so that Aunt Sally would be signed AUNT + S.

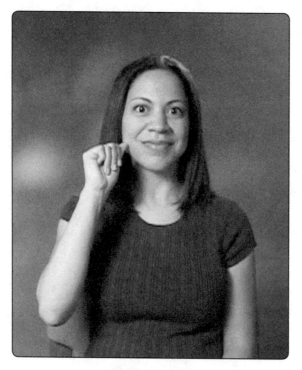

**FIGURE 4-13: AUNT**

The sign for AUNT starts with another familiar sign, the letter A.

1.   Form the manual alphabet letter A.

2.   Hold it beside your cheek, and shake your hand back and forth.

The sign for AUNT can look a lot like the sign for APPLE, particularly when a baby is signing it. By looking for context clues, though, you can likely determine which sign your baby is trying to form.

# UNCLE

If your baby has more than one uncle, you can add an initial after the sign to differentiate between uncles.

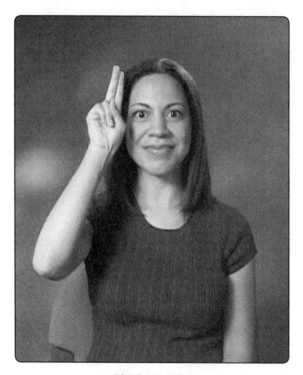

FIGURE 4-14: UNCLE

The sign for UNCLE, as shown in FIGURE 4-14, is similar in form to the sign for AUNT.

1.   Form the manual alphabet letter U.

2.   Hold it beside your forehead, and shake it slightly back and forth.

Because the sign for UNCLE requires that your baby extend his index and middle fingers, he may find it difficult while he is still young. Until he is well into toddlerhood, he may form the sign by extending *all* of his fingers and then shaking his hand at the side of his forehead.

# GRANDMA

Not only does this sign give a baby the opportunity to "talk" about one of her favorite people, Grandma will be thrilled to know that baby can sign her name.

Once your baby has learned the sign for MOMMY, the sign for GRANDMA will be easy to pick up.

1. **Start by signing MOMMY with your thumb resting on your chin.**

2. **Move your hand away from your face, drawing two invisible humps in the air.**

At first, your baby may have some trouble managing to form the humps. He may simply move his hand away from his face in a straight line or in one big arc. He will probably figure out the humps eventually and in the meantime, Grandma will still be ecstatic.

# GRANDPA

Like Grandma, Grandpa will likely be proud as can be when baby signs his name.

In the same way that MOMMY and DADDY are similar signs, so are GRANDMA and GRANDPA. To make the sign for GRANDPA you will start with the sign for DADDY.

1. **Start by signing DADDY, with your thumb resting on your forehead.**

2. **Move your hand away from your face, drawing two invisible humps in the air.**

Similar to differentiating between multiple aunts and multiple uncles, you may want to find a way to differentiate if your baby has more than one grandmother and grandfather. One possibility is to add the grandparent's first or last initial to the sign. Therefore, Grandpa Simpson could be signed using GRANDPA + S.

# GIRL

Your baby can use the sign for GIRL to help differenti-ate between one friend and another.

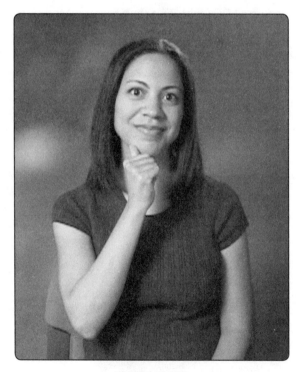

FIGURE 4-15: GIRL

The sign for GIRL, as shown in FIGURE 4-15, is meant to represent the tie of a bonnet.

1.   Form the "A" hand shape.

2.   Run your thumb down from your cheek to your chin two times.

Young boys and girls physically look pretty much the same and have a similar voice pitch. As a result, your baby may have difficulty differentiating between the two. If this is the case, you may want to simply use the sign for CHILD for all children, at least until he is a little older.

# BOY

BOY is another sign that your baby can use to help identify one child versus another.

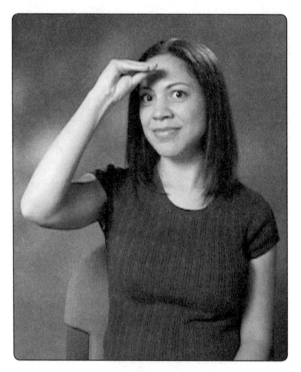

FIGURE 4-16: BOY

To form the sign for BOY, as shown in FIGURE 4-16, it's helpful if you can visualize a little.

1. Imagine you are wearing a baseball cap.

2. Reach up with one hand and grasp the visor of the cap. (The tips of all your fingers and thumb should be pressed together as if operating a hand puppet with its mouth closed.)

That's it. You have just made the sign for BOY. This sign is most commonly recognized as BOY, however it is actually a sign for males in general. It could be used to express GUY or MAN (in addition to BOY), though each of those has its own variation that is more commonly used and understood.

# BABY

Babies and toddlers tend to have an early fascination with other babies. This sign enables them to express their delight at seeing their peers.

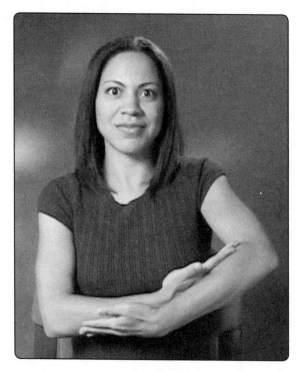

**FIGURE 4-17: BABY**

When your child develops an understanding of what a baby is, he will probably go out of his way to point babies out to you. The sign for BABY, as shown in FIGURE 4-17, will help him to do that.

1.   Put your arms in front of you and place one arm on top of the other, as if you were forming a cradle.

2.   Sway your arms in front of you as if rocking a baby.

When you first set out to introduce this sign, try practicing it with a doll in your arms, particularly a realistic one that looks like a baby. This will help your child to make the connection in his mind.

# CHILD

As fascinated as your baby may be with other babies, he is likely even more excited by children. Use this simple sign instead of the signs for BOY and GIRL to apply to any child.

**FIGURE 4-18: CHILD**

The sign for CHILD is one that may not be very recognizable when your baby demonstrates it.

**1.    Pat the air in front of you, as if patting the head of a child.**

Because it may appear that your baby is simply waving his arm, you may not realize that he is signing at first. Take note of any children who may be in your baby's line of sight and look for any possible resemblance to this sign.

# FRIEND

Teach this sign to your baby to refer to one friend or to playmates in general.

FIGURE 4-19: FRIEND

The sign for FRIEND, as shown in FIGURE 4-19, is meant to indicate the closeness of two friends.

1. **Bring both hands in front of the chest.**

2. **Link both of your index fingers together.**

Because older infants and younger toddlers are just learning to socialize with their peers, the meaning of friendship will be lost on them. Therefore, consider using the sign for FRIEND to indicate "playmate." For instance, when you go to playgroup or to the park, use the sign for FRIEND to introduce your child to another baby. This will let your little one understand that the other baby is someone with whom he can play.

# DRINK

This is a simple sign that your baby can use to express thirst or to ask for any beverage.

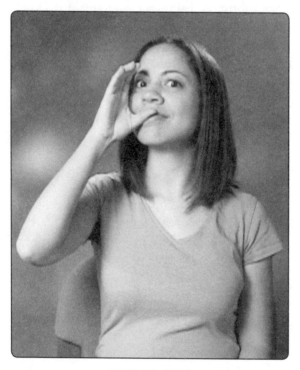

FIGURE 4-20: DRINK

When your baby begins to use a cup, you may want to introduce the sign for DRINK, as shown in FIGURE 4-20. This sign should be fairly simple for your baby to sign.

1.  **Cup your hand as if holding a glass.**

2.  **Raise it to your mouth as if drinking.**

If your child has already learned the sign for MILK, you may find that he uses MILK and DRINK interchangeably. MILK may become his sign of choice for juice, water, and any other beverage. Conversely, he may also use the sign for DRINK when requesting MILK. If you are able to understand what he is signing, respond to his request, but continue to model the correct sign. In time, your baby will be able to differentiate between the two signs.

# BOTTLE

This is an easy sign as it isn't much different than thumb sucking.

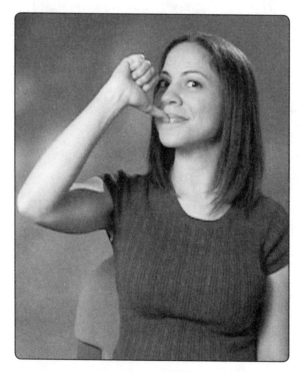

FIGURE 4-21: BOTTLE

The sign for BOTTLE, as shown in FIGURE 4-21, is simple to form. Simply pretend your hand is a bottle and your thumb the nipple.

1.  Form a fist and extend your thumb upward (like the "A" hand shape).

2.  Bring your thumb to your mouth, simulating sucking on a bottle.

Because a baby who is still drinking out of a bottle is usually drinking milk or formula, you will need to differentiate between the signs for MILK and BOTTLE.

**Essential Tip**

If your baby is particular about what she drinks, labeling each individual beverage makes more sense. That will allow her to specifically request milk or juice or water. However, if your baby is willing to drink just about anything you give her, it may be unnecessary for you to introduce her to any signs other than BOTTLE and/or CUP.

# CUP

When your baby transitions from a bottle to a cup, acknowledge the achievement by teaching him this sign.

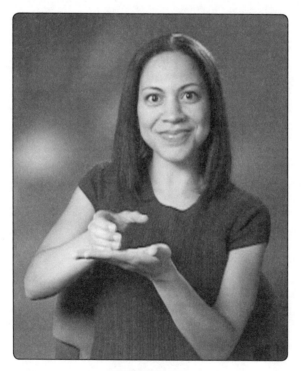

FIGURE 4-22: CUP

If you and your baby have already learned the sign for DRINK, the sign for CUP, as shown in FIGURE 4-22, will be easy to master.

1.   With one hand, form the letter C.

2.   Rest it in the palm of your opposite hand.

This similarity between the signs means that you could allow your baby to use the signs interchangeably if you wish. After all, a baby who is signing for a cup is obviously requesting something to drink. With that in mind, you might find it unnecessary to use both signs with your child and instead may find it better to focus on only one.

# MILK

The sign for milk is an easy one for babies to master.

FIGURE 4-23: MILK

MILK is commonly one of the first signs used with babies. It is easy to remember as it resembles the act of milking a cow, and it will likely be exciting to your baby. After all, what preverbal baby would not want to communicate his desire for milk?

1.  **Use one hand to demonstrate a squeezing motion.**

2.  **Alternate an up-and-down motion to imitate the milking of a cow.**

As you will have many opportunities throughout the day to demonstrate this sign, be sure to do so at every feeding—even in the middle of the night. You may be amazed at how quickly your baby picks up this sign. If you are unsure that your baby is actually signing, simply offer him a bottle or the opportunity to nurse. If he feeds eagerly, chances are he was trying to tell you something.

# JUICE

Some parents opt to use the sign for CUP as a generic drinking sign; however, you may find that teaching individual beverage signs eliminates tantrums from a baby who wanted juice but received water or milk instead.

If you already know the sign for DRINK, you will have no trouble learning the sign for JUICE.

1.  Form the sign for DRINK. (Cup your hand as if holding a glass. Raise it to your mouth as if drinking.)

2.  Finger-spell the letter J.

When you first introduce the sign for JUICE to your child, he may use it as a generic request for something to drink. In fact, you may discover that he uses it interchangeably with other beverage-related signs, including MILK, CUP, or DRINK. If you want your baby to have the ability to specify his drink choice, just continue to model the sign for each drink. He will eventually be able to differentiate between them.

# WATER

Although juice or milk may be the preferred beverage of many little ones, older babies and toddlers who are given water regularly may learn to ask for it when they are truly thirsty.

The sign for WATER is one that many children learn easily. This can be attributed to the fact that there are many opportunities to demonstrate the sign, and it represents something that is often exciting to young children.

1.  Form the letter W with your fingers.

2.  With your fingers facing to the side, tap them to your chin.

Water is certainly an important beverage, but it serves many other functions as well. Babies like to splash in the sink, stomp in puddles, and play in the bath. All of these give you the opportunity to reinforce the sign. Of course, with so many purposes for water, it may not be clear what your baby is asking for when he signs it. Is he thirsty? Does he hear running water? Would he like to take a bath? As with so many other signs, it is important to read this sign in context. That should give you clues to the sign's meaning.

# EAT

Although there are a few specific food signs that are good to teach your baby, EAT is a sign she can use whenever she is hungry.

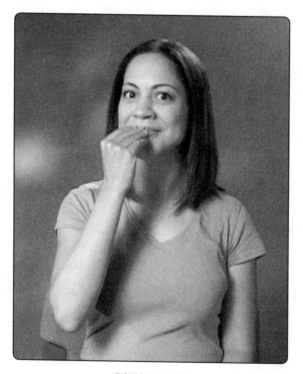

FIGURE 4-24: EAT

For babies who have graduated to baby food, EAT, as shown in FIGURE 4-24, is another highly motivating sign. It may not be the easiest one for your baby to sign perfectly, but he will likely adapt it to work for him.

1. Draw the tips of all of your fingers and thumb together as if operating a hand puppet with its mouth closed.

2. Bring your hand up to your mouth and touch your fingertips twice to your lips.

You may notice that your baby begins to point to his mouth with one or two fingers at mealtimes. If so, congratulations! He is signing! Give it time, and continue to model the actual ASL sign (unless you are practicing modified ASL). Eventually he will form it correctly.

**Essential Tip**
Because infants still get the majority of their calories and nutrition from milk or formula, that is what they typically want when they are hungry. Do not be surprised if your baby only signs EAT while he is actually eating and MILK when he is hungry. In time, this will change.

# PLATE

This sign requires a small amount of dexterity, but your baby will probably eagerly attempt it once she grasps its meaning.

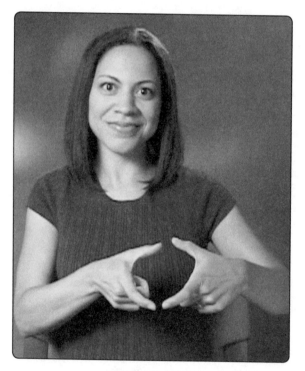

FIGURE 4-25: PLATE

Although there is more than one accepted version of the sign for PLATE, as shown in FIGURE 4-25, this version is an easy one for your baby.

1. Start with your thumbs and index fingers spread wide.

2. Hold your hands about a plate's width apart in front of you and bounce your hands twice as if you are emphasizing the plate.

To give your baby a visual demonstration, position your outstretched fingers around the rim of a plate to help promote understanding of the sign.

> **Essential Tip**
> In addition to a distraction from mess-making, the signs for PLATE and BOWL will provide your baby with labels for some very important everyday objects. She may also use these signs to indicate her desire to eat. Although the signs are simple, it may take a little time for your child to differentiate one from the other. Just be patient, and give her as many opportunities as possible to see and practice the sign.

# BOWL

This is an intuitive sign that your baby will likely pick up quickly.

FIGURE 4-26: BOWL (STEP ONE)

FIGURE 4-27: BOWL (STEP TWO)

The sign for BOWL, as shown in FIGURES 4-26 and 4-27, is an easy one to both remember and form.

1. Cup both hands together in front of your body (see Figure 4-26).

2. Bring your hands up as if feeling the outside of a bowl (see Figure 4-27).

An excellent way to illustrate this sign is by placing an actual bowl into your baby's cupped hands. This will help her to associate the sign with the object. Of course, it is best to do this with an empty bowl to avoid the inevitable mess that a full bowl would create.

# FORK

Once your toddler begins using a fork and learns the sign for it, don't be surprised if she asks for one at every meal.

The sign for FORK resembles the act of spearing a piece of food.

1.   Form the letter V with your first and middle fingers.

2.   With the tips of those fingers, tap the palm of your other hand twice as if your fingers are the tines of a fork and your palm is a plate.

For the sake of demonstration, you could actually hold a piece of food in your hand, tapping it with the first two fingers of the other hand.

> **Essential Tip**
>
> Don't be surprised to find that your baby does not learn the sign for FORK as quickly as she learns the sign for SPOON. Babies and toddlers generally use spoons more often than forks and therefore have more opportunities to see the sign modeled. You may also find that your baby uses one sign to indicate both fork and spoon.

# SPOON

A spoon is a baby's first eating utensil. Teach the sign to him early and you can use it to remind him to use his spoon instead of his fingers.

Because a spoon is probably the first eating utensil your baby will encounter, he will be familiar with its shape early on. This familiarity will motivate him to want to demonstrate the sign.

1. Form the letter U with your index and middle fingers.

2. Curve those fingers slightly and use them to scoop imaginary food out of your other palm.

Try to expose your child to many different kinds of spoons, such as wooden spoons, slotted spoons, iced-tea spoons, and measuring spoons. Your baby will enjoy playing with the spoons and will gain a better understanding of both the object and the sign.

# CEREAL

Babies everywhere love to snack on cereal (namely Cheerios) and because dry cereal is so portable and easy to keep on hand, this is an ideal snack sign for your baby to learn.

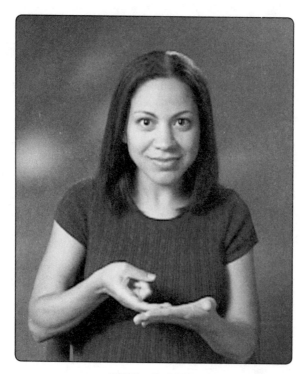

**FIGURE 4-28: CEREAL**

There are actually a couple of accepted American Sign Language signs for CEREAL. The one that will probably be the easiest for your baby to form is shown in FIGURE 4-28.

1.   Hold your left hand in front of your body, palm up.

2.   Use your right first and middle fingers to "scoop" something out of your palm and bring it to your mouth.

Since the sign for CEREAL mimics the act of eating, don't be surprised if your baby uses it to ask for all kinds of foods at first. In time, she will learn to use the sign only when she wants cereal.

**Essential Tip**

Signs like CEREAL are especially good for toddlers who are learning to speak but have not yet been able to master multisyllabic words.

# CRACKER

Although the sign for CRACKER is a little complex, consider creating your own modified version of the sign as crackers are another very popular baby snack.

FIGURE 4-29: CRACKER

CRACKER, as shown in FIGURE 4-29, may be a little difficult for a baby or toddler to form, but with a little practice it will surely become a favorite sign.

1. Cross your left forearm over your chest so the elbow faces forward.

2. Form your right hand into a fist.

3. Tap your left elbow twice with your right fist.

It is acceptable for your forearm to cross your chest diagonally, as in the picture, or horizontally across your abdomen.

> **Essential Tip**
>
> As mentioned, this sign may be difficult at first, so look for variations on this sign from your child. He may simply pat his elbow or touch his shoulder. If you are unsure that he is really signing CRACKER, just ask him. An excited reaction will be your answer.

# COOKIE

The sign for COOKIE is somewhat complex but the hope of cookies will be great incentive for him to try it.

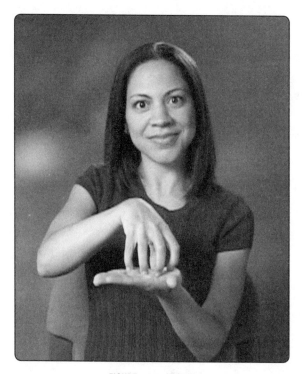

FIGURE 4-30: COOKIE

To form COOKIE, as shown in FIGURE 4-30, imagine that your left hand is cookie dough that has been rolled out flat.

1.  Hold your left palm upward in front of your body.

2.  Place the fingertips of the right hand onto the left palm as if the right hand was a round cookie cutter.

3.  Rotate the right hand on the palm of your left hand as if cutting out a cookie.

Want to bring this sign home for your child? Make cookies and allow him to help you cut them out of the dough with cookie cutters. As an added bonus, you can make the cookies in a variety of shapes, giving your child a bonus lesson in shapes.

## MORE

This may well be one of your baby's favorite signs. When he realizes he can use it to ask for more, you will probably see a lot of it.

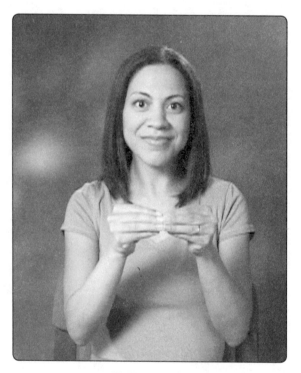

FIGURE 4-31: MORE

MORE is a favorite sign for many babies and is an easy one to form.

1.   Hold both hands in front of you, fingers on each hand held together and thumbs tucked in.

2.   Bring the fingertips of both hands together, as shown in Figure 4-31.

When preverbal babies want more of something, they usually whine, cry, grunt, or point in an effort to make their desires known. You are probably quite familiar with your baby's usual "sign" for more. To reinforce the American Sign Language sign for MORE, simply model it each time she asks for more of anything. On the other hand, if your child's current method for asking for more is acceptable to you, continue to use it. There is no reason to use signs that your child does not need.

# BIB

Although your baby may not frequently ask for a bib, teaching her this intuitive sign is a simple way to expand her signing vocabulary.

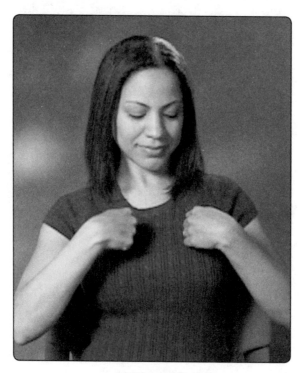

FIGURE 4-32: BIB

The sign for BIB, as shown in FIGURE 4-32, is an iconic one.

1.   Touch your fingertips to your lips as you do in the sign for EAT.

2.   Form both hands into fists and "draw" a bib from your shoulders down to your chest with your hands.

3.   Your hands should meet in the middle of your chest.

BIB is not a commonly used sign. You may even find that in some signing circles, the sign for napkin is used in place of the sign for BIB. Because the sign is so iconic, however, there is really no reason not to use it with your child.

**Essential Tip**

Because babies are such creatures of habit, even those who struggle against the bib may begin to look for you to sign BIB at the start of the meal. In fact, if you forget your baby's bib, don't be surprised if she signs and reminds you. This does not mean that she wants to wear the bib, of course. It simply means that she has become accustomed to the routine.

# CHAIR

Although the sign for CHAIR has several steps, it is worth the extra effort. Your child can use it to let you know when he has had enough walking or standing.

**FIGURE 4-33: CHAIR**

The sign for CHAIR, as shown in FIGURE 4-33, uses both hands to illustrate the act of sitting.

1.  Extend the index and middle fingers of your left hand horizontally in front of your body.

2.  Curve the same fingers on your right hand and have them "sit" on your left fingers.

3.  Lift your right fingers and have them sit again to complete the sign.

Remember to use the sign for CHAIR for any kind of chair, not just the upholstered kind in your living room. Use it for dining room chairs, high chairs, lawn chairs, and rocking chairs. This will help your baby to understand that a chair is simply something to sit in and that the sign does not refer to one chair in particular.

# TABLE

Your baby can use the sign for TABLE to identify her surroundings, request a meal, or to ask for some other tabletop activity.

FIGURE 4-34: TABLE

The sign for TABLE, as shown in FIGURE 4-34, can also be used to indicate DESK.

1.   Hold your left forearm horizontally in front of your body, with your right forearm hovering directly above it.

2.   Bring your arms together twice. This represents resting your arms on a table or other flat surface.

Remember that a table is not only used for mealtimes. If you and your child sit down at the table to color or put together a puzzle, be sure to model the sign for TABLE. This will help your child to recognize the table as a multifunctional piece of furniture.

# TELEPHONE

These days, it seems that we are never without our phones. Chances are good your baby is well aware of this device and will probably use the sign often.

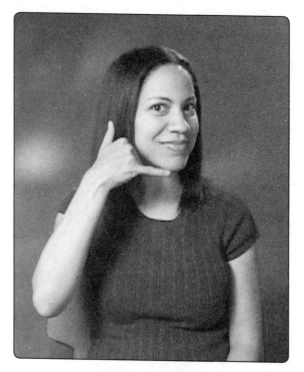

FIGURE 4-35: TELEPHONE

The sign for TELEPHONE, as shown in FIGURE 4-35, is probably what you would expect it to be.

1.  Form the "Y" hand shape by extending your thumb and pinkie finger.

2.  Bring your hand up to the side of your face and touch your thumb to your ear and your pinkie to your mouth.

3.  Repeat to complete this sign.

A fun way to help your child understand this sign is to give him a phone to play with. This can be a toy phone, a cellular phone that is no longer activated, or a home phone with the cord removed. In addition to using this playtime to reinforce the sign, try holding phone conversations with your child. He will likely find this amusing and want to do it again and again.

> **Essential Tip**
> Noises around the house can be fun, but they can also be scary. Babies are usually most afraid of the things they do not understand. Introducing your baby to the TELEPHONE sign will help him to understand what that sound is, so it will stop being scary.

# MUSIC

Preverbal babies learn to ask for things by pointing or picking up the objects they want. Unfortunately, music isn't a tangible item, which is why this sign comes in handy so often.

FIGURE 4-36: MUSIC

The sign for MUSIC resembles the act of conducting an orchestra.

1. Hold one arm in front of your torso.

2. Move the other hand back and forth above your arm in a rhythmic fashion as if conducting.

Don't be surprised if your baby makes this sign without the use of her still arm. She will likely pick up on the conducting part first, and the other may have to come later.

# BOOK

Reading to your little one is a wonderful way to spend quality time with him. Don't be surprised to find he makes this sign often.

FIGURE 4-37: BOOK (STEP ONE)

FIGURE 4-38: BOOK (STEP TWO)

The sign for BOOK, as shown in FIGURES 4-37 and 4-38, actually looks like a book.

1. Start with your palms together.

2. Now open your hands as if they were hinged on one side, like you are opening a book.

3. Repeat the motion to complete the sign.

Books are exciting to children of all ages, and babies are no different. Reading daily to your baby can improve her vocabulary and give her a better command of spoken English.

# OPEN

Your child will likely use this sign frequently as he asks you to open all sorts of things he can't get into by himself.

FIGURE 4-39: OPEN (STEP ONE)

FIGURE 4-40: OPEN (STEP TWO)

Obviously, a great way to demonstrate the sign for OPEN is by opening a door repeatedly and forming the sign.

1.  Hold your hands in front of your body, palms down, index fingers touching, as shown in Figure 4-39.

2.  Pull your hands apart, flipping them over as you do so, as shown in Figure 4-40, to demonstrate something opening.

Of course, doors aren't the only things to be opened. Open jars, boxes, cabinets, and books to help your child grasp the concept of opening something.

# TOY

Every child has a favorite toy and this sign will help identify when she wants to play.

The sign for TOY is simple enough that it could be used for any favorite toy or to refer to your baby's toys as a group.

1.  Form the "T" hand shape with both hands, which is a fist that has your thumb between your middle and index fingers.

2.  Holding both hands in front of you, shake your hands.

The sign for TOY can also be especially useful when teaching your baby to pick up her toys. In fact, you could even reserve this sign exclusively for cleanup time. After a while, your child will understand that she must put her toys away when you demonstrate this sign.

> **Essential Tip**
>
> The sign for PLAY is almost identical to the sign for TOY. Instead of using the "T" hand shape as you do in TOY, you simply shake your hands with the "Y" hand shape to indicate PLAY. If you find that your child is able to form one more easily than the other, you may want to use that sign for both TOY and PLAY.

# PACIFIER

If your baby uses a pacifier, do yourself a favor and teach him this sign. It will lessen the frustration for both of you when he is longing for his binky.

PACIFIER is a two-motion sign that accurately represents the word it stands for, but it may be too complex for an infant.

1. **Rock your arms as if holding a baby.**

2. **With a closed fist, touch the tip of your thumb to your lips.**

Some babies confuse the signs for BOTTLE and PACIFIER. The signs are quite different, but because they both involve the act of sucking, some babies will use the signs interchangeably. If it is likely that your baby is hungry, he is probably requesting a bottle.

# SHOES

Babies and toddlers either love shoes or they hate them. Either way, they can use this sign to express what they want—or don't want—on their feet.

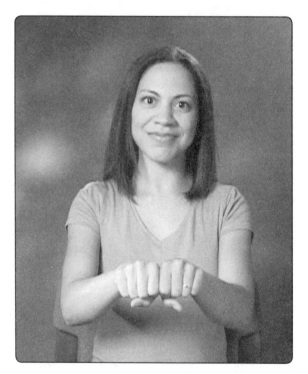

FIGURE 4-41: SHOES

*There's no place like home. There's no place like home.* No, you won't be clicking the heels of your ruby slippers together to indicate SHOE.

1. **Make a fist with both hands.**

2. **Tap the thumb sides of your hands together twice.**

SHOE is one of several signs that use the motion of bringing both hands together in front of the body. It is similar to the sign for MORE. You may have to be particularly observant in the beginning to determine which of these signs your child is trying to form.

> **Essential Tip**
>
> Although there are specific signs for different types of shoes, it is unnecessary to model them for your baby, as this would likely confuse her and weigh her down with unnecessary signs. Additionally, she is unlikely to differentiate between shoe types at this stage.

# SHIRT

If your baby prefers to be naked, don't be surprised if she uses this sign to let you know she wants her shirt off.

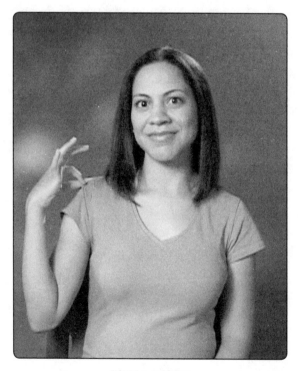

**FIGURE 4-42: SHIRT**

The sign for SHIRT, as shown in FIGURE 4-42, is a simple one that should come easily to your baby. In fact, she may use it already without even knowing it.

1.  Use your index fingers and thumbs to pinch your shirt on each side near the upper part of your chest.

2.  Then tug at it a few times.

This one will probably be a fun sign for your baby to make and she may do it already, even if she isn't trying to tell you anything.

# DIAPER

You may see this sign more often than you'd like but it is a great one for your baby to know. A prompt diaper change will reduce the likelihood of discomfort and diaper rash.

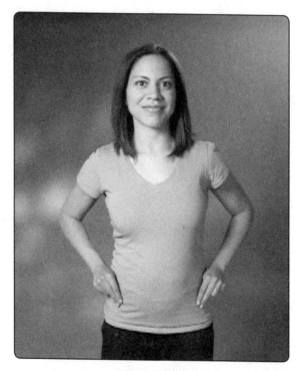

FIGURE 4-43: DIAPER

The sign for DIAPER, as shown in FIGURE 4-43, comes from the act of pinning a diaper closed.

1.  Hold your hands in front of your waist and your fingers pointed downward.

2.  Make a pinching motion with your index and middle fingers against your thumbs.

This motion may seem foreign to your baby, so if you notice that he seems to be scratching at his diaper, he may actually be signing.

# BATH

If your baby enjoys bath time, the sign for BATH is a signing essential. You may find that she soon requests baths on a regular basis.

Babies either seem to love the water or hate it. The baby who loves to bathe will be eager to form this sign when she realizes that she can request bath time whenever she wants it. Those who are not as fond of the water will probably be hesitant to form this sign, at least once they realize that it will result in a bath.

1. Curl up the fingers of both hands and bring them to your chest.

2. Move your fists in tandem up and down your chest twice.

The sign should resemble washing your chest. If getting your child into the bathtub is a struggle, you may want to wait until after she is in the water to form the sign. It will not take very long before she associates the sign with the action, and seeing you make the sign might cause an unnecessary temper tantrum.

# BLANKET

Many babies and toddlers find comfort in their blankets. Teaching them this sign will reduce the panic and frustration they feel when they want, but are unable to ask for, their blankets.

The sign for BLANKET is one that will become quite familiar, and it is easy to learn.

1. Hold your hands out in front of you as though you are holding a blanket with your fingertips.

2. Pretend to cover yourself with that blanket.

This may be an easy sign for your baby to learn although you may not recognize it when he first attempts it. If you suspect that your baby is forming the sign for BLANKET, offer one to him and see if it appeases him. It is always better to assume your child is signing and react appropriately than to risk missing the opportunity for praise and acknowledgment.

# BED

Choose the sign for BED instead of the sign for SLEEP, as it will be easier for your baby to form.

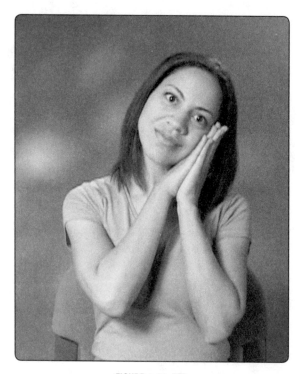

FIGURE 4-44: BED

The sign for BED, as shown in FIGURE 4-44, is familiar to most people and is easy for baby to form.

1.   Tilt your head to one side.

2.   Press both palms together in a "prayer" pose and bring them up to your head.

3.   Rest your head against your hands.

Another variation is to rest your head against the open palm of just one hand. Toddlers seem to love this sign and may occasionally form it even when they are not tired. If your child forms the sign and it is not his usual bedtime or naptime, you may want to simply try cuddling with him for a bit to see if he is truly tired.

# LIGHT

Once your child learns the sign for LIGHT, she may use it to ask for the light to be turned either off or on.

FIGURE 4-45: LIGHT (STEP ONE)

FIGURE 4-46: LIGHT (STEP TWO)

There are a few different ways to sign LIGHT. Your baby will probably most often be referring to overhead lights when he signs LIGHT. Fortunately, this version, as shown in FIGURES 4-45 and 4-46, is one of the easiest versions to form.

1.  Hold your hands up in the air near your head with your fingertips and thumb touching and pointed downward.

2.  Open your hand up wide as if indicating a flash.

This sign does double duty as it can also mean SUN.

# IN

This sign allows your baby to ask to go inside when he has had enough of playing outdoors.

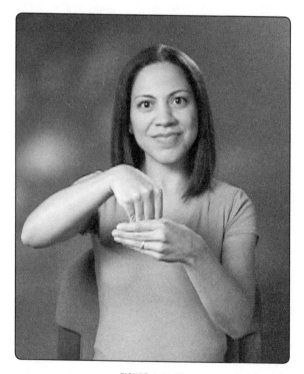

**FIGURE 4-47: IN**

The sign for IN, as shown in **FIGURE 4-47**, is formed by inserting one hand into the other.

1. Hold your hand in front of your body, palm facing toward you.

2. Bring your other hand up, and with fingers together, insert it into the palm of the first hand.

This sign will be especially useful to your baby when she begins filling up containers for fun. Babies love to fill boxes, buckets, and bins with almost anything that will fit inside. Use this to your advantage, and instruct your child to put her toys in her toy box.

> **Essential Tip**
>
> Another good way to demonstrate this sign is by using it when going indoors after playing outside. Announce to your child that it is time to go in, putting emphasis on the word "in" and signing it simultaneously. Then immediately take her inside.

# OUT

Similarly, the sign for OUT gives your baby a "voice" when she wants to go outside. It is much easier to learn than the sign for DOOR, making it a better choice.

The sign for OUT is simply the opposite of the sign for IN.

1. **Start with one hand enclosed in the other, as described in the previous section for the sign for IN.**

2. **Separate your hands from each other.**

In the same way that babies love to fill containers, they also (and perhaps even more so) love to empty them. Each time she pulls the blocks out of the block box or the socks out of her dresser drawer, demonstrate the sign for OUT.

> **Essential Tip**
>
> In the same way that you might sign IN to tell your child that it is time to go inside, you can also use the sign for OUT to let her know it is time to go outside. When she is ready to go, simply tell her that it is time to go out, and form the sign. She will undoubtedly use OUT by itself to mean both "out of" and "outside."

# FLOWER

Flowers are bright and colorful and likely to capture your baby's attention from an early age—so this is a great, high-impact sign.

The sign for FLOWER displays the correlation between flower and scent.

1. Draw the tips of all your fingers and thumb together as if operating a hand puppet with its mouth closed, as you did with the sign for EAT.

2. Touch the tips of those fingers first to one side of your nose and then to the other.

When you first introduce this sign, try to expose your child to as many types of flowers as possible. This will prevent her from understanding the sign to mean one specific type of flower. Be sure to let her see you sniffing the flower. Let her know how good it smells, and hold it up to her nose. This will help her to see a correlation between the flower and her nose. That, in turn, will help to reinforce the sign.

**Essential Tip**

Using the signs for things that interest your baby is a great way to motivate her as she begins her signing journey. Choosing high-impact signs for your baby's starter words is a good way to encourage her to sign.

# TREE

Trees are so big and impressive that young children are naturally interested in them. This easy sign will give your child the chance to share his interest with you.

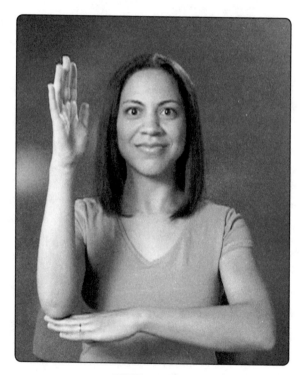

**FIGURE 4-48: TREE**

The sign for TREE, as shown in FIGURE 4-48, is fun to form and is a great representation of an actual tree.

1.  Hold your left arm in front of your body, palm downward.

2.  Rest the elbow of your right arm on the back of your left hand. The fingers of your right hand should be extended.

3.  Twist the right arm twice to complete the sign.

This is another good example of a high-impact sign that will help encourage your baby to sign.

# RAIN

If your child knows the sign for WATER, she may use it when she sees rain or puddles. To avoid confusion on your part, though, consider teaching her this simple sign when water falls from the sky.

**FIGURE 4-49: RAIN**

RAIN is a fairly straightforward sign and might be just what you would expect.

1.  Hold your hands up with your fingers extended, as shown in Figure 4-49.

2.  Bring your hands down to indicate raindrops falling.

3.  Repeat the motion to complete the sign.

The next time a rainy day keeps you and your baby indoors, use the sign in a song as you watch the rain fall. There are plenty of children's rain-related songs you can use, including "The Itsy Bitsy Spider," "Rain Rain Go Away," and "It's Raining, It's Pouring."

# HOUSE

Although the sign for HOUSE is a generic one, it is easier than the sign for HOME, making it the better choice even if you use it to refer to your baby's home.

FIGURE 4-50: HOUSE (STEP ONE)

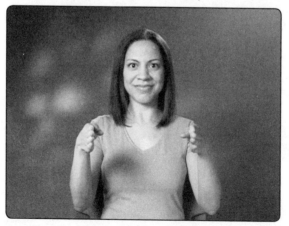

FIGURE 4-51: HOUSE (STEP TWO)

The sign for HOUSE, as shown in FIGURES 4-50 and 4-51, is simple to form. Basically, you trace the outline of a house in the air.

1.   Raise both your arms in front of you and form the top of a triangle by touching your fingertips together. This depicts the roof of a house.

2.   Bring your hands down outlining the shape of a box. This depicts the walls and foundation of a house.

Help your baby to understand this sign by using it in reference to many different houses. Point out houses of different sizes, shapes, and colors so that she understands the sign does not just represent her own home.

# BICYCLE

The sign for BICYCLE is a fun one to form and your baby may seek out extra opportunities to use it.

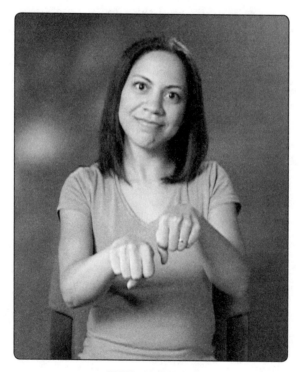

FIGURE 4-52: BICYCLE

The sign for BICYCLE, as shown in **FIGURE 4-52**, resembles feet pedaling.

1.  **Hold both hands in front of your body and make them into fists.**

2.  **Rotate each hand in a forward circle, as if pedaling with them.**

Some babies may be more interested in the person riding the bicycle than in the bicycle itself. If this is the case with your baby, point out bicycles without riders, such as those on a bicycle rack or in a store. Some babies may even confuse a bike for a car when they notice the wheels.

> **Essential Tip**
> Because the sign for TRICYCLE is quite complicated, your baby will probably have some difficulty with it. You may find it easier, though not entirely accurate, to use BICYCLE to describe both a bike and a tricycle.

# CAR

In this day and age, a car is an everyday sight and/ or experience for a baby. He can use this sign both to signify that he sees a car or to express that he's eager to go somewhere in a car.

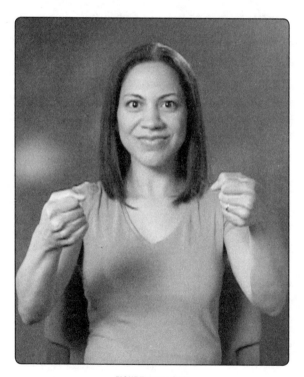

FIGURE 4-53: CAR

CAR may be one of the easiest signs you and your baby will learn.

1.  Hold your hands in front of you as if holding onto a steering wheel, as shown in Figure 4-53.

2.  Move your hands up and down as if turning the wheel.

In the beginning, your baby may use the sign for CAR to describe everything on wheels. If it is important to you that he uses the correct sign, just keep modeling it, but acknowledge his efforts. For example, if a truck drives by and your baby signs CAR, you could say, "You're right, that does look like a car. It is a truck and it is bigger than a car."

# AIRPLANE

Even if your child won't be traveling in an airplane anytime soon, he will probably see plenty of them in the sky.

The sign for AIRPLANE is made with the same hand formation as the sign for I LOVE YOU.

1.   Extend your index finger, pinkie, and thumb of your right hand.

2.   Make a jabbing motion in the air twice with that hand.

You often hear an airplane before it is visible in the sky. This gives you a great opportunity to demonstrate the sign before your baby is too busy watching the plane to notice. As soon as you hear it, ask your baby if *he* hears the airplane. As you say it, form the sign in his line of sight. Soon the plane will be visible, and he will make the connection.

# SWING

Whether in the living room or at the park, babies enjoy swings. Teaching this sign will give him the opportunity to ask to participate in this activity.

Swings are fun for people of all ages. Your baby likely got her first experience in a swing while she was still a very young infant.

1. Extend the first and middle fingers of your left hand horizontally in front of your body. This represents the seat of the swing.

2. Use the same fingers of your right hand, and hook them over the left fingers. This represents legs dangling from the swing.

3. With your fingers hooked together, swing both hands back and forth twice.

It may take a while for your baby to master SWING. In the meantime, you may find that she simply links her hands together and swings them back and forth.

> **Essential Tip**
> When your toddler is old enough to enjoy the playground, she will likely make a beeline for the swings. You can use her interest to your advantage when you introduce this sign. Keep in mind, however, that a playground can be a stimulating place with lots of things for your baby to see, hear, and do. If you can't seem to capture her attention for long enough to demonstrate these signs, just keep trying and waiting for an opportunity.

# STROLLER

Teaching your baby to sign STROLLER gives him the ability to let you know when he's tired of walking or simply when he wants to head outside for a stroll.

STROLLER is an easy sign to form, but as it is difficult to model this sign while your child is riding in the stroller, be on the lookout for other parents pushing strollers. Your baby will probably take notice of them, and that will provide you with an ideal moment to model the sign.

1.  Hold your fists in front of your body as if holding onto the handlebars of a stroller.

2.  Push your fists forward slightly to complete the sign.

Even the youngest toddlers love to push toy strollers around. It gives them a chance to imitate their mothers or fathers and the opportunity to wheel something around, much like driving a car. Giving your toddler a toy stroller is also a great way to teach him about caring for a baby, if he has a sibling on the way.

# WALK

WALK is another sign that your baby can use to ask to go out for a walk. It also adds an element of interest when you are trying to coax your baby into taking her first steps.

To form the sign for WALK, just let your fingers do the walking.

1. Hold your hand out in front of your body and extend the index and middle fingers, curling the remaining fingers into your palm.

2. Point your extended fingers downward.

3. Move your extended fingers back and forth as if they were legs walking.

The best time to demonstrate this sign is not while taking a walk with your child. There are far too many things to see for your baby to pay much attention to your signing efforts. Instead, ask your baby if he would like to take a walk, and then demonstrate the sign. Be sure he already has his shoes and jacket on because you will want to take him outside immediately and go for the walk to help him associate the sign with the action.

# RUN

Your little one may do more actual running than making the sign for RUN, but if he learns to use the sign, you may get forewarning before he makes a run for it.

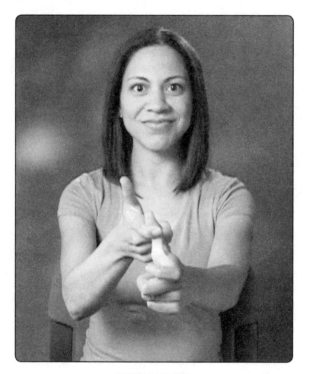

**FIGURE 4-54: RUN**

Obviously, you and your child won't be able to demonstrate the sign for RUN, as shown in FIGURE 4-54, while he is running. Instead, model the sign when you see other children running.

1. Hold both hands in front of the body with index fingers extended and thumbs upward.

2. Hook the index finger of your right hand with the thumb of your left hand.

3. Move the entire formation forward while wiggling the index finger of your left hand and the thumb of your right.

This sign is a bit complex and you may find that your baby modifies it to make it easier right from the beginning. If not, consider modifying it yourself if your child is having trouble with it.

# CAT

If you have a cat at home, this sign is essential. Even if you don't, chances are your baby will encounter cats when visiting friends and relatives.

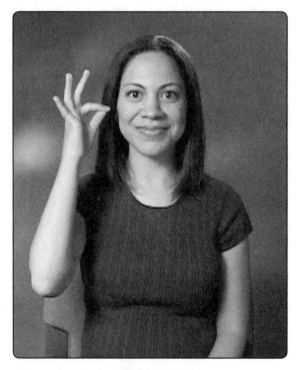

FIGURE 4-55: CAT

The sign for CAT, as shown in FIGURE 4-55, is relatively simple.

1. Bring your thumb and your index finger up to your cheek, very close to your nose. At this point, the fingers should not be touching.

2. Move your fingers out to the side and pinch them together (your remaining fingers will be extended). It should look like you are stroking whiskers on your face.

Pet your cat as you form the sign. This should help your child to make the connection between the cat and the sign. Try not to aggravate your cat, though. With a baby in the house, he is probably aggravated enough as it is.

# DOG

If your family has a dog (or even if you don't), this is another sign that will come in handy.

DOG is another simple sign, though it requires two motions.

1.   **Pat your thigh with your open hand once.**

2.   **Snap your fingers twice.**

If you have a dog in the house, the sign may cause him to come running. This would actually be helpful in reinforcing the sign for your child.

> **Essential Tip**
>
> If you have pets in your home, chances are good that your baby adores them. Unfortunately, your pet may not adore your baby. Many babies point at, or motion toward, pets in an effort to acknowledge them. The signs for CAT, DOG, BIRD, and FISH will give baby a way to acknowledge the pet's presence and to alert you to it, as well.

# BIRD

Even if you don't have a pet bird, our feathered friends are everywhere and will present great opportunities to reinforce signing.

Give your baby the opportunity to talk about them by teaching this easy sign that also doubles as the sign for CHICKEN.

1. Bring one hand up to your mouth and press the index finger and thumb together (the remaining fingers should be tucked in the palm).

2. Snap your thumb and index finger open and closed in front of your mouth, as if you have a beak.

If you plan to use this sign for BIRD, it might be best to avoid using it for CHICKEN, at least until your child is old enough to understand what she is eating.

# FISH

This intuitive sign is a great one for those babies who are mesmerized by fish swimming around in a tank.

There is a more commonly used, two-handed motion to indicate FISH, but the single-hand motion will probably be easier for your child to master.

1. Extend your hand as if offering a handshake.

2. Make your hand "swim" in a zigzag motion like the tail of a fish.

If you plan to use this sign for both the goldfish in the fishbowl and the fish on your baby's plate, your baby may be a little confused. Consider using one form of the sign or the other, but not both, at least until your child is a little older and better able to understand what she is eating.

# HOT

It may be obvious when your child is very hot because of outward appearances such as flushed skin or sweat. However, she can use this sign to let you know she is uncomfortable before she reaches that point.

The sign for HOT is formed by starting with your fingertips at your lips, similar to the sign for EAT.

1.   Draw the tips of all of your fingers and thumb together as if operating a hand puppet with its mouth closed, as in the sign for EAT.

2.   Pull your fingers away and downward as if pulling something from your mouth that is too hot.

As with COLD, you will have plenty of chances to demonstrate the sign for HOT. If you put your baby in the car on a summer afternoon, be sure to tell her how hot it is. If her food is too hot to eat, let her know by forming the sign. It won't be long before she is telling you when something is too hot.

# COLD

Until your child is old enough to tell you that he is cold or hot, keeping him comfortable can be an exercise in trial and error. With this sign, though, he can let you know if he needs another layer of clothing.

FIGURE 4-56: COLD

To form the sign for COLD, imagine that you are, in fact, cold.

1. Draw your shoulders in and bring your forearms up to your chest with your hands balled into fists, as shown in Figure 4-56.

2. Shake your hands as if you are cold.

Seek out opportunities to use this sign to help reinforce its meaning. For instance, if it's cold outside, use the sign when you step out the door. You could also let your baby play with an ice cube while you demonstrate the sign. This will help your baby learn the sign and its meaning quickly. You will find multiple opportunities in your everyday life to use this sign.

# PAIN

The sign for pain is relatively easy to form and can be used to express everything from an injury to pain from an illness (e.g., a sore throat or stomachache).

FIGURE 4-57: PAIN

Introducing a baby to the sign for PAIN, as shown in FIGURE 4-57, can be difficult because he will likely be distracted by the very pain to which you are referring.

1.  Bring your hands in front of your body and point your index fingers at one another.

2.  Twist your fingers in opposite directions.

One effective way to introduce this sign is to demonstrate it when you have hurt yourself. In addition, take advantage of small ouchies (such as a fall on the bottom or a light bump on the head) that your baby experiences. These minor incidents are not likely to be as distracting to your baby, but they will still allow him to grasp the concept of pain. Another opportunity for instruction is during teething, as it will occur frequently and last a while. There are not too many advantages to the pain of teething, but this is one of them.

# DOCTOR

The doctor is probably a familiar person in your baby's life, making this an important sign to know.

**FIGURE 4-58: DOCTOR**

The sign for DOCTOR is shown in FIGURE 4-58.

1. Form the manual alphabet letter D with one hand.

2. Tap it to the inside wrist of the opposite hand to indicate checking for a pulse.

To help distinguish a doctor in your child's mind, point out the doctor's white coat, stethoscope, and other features that are singular to doctors. These visual clues will help your baby to identify doctors, therefore sealing the sign's meaning in his mind.

> **Essential Tip**
>
> Some babies love going to the doctor's office, and some babies hate it. Giving signed names to your child's doctors will help your baby to understand who they are, even if he still cannot understand how they help him. It is also a good way to let your baby know where he is going when it is time for an all-important trip to the doctor.

# CRY

Use the sign for CRY instead of the sign for SAD as crying is a concept babies and toddlers readily understand.

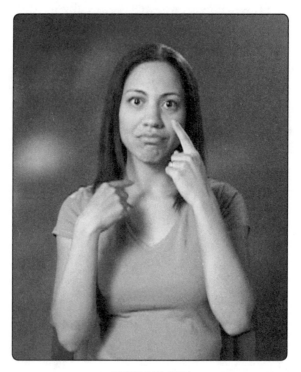

FIGURE 4-59: CRY

The sign for CRY, as shown in FIGURE 4-59, is simple to form and is a good representation of the word.

1. Touch the tips of your index fingers just under your eyes.

2. Move your fingers downward to indicate tears.

As simple as this sign is, and as many opportunities as you will undoubtedly have to demonstrate it, CRY can still be a difficult sign for babies to demonstrate. Why? Most likely because when they are crying, they are preoccupied with the cause of their distress and have no inclination to focus on the sign you are so diligently modeling.

One way to overcome this distraction is to wait until your baby has stopped crying. Touch his tears and then form the sign. He may begin to associate tears with the sign for CRY. Also, be sure to demonstrate the sign whenever your baby witnesses anyone else crying.

# ANGRY

When a little one is angry, he needs an outlet to express that anger. The sign for ANGRY is somewhat intuitive and will give him something to do with his hands instead of hitting or throwing.

FIGURE 4-60: ANGRY

The sign for ANGRY, as shown in FIGURE 4-60, is another sign that benefits from the use of facial expressions.

1.   Hold your hand, palm toward you, in front of your face.

2.   Bend your fingers in and pull your hand away, all the while making an angry facial expression.

To demonstrate this sign, wait for indications that your child is angry, such as when he does not get his way. If he is too angry, of course, he will be unable to focus on the sign, so try to wait until he has calmed down a bit.

# LAUGH

What baby doesn't love smiles and laughter? Once he realizes that he can make the sign for LAUGH to elicit a laugh from you, he may sign it over and over and over again.

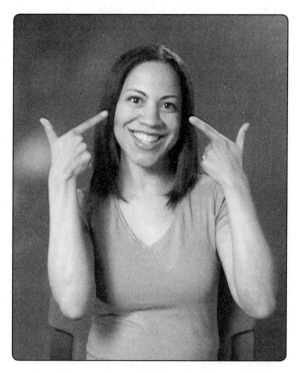

FIGURE 4-61: LAUGH

The sign for LAUGH is shown in FIGURE 4-61.

1.  Form the "L" hand shape with both hands.

2.  Point to the corners of your mouth with your index fingers.

3.  Gesture upward as if indicating a smile, and be sure to smile while you are doing it.

Many babies and toddlers quickly learn that the act of laughing is one that provokes a positive reaction from adults. Many will then start to offer up fake laughs in order to get that same reaction. If your baby does this, it should be quite easy to get him to use the sign for LAUGH. Simply laugh and form the sign. If he laughs in response (real or fake), make the sign again. Keep playing this back-and-forth game, and soon he will be signing while he's laughing.

# HUG

The sign for HUG gives even the youngest children the ability to ask before hugging someone who might not be so receptive—like another child.

FIGURE 4-62: HUG

The sign for HUG, as shown in FIGURE 4-62, is made by simply giving yourself a hug.

1.  **Cross your arms over your chest.**

2.  **Grasp your upper arms, squeezing tightly as if hugging.**

You may find that your baby enjoys this newfound ability to embrace himself, and he may do it frequently. If, after he forms the sign, you offer him a hug and he rejects it, it is safe to assume that he is just having fun with the sign. However, it is still important to try to hug him when he makes the sign to continue to reinforce its meaning.

# CHAPTER 5

# Troubleshooting Common Problems

When your baby is learning to walk, you can expect that she will fall on her diaper-padded bottom many times. You will not be able to prevent it from happening, but knowing that a fall is inevitable will make you better prepared to handle it when it does happen. Likewise, your baby will have many "stumbles" as she acquires the language of sign. Find out about these common signing problems so that you can be prepared when they occur.

## Baby Isn't Paying Attention

Babies are busy creatures. They are constantly checking out the world around them and learning all sorts of new things. They have very short attention spans and are not likely to focus on any given thing for very long. For that reason, you may find that it is sometimes difficult to get your baby to pay attention to your signing efforts.

Unfortunately, you can't force your baby to watch you as you sign. The good news is that you are not missing out on valuable learning time when your baby is unfocused because babies absorb the most information when they are in a state of quiet attentiveness. It is important to watch for these moments of attentiveness in your child. So, for example, if she is not paying attention at the start of her feeding, when you would normally demonstrate the sign, perhaps she will be attentive by the middle or the end of it. If so, use that opportunity to demonstrate the sign. If your baby goes through the entire feeding and doesn't gaze at you for more than a moment at a time, just wait until the next feeding. You will eventually find a time when your baby is attentive and alert and therefore ready to participate.

## Baby Won't Sign

When you first set out to sign with your baby, you may be filled with visions of carrying on fluent conversations with your infant. After a couple of weeks of signing with no reaction from your baby at all, you may find yourself disappointed and convinced that your baby will never sign.

It is important to remember that even under the best of circumstances, it still takes time for a baby to sign. You may have begun signing at just the right stage in your baby's development. You may have started with the perfect first signs. You may demonstrate the signs every time the opportunity arises. Even so, it may be weeks or months before your baby offers you a sign in return.

> **Essential Tip**
>
> Some babies begin walking as early as nine months. Others walk as late as eighteen months. Both extremes are considered to be normal. In the same way, some babies will begin forming their first signs in just a couple of weeks, whereas others may take a few months.

It is understandable that as time wears on, you may begin to grow discouraged. This is the plight of signing parents everywhere. Talk to other signing parents for support and encouragement. Continue to follow the suggestions given in this book, and seek out as many opportunities to sign as possible. As with any other skill your baby has yet to master, this one will take time. Be patient and diligent, and soon your baby will be signing.

## Is Baby Really Signing?

After you have begun to sign with your baby, you may notice that she is making new and unusual gestures that you never noticed before. They don't quite look like the signs you have used with her, though you must admit there may be a slight resemblance. You begin to experience the first stirrings of hope and you think that maybe, just maybe, your baby is signing.

### Just a Coincidence?

As the parent of a baby, you have likely witnessed your child as she tries out her new body, checking to see what it can do. Younger infants, especially, will sometimes test their range of motion by stretching, wiggling, and flexing their limbs. For that reason you may have trouble believing that your child is actually signing. You may worry that you will interpret her spontaneous movements as a deliberate sign.

The good news is that your baby probably *is* signing. At the very least, she is likely trying to imitate the gestures she has watched you make, even if she has yet to comprehend their meanings.

> **Essential Tip**
>
> Be on the lookout for vague movements that resemble a sign. For example, the sign for EAT requires that you bring the tips of your fingers up to your lips and tap twice. Initially, though, your baby might simply bring her entire hand to her mouth. Even without the finger movements, she is still signing.

It is better to give her the benefit of the doubt and react as if you are sure she is deliberately communicating with you. Acknowledge the sign, and then give her what you think she may be asking for. If she *is* signing, you will be showing her that signing is a form of communication. If she is not signing, she may still associate the gestures with getting something she wants. This will take her one step closer to actually signing. And if it turns out that she didn't want the object you thought she was asking for, she will undoubtedly let you know it!

### Handling Early Signs

Because your baby's first signs are likely quite different than their true American Sign Language (ASL) counterparts, you will have to decide if you will encourage the true sign or your baby's version. If you are encouraging modified signs, then you can choose to adopt your baby's adaptation of the sign as the one you will continue to use. Simply begin modeling her version of the sign each time you make it. If you want to adhere to actual ASL signs, however, then continue to model the ASL sign, while still acknowledging and responding to her sign. With enough repetition, your baby's signs will become more and more accurate. They may never be done with the accuracy of an adult, but they will get better and easier to understand.

## Baby Is Making Up Her Own Signs

You feel certain that your baby is actually trying to sign, but now it seems as if she is making up her own signs. This is not only possible but likely. Babies have a natural inclination to gesture to get what they want. Even babies who do not learn to sign quickly figure out that they can lift their arms to be picked up or point to an object they want. A baby who signs is even more aware of the possibilities that gesturing offers her. She is likely to form all sorts of gestures to get her needs met.

> **Essential Tip**
>
> Some babies begin to demonstrate their own gestures as early as six months of age, though many will not actively gesture until they are nine months old or older. Gestures you may see your baby develop on her own include pointing, waving, and clapping.

As with a baby's variations on ASL, the way you use (or choose not to use) these homemade gestures depends on the school of sign you are using. If you are using home signs or modified sign language, then these gestures will fit right into your plan of instruction. If you are strictly adhering to ASL, just continue to demonstrate the ASL signs, and your baby will acquire them in time.

## No One Else Will Participate

You have explained all the benefits. You have shown everyone how easy it can be. Still, though, you can't get your spouse or relatives or child's caregiver to participate. Is it time to throw in the towel?

Not at all. Even babies who only have one person in their lives who signs with them can still benefit greatly. It may require more effort on your part if you are the sole signer, but your child can still acquire all the signs you want her to use. She may be slower to acquire some signs, especially if she spends a great deal of time with other people, but the signs will come. Look for as many opportunities as you can to demonstrate each sign you introduce to her.

> **Essential Tip**
>
> Even if the other adults in your household do not sign with your baby, the other children (if you have any) will probably be eager to. Try to recruit your baby's siblings as your partners in sign.

Many relatives and caregivers are reluctant to practice baby sign language because they are skeptical of its merits and they doubt it can actually be taught. If the other adults in your baby's life share these doubts, they are likely to get excited and jump onboard when they see your baby communicating through sign.

## Baby's Signs Are Indecipherable

She tries and tries and tries to mimic your signs, but you just aren't sure what your baby is saying. Or perhaps she has two or three signs that resemble each other so much that you never know for sure which one she is using. These are common problems in signing families and are almost unavoidable. There are a few things you can do, however, to help translate your baby's signs:

- **Consider the context of the sign.** What is going on in baby's environment? What time of day is it? For example, if it is mealtime and others are eating, your baby might be trying to make the sign for EAT.
- **Watch for visual clues.** Is your baby doing anything else that would indicate her wants or needs? A baby who is alternating signing with rubbing her eyes is possibly trying to indicate bed. One who is signing and pointing at the refrigerator may be asking for juice.
- **Avoid using similar signs.** In the beginning, try to avoid using signs with your baby that closely resemble each other. This will reduce potential confusion for both of you.
- **Ask for verbal verification of the sign.** Babies often understand a spoken word long before they are able to say it. So if you aren't sure you know what your baby might be signing,

just ask. An excited reaction is a good indication that you've interpreted correctly.

The longer your baby signs, the better she will become at forming the signs correctly. Likewise, the more you read her signs, the easier it will become for you. You will learn to interpret the little nuances that make her signs different from the standard formations. Just as you may have to work especially hard to understand your child's speech when she begins to talk, it will take some time to understand her hand speak when she learns to sign.

## Baby Is "Forgetting" Some Signs

Your baby has been signing for weeks and has a growing vocabulary of signs. Suddenly, though, you notice that she is neglecting to use some of the signs she has been using since the beginning. It is as if she has forgotten some of her first signs.

The reality is that once your baby has learned a sign, she is unlikely to forget it so long as you continue to demonstrate it each time you use the word. Instead, she is probably dropping a sign temporarily so that she may turn her attention to other signs. Babies commonly do this as they learn any number of new skills. For instance, a baby may stop waving when she begins clapping. Or she may stop saying "da da" when she learns to say "ma ma." But these skills are not lost. Instead, a baby will pick up the old skill again after she has mastered the new one. In the same way, with continued encouragement, your baby will probably resume using her earlier signs.

> **Essential Tip**
>
> Occasionally, you may encounter a sign that your baby rarely needs and therefore has trouble remembering. You may want to consider whether the sign is one that your baby actually needs in her vocabulary. If not, perhaps you should introduce other signs that she will be more likely to use.

As she grows more comfortable with her expanding repertoire of signs, your baby will eventually start using the old signs again. You can ensure that she does not forget the signs by continuing to model them in her presence, even if she fails to do so. This will keep the signs fresh in her memory, and she will pick them back up before long.

## You Are Forgetting Some Signs

You have been practicing sign language with your child for a while and have developed a signing vocabulary of twenty, thirty, fifty, or more signs. Suddenly you find that you are losing track of which signs are which, particularly those you introduced in the beginning. If you have been consistent in demonstrating both the old and new signs, you probably won't have too much trouble remembering them. A memory lapse can happen occasionally, though, so it is a good idea to have your signs organized for your reference.

One way to keep track of the signs you have taught is to keep a log. This can be a notebook in which you jot down the signs you have taught baby, a photo album with pictures of you or your baby forming the signs, or simply a book (such as this one) in which you have marked each sign as you have taught it.

Another way to keep from forgetting the signs is by keeping a reference sheet with you. Simply write instructions for forming the signs you most commonly use with your baby and tuck it into your purse, pocket, or wallet. Then, no matter where you are, you will have your signs with you.

## Enjoy Speaking with Your Baby

After months of effort, you are finally able to communicate with your baby in a way that would not have been possible without the use of sign. He is sharing with you his wants, feelings, and observations in a way that not all babies can. And while his signing is bridging the existing communication gap, it won't be long before your baby begins to speak. You may find that you have bittersweet feelings as he learns to talk.

When your little one does learn to talk, you will begin a whole new adventure in communication. You will delight in listening to him as he chatters about anything and everything, and the two of you will enjoy new realms of communication. However, you may find that you still miss the days of signing with your baby. So be sure to enjoy this very special time and the intimate conversation that you share exclusively with your baby.

# American Sign Language
# Manual Alphabet

A B C D

E F G H

I J K L

M N O P

**Human Kinetics Publishers**

**Library of Congress Cataloging-in-Publication Data**

Shephard, Roy J.
   Aerobic fitness and health / Roy J. Shephard
      p.   cm.
   Includes bibliographical references (p.   ) and index.
   ISBN 0-87322-417-5
   1. Physical fitness.   2. Exercise.   3. Health.   I. Title.
   QP301.S468      1994
   613.7--dc20                                                      93-457
                                                                     CIP
ISBN: 0-87322-417-5 (case)
      0-88011-725-7 (paper)

**Managing Editor:** Julia Anderson, **Assistant Editors:** Julie Lancaster, Dawn Roselund, and John Wentworth, Copyeditor: **Dianna Matlosz, Proofreader: Kathy Bennett, Production Director:** Ernie Noa, **Typesetting and Text Layout:** Julie Overholt, **Text Design:** Keith Blomberg, **Cover Design:** Jack Davis, **Interior Art:** Jim Hampton, **Printer:** Braun-Brumfield

Printed in the United States of America      10  9  8  7  6  5  4  3  2  1

**Human Kinetics**
Web site: http://www.humankinetics.com/

*United States:* Human Kinetics, P.O. Box 5076, Champaign, IL 61825-5076
1-800-747-4457
e-mail: humank@hkusa.com

*Canada:* Human Kinetics, Box 24040, Windsor, ON N8Y 4Y9
1-800-465-7301 (in Canada only)
e-mail: humank@hkcanada.com

*Europe:* Human Kinetics, P.O. Box IW14, Leeds LS16 6TR, United Kingdom
(44) 1132 781708
e-mail: humank@hkeurope.com

*Australia:* Human Kinetics, 57A Price Avenue, Lower Mitcham, South Australia 5062
(088) 277 1555
e-mail: humank@hkaustralia.com

*New Zealand:* Human Kinetics, P.O. Box 105-231, Auckland 1
(09) 523 3462
e-mail: humank@hknewz.com